Psychodynamic Therapy Techniques

Psychodynamic Therapy Techniques

A Guide to Expressive and Supportive Interventions

BRIAN A. SHARPLESS

OXFORD
UNIVERSITY PRESS

Oxford University Press is a department of the University of Oxford. It furthers
the University's objective of excellence in research, scholarship, and education
by publishing worldwide. Oxford is a registered trade mark of Oxford University
Press in the UK and certain other countries.

Published in the United States of America by Oxford University Press
198 Madison Avenue, New York, NY 10016, United States of America.

Library of Congress Cataloging-in-Publication Data
Names: Sharpless, Brian A., author.
Title: Psychodynamic therapy techniques : a guide to expressive and
supportive interventions / Brian A. Sharpless.
Description: New York, NY : Oxford University Press, [2019] |
Includes bibliographical references and index.
Identifiers: LCCN 2018039422 (print) | LCCN 2018050440 (ebook) |
ISBN 9780190676285 (UPDF) | ISBN 9780190676292 (EPUB) |
ISBN 9780190676278 (paperback : alk. paper)
Subjects: LCSH: Psychodynamic psychotherapy—Technique.
Classification: LCC RC489.P72 (ebook) | LCC RC489.P72 S53 2019 (print) |
DDC 616.89/14—dc23
LC record available at https://lccn.loc.gov/2018039422

9 8 7 6 5 4 3 2 1

Printed by Webcom, Inc., Canada

This book is dedicated to the continued inspiration—literary or otherwise—of Friedrich Nietzsche, Jimi Hendrix, Arthur Schopenhauer, Indiana Jones, Søren Kierkegaard, Christopher Hitchens, Mark Manning, John Waters, and the Ramones.

CONTENTS

I begin this book with a personal confession: I *love* psychodynamic psychotherapy. However, mine is not a young, wide-eyed love where I only see the good. Instead, it is a mature and nuanced love where, as Freud might say, I have *owned my ambivalence*. To be perfectly blunt, there are aspects of psychodynamic therapy that I hate with the white hot heat of a thousand suns.[1] For instance, I hate the unnecessary obscurantism found in some of our books and constructs. I dislike the fact that some psychodynamic therapists remain uninterested in testing our most cherished beliefs.[2] I also hate the nasty, reductionistic side of certain theories that view people through myopic eyes. But despite these criticisms, there is also so much to love. My hope is that the remainder of this book will more fully explain this pronouncement.

I have gravitated toward psychodynamic therapy's *realistic* view of people since my undergraduate days. It is neither optimistic nor pessimistic. Though it may not be fun to think about, I fear that Freud, Nietzsche, Schopenhauer, and other depth psychologists were correct in realizing that there were practical limits for how well we can really know ourselves and others. Whatever progress we make in these regards is hard won. As one example, people often desire and dread the exact same thing and sometimes at the exact same moment.[3] These confusing experiences do not make self-understanding easy. We are also fantastically good at deceiving ourselves.

Psychodynamic theory assumes this to be the case, and, in fact, some of its main techniques are predicated upon it. For example, *interpretations*—the most "psychodynamic" of psychodynamic techniques—presuppose that patients are unaware of at least one aspect of their subjective experience (see Chapter 13). The therapist helps remedy this state of affairs by presenting them with an interpretive hypothesis. Further, one subtype of *confrontation* encourages patients to resolve their personal inconsistencies (see Chapter 12). Through these and other efforts, psychodynamic therapy helps people become more transparent to themselves. Regardless of how sick or healthy we are, all of us could use a bit of help in this area.

However, as anyone who studies the subject knows, it is difficult to write anything general about psychodynamic therapy (e.g., a book on techniques) without alienating large portions of the field.[4] This text, though intended to be as neutral as possible, will nevertheless reflect my own preferred theories and prior training.[5] However, my hope is that the descriptions of techniques, and the procedures for formulating them, will be applicable across the many forms of psychodynamic therapy. At present, all these viewpoints are needed, as they each provide a slightly different conceptual lens through which to view people and pathology. Psychotherapy is no small task. Given the sheer range and intricacy of human suffering, a plurality of views seems far preferable to a hegemony.

After all, humans are nothing if not complex and full of contradictions. This is strikingly apparent to me at the present moment. I drafted this preface while walking around the crumbling ruins of a castle owned by a long dead 16th-century countess. By all accounts she was a brilliant woman, a polymath, a patriot, and a very good mother. However, she was also a sexual sadist and a serial killer—perhaps the most prolific in all recorded human history. If the trial records are to be believed, she may have been responsible for the deaths of up to 650 women and girls.[6] Again, people are nothing if not complex and full of contradictions.

Regardless of the person or the patient involved, psychodynamic therapy is a useful, albeit imperfect method for peeling back the light, dark, and gray layers of human existence. A possibility for better relationships and an end to old patterns could result from using its techniques. More generally, psychodynamic therapy is a means to help people move forward in their lives or, at least, to better understand themselves and their many confusing contradictions.

—Čachtice, Slovakia, 2018

NOTES

1. The reader will hopefully forgive me for adapting this particularly dramatic quote from the *Bhagavad Gita* (2009, p. 464).
2. However, as described in Chapter 2, there are a number of top-notch psychodynamic researchers currently hard at work.
3. For instance, see Sharpless (2013).
4. Jacques Barber and I (2015) recently argued that these internecine struggles might be a legitimate danger to the future of psychodynamic therapy.
5. This includes the broad suborientations of ego psychology and object relations as well as the more specific approaches of *supportive–expressive therapy*, *transference-focused psychotherapy*, and *mentalization-based treatments*. I also have experience in cognitive-behavior and existential approaches.
6. See McNally (1983) and Craft (2014).

ACKNOWLEDGMENTS

A number of people contributed to making this book a reality. I would first like to express my gratitude to Sarah Harrington at Oxford University Press. Sarah is not only great at her job, but a lot of fun to work with. Second, I would like to thank all of my patients and clinical supervisors. Next, I would like to thank my colleagues, friends, and students at the American School of Professional Psychology, the University of Pennsylvania, Pennsylvania State University, and Washington State University. And last, but certainly not least, I would like to individually thank Gary Sharpless, Linda Sharpless, Jamie Weaver, Peter Arnett, Jason Baker, Jacques Barber, Larry Blum, Thomas Borkovec, Louis Castonguay, Dianne Chambless, Amanda Cummings, Homer Curtis, Dan Denis, Mariana Dobre, Karl Doghramji, Christopher French, Reed Goldstein, William Gottdiener, Alice Gregory, Laena Huffaker, Michael Kowitt, Ken Levy, Peter Lilliengren, James Martin, Dakota Mauzay, Kevin McCarthy, Victoria Merritt, Jessie Meyer, Barbara Milrod, the Nationals Capital Area Skeptics, Niels Nielsen, Debra O'Connell, Desmond Oathes, Aaron Pincus, the Psychodynamic Research listerve, the Ratio Organization of Popular Science, Michael Roche, Gowen Roper, Matt Rothrock, Ayelet Ruscio, Jeremy Safran, Debbie Seagull, Skeptics in the Pub UK, Christina Temes, Sandra Testa, Joseph Tse, Bo Vinnars, Deborah Wachter, Ernest Wachter, Kenneth Wachter, Thomas Wachter, and Jacob Zimmerman.

Psychodynamic Therapy Techniques

Introduction

Psychotherapy is a strange business. It is also very hard to do well. Both these statements make sense if you consider what psychotherapy really entails. At its core, psychotherapy is intended to alleviate human suffering through only a com- bination of *words* and *a relationship*. Other fields may use drugs, surgeries, deep brain stimulation, etc., but this is not the case in psychotherapy. For better or worse, it has always been a "talking cure" (Breuer & Freud, 1955, p. 30) and re- mains so to this day. The various modalities—psychodynamic therapy included— just tend to speak a bit differently and create different types of relationships.

Given these limited tools, good therapists need to know not only *what to in- tervene on* (i.e., a problem derived from a good case formulation) but also *how to intervene* (i.e., which techniques to use and when to use them).[1] Both are viewed as necessary pieces of the psychotherapy puzzle (Anderson & Hill, 2017; Caspar, 2017). For instance, technical skill will be unlikely to help patients unless guided by a good case formulation. This is because techniques are believed to be most beneficial when applied in a deliberate manner using a long-term time horizon (i.e., not haphazardly or reactively). Similarly, even the best of case formulations will be of limited value unless therapists know how to use them when they are in the room with patients. Building upon a famous quote from Immanuel Kant (1996, p. 107), *formulations without techniques are empty; techniques without formulations are blind.*

But how can therapists best learn these skills? A number of readable and "experience-near" introductory psychodynamic texts are fortunately available (e.g., Cabaniss, Cherry, Douglas, & Schwartz, 2011; Gabbard, 2014; McWilliams, 2011; Summers & Barber, 2010). When used in conjunction with appropriate su- pervision, they provide useful introductions to psychodynamic practice (e.g., case formulation, use of countertransference) and help beginning therapists feel more comfortable with patients. Given the breadth of their coverage, though, it is understandable that they are unable to devote extensive attention to every topic. Therefore, the present work has the narrower aims of (a) describing many of the techniques of psychodynamic psychotherapy and (b) explaining how to prepare them for clinical use.

ON THE DEFINITIONS OF SPECIFIC PSYCHODYNAMIC TECHNIQUES

However, these two simple goals quickly became complicated. The long history of our field is in many ways a strength,[2] but it also has some unintended consequences. For example, a number of techniques have been defined inconsistently across authors. One person's *confrontation* might be another author's *clarification,* or vice versa (see Chapters 11 and 12). Making the matter even more complex, certain technical terms have undergone such heavy theoretical modification over the years that they are viewed quite differently in 2019 than they would have been in the early days of psychoanalysis (e.g., *evenly-hovering attention* as described in Chapter 8). A solution to these conceptual difficulties—imperfect though it may be—was to separate the main techniques according to their therapeutic *intentions.*[3] Therefore, all the specific psychodynamic interventions were distinguished from one another according to their specific *a priori* clinical functions. This will hopefully make the book easier to use.

BACKGROUND TRAINING

This book was primarily written to be an intermediate-beginner level text for graduate students and psychiatric residents. It may also be useful for practitioners of other orientations, those interested in psychotherapy integration (Stricker, 2010), and psychotherapy researchers. Regardless, proper use of these techniques presupposes:

- experience with psychodynamic case formulation;
- a basic knowledge of psychodynamic theories and concepts;
- diagnostic interviewing skills;
- comfort assuming a therapist role with patient; and
- knowledge of risk assessment (e.g., how to assess for suicidal or homicidal risk).

If any of these knowledge bases have not yet been acquired, this book might best be supplemented with one of the previously mentioned psychodynamic texts and other relevant resources. Of course, it is also strongly recommended that readers receive clinical supervision from licensed providers intimately familiar with these techniques (i.e., trained psychodynamic psychotherapists or psychoanalysts). The process of psychodynamic therapy has a steep learning curve, and it will take time, patience, repetition, and careful self-observation to effectively use these interventions. Therefore, therapists may want to begin this process by working through any suggested technical procedures (e.g., the six steps in the process of interpretation listed in Chapter 13) until each technique begins to feel more effortless and "natural."[4]

OVERVIEW OF THE BOOK STRUCTURE

This book is divided into three sections and one appendix. The first section focuses on information relevant to understanding and applying psychodynamic techniques. It begins with a chapter on the empirical status of psychodynamic therapy and makes the case for its importance in the contemporary clinical landscape. Next, individual chapters describe psychodynamic treatment goals, components of the psychodynamic *stance*, and the "supportive–expressive" continuum of techniques/treatments. The last two chapters detail the characteristics of good psychodynamic interventions and suggest ways to assess clinical impacts during session (i.e., were they effective?).

The second section of this book focuses on what many practitioners consider to be the classic psychodynamic techniques (e.g., Yeomans, Clarkin, & Kernberg, 2015).[5] Eleven *foundational techniques* are described first (e.g., how to listen in a psychodynamic manner, abstinence, technical neutrality). They are considered foundational because they lay the groundwork for more specific interventions. Next, individual chapters are devoted to each of the "big four" techniques of questions, clarifications, confrontations, and interpretations. Clinical vignettes[6] are interspersed among the historical, theoretical, and practical discussions. Methods for formulating these techniques are suggested along with tips on phrasing.

Section III focuses on the expanded range of psychodynamic practice by outlining *supportive therapy techniques.* As is well known, not every patient is appropriate for traditional, insight-oriented therapy. In fact, this approach may even be contraindicated for sicker patients (especially for those with a psychotic personality organization or those in a state of acute crisis; see Rockland, 1989). Six sets of supportive techniques are described. The intentions of these range from supporting self-esteem and reducing patient anxiety to improving adaptive life skills. The final chapter focuses specifically on ways to identify and repair therapeutic alliance ruptures. These events, common to all forms of therapy (i.e., expressive, supportive, or otherwise), can lead to poor therapy outcome and premature termination (Eubanks-Carter, Muran, & Safran, 2015). However, if managed properly, ruptures can also serve as an impetus for meaningful clinical change (Safran & Muran, 2000).

Finally, the appendix, co-authored with Peter Lilliengren, serves as a resource for those interested in exploring the empirical literatures or locating specific clinical tools. It lists psychodynamic *models* (e.g., *supportive-expressive therapy*) as well as disorder-specific *manuals* (e.g., *panic-focused psychodynamic psychotherapy*) and compiles their corresponding references. As discussed more fully in the next chapter, psychodynamic researchers have made significant contributions to psychotherapy research. Manualized treatments were—and continue to be— a useful means to this end. Further, many of these manuals can also serve as helpful guides for therapists interested in learning how to apply psychodynamic techniques to specific patient populations.

NOTES

1. This also presupposes some skill in managing therapeutic relationships.
2. For example, this long history resulted in the many subfields we have today (e.g., object relations, self psychology) and the different clinical viewpoints that they each provide.
3. Therefore, for the sake of consistency, certain authors are prioritized over others.
4. There is obviously not only one "correct" way to enact psychodynamic techniques. The suggested procedures are included for didactic purposes. Responsiveness to a particular patient is key.
5. The majority of these have been in use since the earliest days of psychoanalysis.
6. To preserve patient and supervisee confidentiality, clinical vignettes are a combination of de-identified (i.e., their identities and details have been heavily distorted), aggregated (i.e., blends of actual people), and hypothetical patients/supervisees.

Background Information for Psychodynamic Therapy Techniques

Do We *REALLY* Need Psychodynamic Therapy?[1]

INTRODUCTION

I do not assume that everyone reading this book is a fan of psychodynamic psychotherapy. When I began teaching and supervising in 2006, I soon noticed that a not insignificant proportion of students came to graduate training with negative preconceptions. Given some of the depictions found in movies, television, and undergraduate textbooks (Habarth, Hansell, & Grove, 2011; Redmond & Shulman, 2008), I do not blame them for their skepticism. If these were my only exposures to psychodynamic therapy, I might feel similarly.

Along with misinformation, though, the field itself is partially to blame for bad public perceptions. As noted by Shedler (2010), "one potential source of bias is a lingering distaste in the mental health professions for past psychoanalytic arrogance and authority. . . and . . . a dismissive stance toward research" (p. 98). It is an unfortunate historical fact that psychodynamic therapists indeed arrived late to the game of traditional empiricism. Other orientations (i.e., humanistic, behavioral, and cognitive modalities) developed "rules" for the never-before-existing field of psychotherapy research, and, perhaps not surprisingly, these rules were not focused on traditional psychodynamic constructs (Barber & Sharpless, 2015). Early psychoanalytic scholarship focused not on clinical trials and the study of groups of people, but on the intensive study of *individuals* (Boswell et al., 2010).[2] This emphasis on case studies, though valuable in a number of ways, was not viewed by some scientists as "rigorous enough" or scientifically convincing. However, as will be demonstrated in the following discussion, the situation has changed considerably in recent years, and a number of different research methodologies are currently in operation. I echo the sentiments of Thomä and Kächele (1992) who noted, "The more strictly rules are laid down and the less their impact on therapy is *investigated empirically*, the greater the danger of creating orthodoxy" (p. 7; emphasis added).

Therefore, throughout the remainder of this chapter, I will detail the reasoning behind an affirmative answer to the question posed in the chapter title. To be clear, my intention is not to criticize other approaches and, in a sense, argue for psychodynamic therapy's superiority. That would be unreasonable, inconsistent with my own training[3], and intellectually myopic. I instead hope to make the far more reasonable claim that a *multiplicity* of orientations is needed and that psychodynamic therapy has an important role to play in contemporary science and practice.

REASONS THAT WE STILL NEED PSYCHODYNAMIC THERAPY

It Is a Flexible Treatment Approach

As will be demonstrated in Sections II and III, psychodynamic therapy is an extremely flexible and responsive treatment approach. It also offers a unique perspective on the alleviation of human suffering (Blagys & Hilsenroth, 2000; also see Chapter 4). Though Freud began his work with a fairly narrow procedure and very specific patients, the "scope" of psychodynamic therapy has massively expanded over the past 120 years. No longer even an exclusively "Western" approach, over 130 psychoanalytic training centers can be found dispersed across six continents (i.e., including Asia and Africa; International Psychoanalytic Association, 2018). Dynamic therapy can now be applied to individuals, couples, and groups at many different ages and in many different treatment settings (Gabbard, 2014; Midgley, O'Keefe, French, & Kennedy, 2017; Summers & Barber, 2010).

However, the majority of *empirical* attention has been devoted to individual dynamic therapy with adult patients. It has been used to treat a number of psychiatric diagnoses (Gabbard, 2014) at any of the three levels of personality organization (i.e., neurotic, borderline, and psychotic; Kernberg, 1984). Just to give a small sampling of this range (see the appendix; Rockland, 1989), psychodynamic therapy has been successfully applied to "neurotic" conditions (e.g., social anxiety disorder; Leichsenring et al., 2014), personality disorders (e.g., borderline personality disorder; Clarkin, Levy, Lenzenweger, & Kernberg, 2007), somatic complaints (e.g., medically unexplained pain; Chavooshi, Saberi, Tavallaie, & Sahraei, 2017), and eating disorders (e.g., anorexia nervosa; Dare, Eisler, Russell, Treasure, & Dodge, 2001).

The time-frame of contemporary psychodynamic therapy is also more flexible than it was in 1900. Whereas the duration of classical psychoanalysis was often measured in years and required three to six visits per week,[4] many current treatments last from weeks to months. In fact, the majority of outcome trials have focused on time-limited approaches (i.e., 8–24 sessions). These shorter therapies required a heavy modification of standard psychodynamic processes (e.g., free association as discussed Chapter 7), shifts in therapist activity, and responsiveness to the needs of specific patients. They also presupposed an ability to "focus" the treatment, and researchers have developed several ways to do this.

For example, therapists with very little training[5] can reliably derive a *core conflictual relationship theme* (CCRT; see Chapter 3) from patient material (e.g., Book, 1998). A CCRT essentially distills a patient's problematic relational patterns down to its essence. This information is then shared with the patient in "experience-near" language. The CCRT method, which forms the basis of *supportive-expressive psychotherapy* (Luborsky, 1984), has been used in numerous empirical studies (see the appendix) and is both clinically useful and empirically defensible (Crits-Christoph, Gibbons, & Mukherjee, 2013; Leichsenring, Steinert, & Crits-Christoph, 2018). Methods such as these allow complex and individualized psychodynamic work to take place under stringent time constraints.

All Existing Treatments Have "Nonresponders" and "Nonremitters"

By way of broad summary, psychotherapy is clearly an effective treatment for any number of psychiatric conditions (Roth & Fonagy, 2005). To say otherwise would require a massively distorted reading of the outcome literatures. However, this does not imply that there is no room for improvement. Even in the best and most well-controlled clinical trials, remission rates are not terribly high (Roth & Fonagy, 2005) and, even more troubling, approximately 5% to 10% of patients actually *get worse* during treatment (i.e., they deteriorate; see Lambert, 2013).[6] This is the case with *all* major treatment modalities, and psychotherapy is not unique in having these challenges.

The efficacy of *psychopharmacology* has also been questioned. As one example, consider the use of antidepressant medications for major depressive disorder. Though widely used and considered efficacious, a recent review in *World Psychiatry* concluded that the efficacy of antidepressants was "less than impressive" (Khan & Brown, 2015, p. 294). This is not to say that they are useless, obviously, but their efficacy is more limited than previously thought. Other research indicates that antidepressants may be more helpful for patients with severe depression than those with mild or moderate cases (Fournier et al., 2010). Further, medication treatment gains may not be as long-lasting as those caused by psychotherapy (Hollon et al., 2005; Spielmans, Berman, & Usitalo, 2011). Interestingly, and despite these limitations, medications are on the rise whereas the use of psychotherapy is in decline (Clay, 2011).

Regardless of treatment modality or the specific disorder being treated, the reasons for nonresponse, nonremission, and deterioration are not yet fully understood. As patients are quite heterogeneous—even those ostensibly suffering from the same disorder—it only makes sense that not every treatment will be effective for every patient or every problem. Therefore, previously summarized findings imply a clear need for *multiple* treatment options.

Psychodynamic Therapy Is Efficacious

Individuals less familiar with the therapy outcome literatures are often surprised by the evidence base for psychodynamic approaches.[7] Though getting a "late start" compared to cognitive behavioral therapy (CBT), the past two decades in particular witnessed an increase in high-quality psychodynamic research. This resulted in an ability to conduct meta-analytic studies[8] that compared and contrasted the overall efficacy of psychodynamic therapy with other modalities.

In general, psychodynamic therapies are no more or less effective than others.[9] A well-conducted and very wide-ranging meta-analysis found that psychodynamic therapy was clearly better than no treatment (i.e., controls or "treatment as usual") and not significantly different from alternatives (e.g., CBT) at posttreatment or follow-up assessments (Barber, Muran, McCarthy, & Keefe, 2013). These findings held for mood disorder, anxiety disorder, and personality disorder studies (see also Driessen et al., 2015; Leichsenring & Leibing, 2003; Leichsenring, Rabung, & Leibing, 2004). However, this is not to say that no differences exist. For instance, the limited comparisons indicated that dynamic therapy may be *less* effective for generalized anxiety disorder than CBT (Barber et al., 2013).[10]

The results of one recent meta-analysis are particularly compelling. Steinert, Munder, Rabung, Hoyer, and Leichsenring (2017) took the unique approach of using adversarial collaboration to control for potential *allegiance effects*. Allegiance effects are one of many forms of bias that can inadvertently creep into meta-analyses (Cuijpers, 2016). In this case, the research team included representatives of psychodynamic and CBT approaches during all phases of the study (e.g., study selection, analysis). Their overall findings, like those previously mentioned, suggested equivalence of psychodynamic therapy to the more well-established CBT.[11]

Finally, there is limited evidence that more intensive treatments may be better than those that are less rigorous. For instance, Leichsenring and Rabung (2008) found that longer-term psychodynamic treatments (i.e., at least 50 sessions) were superior to approaches of shorter duration.[12] Further, in a study comparing long-term psychodynamic therapies, Blomberg, Lazar, and Sandell (2001) found that higher weekly session frequencies ($M = 3.5$) were better than lower ($M = 1.4$ sessions per week).

Psychodynamic Therapy May Have Other Important Clinical Benefits

Although outcomes may be equivalent when averaged across studies, there is an increasing body of evidence that psychodynamic therapy is associated with other positive clinical gains. Some of these may be unique[13] and could be particularly helpful for patients who have corresponding deficits. However, given the limited state of the research, additional replications are needed to increase confidence that these effects are not found in other modalities.

For instance, psychodynamic therapy leads to increases in *mentalization/reflective functioning* (Bo et al., 2017; Maxwell et al., 2017; Meulemeester, Vansteelandt, Luyten, & Lowyck, 2018; Rudden, Milrod, Target, Ackerman, & Graf, 2006). Mentalization is the crucial human capacity to understand oneself and other people in terms of internal mental states such as feelings and desires (Fonagy, Target, Steele, & Steele, 1998). It is considered to be an important form of social cognition with a wide range of clinical applicability (e.g., individuals, groups, caregivers, and therapists; Bateman & Fonagy, 2016). Certain types of patients— especially those with borderline personality disorders—have deficits in this area (Bateman & Fonagy, 2006). To the best of my knowledge, only dynamic treatments have been found to increase mentalization (Levy et al., 2006), but it would not be surprising if other approaches also improved this capacity (e.g., CBT).

Psychodynamic therapy also fosters changes in patient *insight/self-understanding*.[14] This has been a therapeutic target and proposed mechanism of change since the earliest days of psychoanalysis (see Chapter 3) and, indeed, levels of self-understanding increase with successful treatment (Connolly et al., 1999; Kivlighan, Multon, & Patton, 2000). However, with one exception (Hoffart, Versland, & Sexton, 2002), this was not found in other orientations. Interestingly, the Hoffart et al. study used *schema therapy*. This integrative variation of CBT shares some degree of overlap with psychodynamic therapy (Riso, du Toit, Stein, & Young, 2007).

Patients also seem to improve their *quality of object relations*.[15] The unfortunate (and ponderous) phrase "object relations" refers to the way that we internalize and symbolize our relationships with others (Blatt, 1974). Individuals with good object relations tend to have stable connections with others that are reliable, satisfying, nuanced, and reciprocal. Those with poorer object relations have unstable relationships characterized by such things as superficiality, neediness, preoccupation with potential loss, and so on (Azim, Piper, Segal, Nixon, & Duncan, 1991). Several trials indicated that psychodynamic treatment improves patients' overall quality of object relations (Lindgren, Werbart, & Philips, 2010; Mullin, Hilsenroth, Gold, & Farber, 2017, 2018; Vermote et al., 2010), but this has yet to be assessed in nondynamic modalities (Barber et al., 2013). Therefore, more data are needed to determine whether this is indeed a psychodynamic-specific impact.

Other psychodynamic constructs have been found to change with treatment and in the expected directions. However, limited data indicate that they are not "unique" but manifest in other modalities as well. For instance, it is difficult to identify a more "classic" psychodynamic construct than patient *defense mechanisms* (Freud, 1966; Reich, 1990)[16]. Defenses have played a key role in treatment since the very founding of psychoanalysis, and their importance continues to the present day (McWilliams, 2011).

As expected, defensive functioning improves over the course of psychodynamic treatment. Successful therapy results in the decreased use of immature defenses

(Akkerman, Carr, & Lewin, 1992; Roy, Perry, Luborsky, & Banon, 2009) and an increased use of mature defenses (Johansen, Krebs, Svartberg, Stiles, & Holen, 2011; Kramer, Despland, Michel, Drapeau, & de Roten, 2010) but appears to have little impact on the neurotic defenses (Akkerman, Lewin, & Carr, 1999). Therefore, defenses at the "extremes" may be more malleable. Interestingly, CBT improves defensive functioning as well (Heldt et al., 2007; Johansen et al., 2011). Given the conceptual overlap between cognitive distortions (Beck, 2011) and certain defense mechanisms, this makes a good bit of theoretical sense. Future research may help determine whether individual defenses might be modified more easily through one approach or the other.

Another nonunique construct is *relationship rigidity*. As is well-known, psychodynamic theories assume the reliable repetition of interpersonal patterns (e.g., as in transference). This is especially the case for those that were established during formative developmental periods. Everyone manifests relational patterns, therapists included, but some are more inflexible and problematic than others. Since psychodynamic therapy focuses on confronting and understanding these repetitions of behavior (see Section II), it is perhaps not surprising that reductions in relationship rigidity occur (Salzer et al., 2010; Slomin, Shefler, Gvirsman, & Tishby, 2011). However, this has been somewhat inconsistent across studies (Wilczek, Weinryb, Barber, Gustavsson, & Asberg, 2004), and differences in the measurement of rigidity may explain these discrepancies (McCarthy, Connolly Gibbons, & Barber, 2008). These reductions in rigidity may not be unique to psychodynamic therapy (e.g., Ruiz et al., 2004), but more research is needed.

Finally, mention should be made of changes to *attachment* patterns. Attachment theory has grown far beyond its original confines as a psychoanalytic concept (for certain anticipations of attachment theory, see Fairbairn, 1994, 1994; Klein, 1949) and has entered the field of psychology more generally through the pioneering work of John Bowlby and Mary Ainsworth (Cassidy & Shaver, 2016). Psychodynamic therapy, with its emphasis on interpersonal needs and patterns, has been shown to move patients closer to secure attachment (Levy et al., 2006). However, improvements in attachment have also been found with CBT (Zalaznik, Weiss, & Huppert, 2017). I would not be surprised if this occurred in other modalities as well (e.g., humanistic therapy).

In ending this section, it may be important to note that all the changes previously detailed are consistent with what psychodynamic theory would predict. Even if some of these constructs and potential mechanisms of change are not unique, it is nonetheless important to document both the supportive and disconfirming data and encourage further empirical inquiry.

Psychodynamic Therapy Leads to Significant Reductions in Healthcare Costs

In addition to symptom reduction and other positive clinical impacts, psychotherapy reduces healthcare costs (American Psychological Association, 2012).

This finding may be particularly attractive to policymakers and insurance companies but carries a practical significance for society as well. Few could argue that mental health issues are not a severe burden on limited healthcare resources. The situation may be even more dire than it appears, though, as a recent study in *The Lancet* argued that previous calculations actually *underestimated* the true cost of the problem (Vigo, Thornicroft, & Atun, 2016).

Fortunately, data on the specific cost-effectiveness of psychodynamic therapy exist. As one example, Abbass and Katzman (2013) conducted a review of 13 trials of *intensive short-term dynamic psychotherapy*[17] that also assessed health-care utilization. Though the studies were heterogeneous in terms of patients (e.g., treatment-resistant depression, personality disorders) and treatment durations (i.e., 1–28 sessions), the results were nonetheless compelling. In the seven studies that assessed medication use, patients on pretherapy medication reduced their overall number of prescriptions, and almost 60% stopped using them altogether. The authors also assessed cost-effectiveness in terms of the percentage of patients returning to work. These rates ranged from 14.3% (i.e., the one-session treatment) to 100% in a sample of patients treated for chronic headaches.

Two other individual studies deserve mention. First, Lilliengren et al. (2017) recently published a trial of *intensive short-term dynamic psychotherapy* for generalized anxiety disorder. They identified significant reductions in posttherapy physician costs following treatment. These reductions continued in a linear fashion for four consecutive years. By year two of the follow-up, the mean patient physician costs fell below the national average (Lilliengren et al., 2017, pp. 5–6). Second, a comparative outcome trial of anorexia nervosa patients found that *focal psychodynamic therapy* was *more* cost-effective than enhanced treatment as usual and enhanced CBT (Egger et al., 2016). The authors reported that this was primarily due to less patient use of hospitalization.

Constructs Derived from Psychodynamic Theory Are Useful and Have Been Adopted into Other Orientations

It will probably come as no surprise to learn that ideas derived from psychodynamic theory have been incorporated into other modalities. After all, from a purely historical perspective, how could this *not* happen? Psychoanalysis preceded cognitive, humanistic, gestalt, and existential approaches to therapy by many years, and the founders of these systems were all initially trained as analysts (i.e., Aaron Beck, Albert Ellis, Carl Rogers, Fritz Perls, Ludwig Binswanger). Even if they disagreed with certain fundamental psychodynamic principles, they were intimately familiar with them.

Three constructs in particular have been so widely adopted that they are no longer even seen by most people as psychodynamic constructs, but instead as general *psychological* constructs. First, consider the therapeutic alliance. Emerging from the early work of Ralph Greenson (Greenson, 1967) and other analysts, this extremely intuitive construct is now viewed as a *sine qua non* of contemporary psychotherapy. It would be difficult to imagine an outcome trial being funded today if the alliance was not measured (for a review, see Muran & Barber, 2010). Second, the idea of unconscious processing (also known as automatic processing) is another widely accepted psychological construct that reaches far beyond clinical psychology (Bargh, Schwader, Hailey, Dyer, & Boothby, 2012). To be clear, the Freudian unconscious and its vicissitudes (Freud, 1964) differ from the nondynamic variants in important ways, but overlap nonetheless exists (see also Beck, 2011; Huprich, 2009). Finally, research on attachment theory has exploded since Bowlby's early work (Bowlby, 1969; Bowlby & King, 2004). Attachment has influenced many subdisciplines of psychology (e.g., developmental) as well as certain CBT approaches (Gilbert, 2014). More generally, though, it continues to yield empirical data with direct clinical applicability to psychotherapy in general (Cassidy & Shaver, 2016) and psychodynamic therapy in particular (Target, 2018).

Constructs Derived from Psychodynamic Theory *Continue* to Be Adopted into Other Approaches

Psychodynamic constructs continue to be used in other approaches.[18] I will only provide two brief examples, but I imagine that there are more. First, Franz Alexander's idea of a *corrective emotional experience* (CEE; Alexander & French, 1946) recently received an uptick in attention. His original definition of a CEE as the patient "reexperiencing the old, unsettled conflict but with a new ending" (p. 338; also see Chapter 7) could potentially happen in any relationship, including with a therapist. Interestingly, the new-found interest in CEEs can be found across orientations. As evidence for this, a series of conferences on this topic were held at Pennsylvania State University between 2007 and 2011. The meetings resulted in an edited book with chapters authored by representatives of each major theoretical orientation (Castonguay & Hill, 2012). Although there was disagreement on certain aspects of CEEs, no author questioned their importance. Given the strong negative reactions that Alexander's idea initially garnered from his psychoanalytic peers (i.e., Sharpless & Barber, 2012), this interorientation agreement was all the more striking. Section II of that same book (pp. 159–352) included seven empirical studies, and more have been conducted since publication (Friedlander et al., 2012; Mallinckrodt, Choi, & Daly, 2015). It is possible that, as research accrues, the CEE may become another clinically useful, yet transtheoretical construct.

Second, reflective functioning/mentalization also appears to be leaving the psychoanalytic "nest." Firmly rooted in attachment theory, mentalization has a long history in psychoanalytic thought (for a review, see Fonagy et al., 1998) and, as previously noted, has been assessed in numerous psychodynamic trials. Recently, Swedish researchers (Ekeblad, Falkenstrom, & Holmqvist, 2016) assessed pretherapy levels of reflective functioning/mentalization within the context of two *nondynamic* treatments for depression (i.e., CBT and interpersonal psychotherapy). They identified a moderating effect such that lower levels of reflective functioning predicted a worse outcome and poorer working alliance in both treatments. These results have practical implications. Namely, it may be important to differentiate between patients with lower and higher levels of mentalization to better determine their appropriateness for either of these two treatments. From my perspective, interesting and high-quality research like this can only help therapists improve their ability to help patients and also foster mutual influence among "competing" orientations (see also Barber & Sharpless, 2015).

A CASE FOR THEORETICAL PLURALISM

I hope to have made a reasonably compelling case for psychodynamic therapy to retain an important position among the ever-growing panoply of psychological treatments. While I am generally optimistic for the future, it would be naïve to say that it looks entirely rosy. There are some important challenges that the field will be forced to face sooner rather than later. Jacques Barber and I summarized three of these in a special issue of *Psychotherapy Research* (Barber & Sharpless, 2015). The first two affect psychotherapy as a whole.

First, and as previously mentioned, there has been an increased medicalization of the mental health field. Despite the clear benefits of psychotherapy, the use of psychopharmacology is rising. According to the National Center for Health Statistics (2016), 10.7% of the US population (all ages) between 2011 and 2014 used at least one antidepressant in a 30-day period, and 5.3% used at least one anxiolytic, sedative, or hypnotic (p. 295). From 1988 to 1994, these rates were only 1.8% and 2.8%, respectively. Needless to say, that is quite an increase.

Second, there has been a drastic reduction in the availability of funding for psychotherapy research. Though some European countries may be faring better than North America in terms of governmental support, there appears to be a nearly universal decline. Although these restraints will force researchers to come up with creative (and cheaper) ways to test novel hypotheses, they also limit the number of high-quality (i.e., expensive) randomized controlled trials that can be conducted. This would obviously curtail the field's ability to answer certain questions that are crucial to the public interest. So, in a nutshell, things could be better.

There is an even more uniquely troubling issue facing dynamic therapy, though. If existing trends continue there will be fewer and fewer opportunities for psychodynamic training. This is especially the case in academic psychology departments. As one example of this, the number of core faculty in North American clinical psychology programs who consider themselves to be psychodynamic has been steadily declining (Levy & Anderson, 2013). This trend does not appear to be present in counseling psychology programs (Sharpless, Tse, & Ajeto, 2014), but the reasons for this are unclear.

Postgraduate psychoanalytic training centers are also experiencing difficulties. As noted by Robert Pyles (first president of the Psychoanalytic Society of New England, East), "the evidence is clear. Our recruitment is dwindling. Our membership is declining. Our members are divided. And more than a third of our institutes are on a course to fail" (Pyles, 2014, p. 3). So, again, this does not exactly engender unbridled optimism.

Along with the general decrease in psychodynamic faculty, there has been an increased homogenization of individual clinical psychology PhD training programs. The number of North American programs espousing a 100% CBT orientation of faculty members is on the rise (i.e., approaching 13% as of 2012) whereas the number of psychodynamic programs doing the same was nearly nil (Sharpless et al., 2014). Though some may not view this as a problem, the potential consequences are easy to envision. Over time, fewer and fewer students—especially in PhD programs—will have significant exposure to psychodynamic theories, methods of inquiry, and therapies. As these students move on and become the next generation of researchers, professors, practitioners, and supervisors, the situation will become even grimmer. Interestingly, psychiatric residents might be in a better position than psychologists in terms or receiving diverse psychotherapy training. This is because, at present, the Accreditation Council for Graduate Medical Education and the American Board of Psychiatry and Neurology (2015) require residents to display competency in psychodynamic therapy, cognitive behavioral therapy, and supportive therapy. No such competency requirement is mandated by either the American or Canadian Psychological Associations.

In closing, given the enormously complex task of trying to alleviate psychological problems through a combination of only words and a human relationship, the potential winnowing of psychodynamic approaches from the psychotherapy field is problematic. All the main forms of psychotherapy (i.e., existential, humanistic, systems, CBT) are far more than just an assortment of techniques. They also provide unique perspectives—even unique *world views*—on the nature of human health and suffering. Therefore, given (a) the incomplete state of our psychological knowledge and (b) human beings' well-known tendencies toward fallibility, it seems prudent to support and encourage theoretical *pluralism* instead of theoretical hegemony (see also Barber & Sharpless, 2015; Koch, Finkelman, & Kessel, 1999; Leichsenring et al., 2018).[19] This should especially be the case if the theory in question is considered to be what Lakatos and Musgrave (1970) would term a "progressive" (i.e., productive) research program where novel predictions are made and additional explanations are forthcoming. I would argue that psychodynamic therapy, as currently practiced, meets these requirements.

NOTES

1. An earlier version of this chapter was presented at the Psychotherapy Training Program of the Karolinska Institute in Stockholm, Sweden (February 2016).
2. Interestingly, the case study methodology of Freud was similar in a number of ways to the psychological explorations of Soren Kierkegaard (e.g., Sharpless, 2013).

3. In the interest of full disclosure, I was trained in both psychodynamic therapy and CBT, have published in both areas (e.g., a CBT treatment manual; see Sharpless & Doghramji, 2015) and value both approaches.

4. Thus, as a treatment modality, it was not appropriate or realistic for many patients.

5. However, to be clear, the effective *use* of the CCRT requires a great deal of psychodynamic training.

6. The child therapy data cited by Lambert (2013) are even worse, with 14% to 24% deteriorating during therapy trials.

7. A number of these studies and their corresponding treatment approaches can be found in the appendix.

8. A meta-analysis is essentially a study of other research studies (e.g., psychotherapy trials for depression). Meta-analyses require a common metric/effect size (e.g., a Hedge's g) so that studies using different measures or procedures can be compared to one another.

9. In other words, the "dodo bird verdict" largely remains unaltered.

10. A new psychodynamic approach to treating generalized anxiety disorder was recently piloted and appears promising (Lilliengren et al., 2017).

11. There are some methodological dangers inherent to meta-analyses. For example, the heterogeneity of studies can make interpretation difficult, especially if there are significant differences in study quality across comparison groups. Unfortunately for the field, study quality has been inconsistent (i.e., lower than desirable) in both psychodynamic (Gerber et al., 2011) and CBT (Thoma et al., 2012) trials. However, study quality between the two approaches was not found to differ (Thoma et al., 2012).

12. It may be important to note that even longer-term psychodynamic therapies (e.g., 40 sessions) can be guided by manuals (e.g. Vinnars, Barber, Noren, Gallop, & Weinryb, 2005).

13. For a more extensive review of this literature, see Barber et al. (2013).

14. It may be important to note that insight and self-understanding have been operationalized differently over time and across measures. See Connolly Gibbons, Crits-Christoph, Barber, and Schamberger (2007) and Chapter 3 for reviews.

15. For an extensive review of object relations in psychodynamic therapy, see Greenberg and Mitchell (1983).

16. Interestingly, a number of defense mechanisms were identified by other 19th century continental philosophers such as Nietzsche and Kierkegaard.

17. This is a time-limited approach based on the work of Habib Davanloo.

18. To be fair, this influence has gone in both directions. The psychotherapy integration movement has been very generative (e.g., Stricker & Gold, 2005).

19. This line of argumentation was influenced by the philosopher of science Paul K. Feyerabend (Feyerabend, 2010).

3

Goals of Psychodynamic Therapy

In psychotherapy, as in life more generally, it is usually a good idea to know where you want to go and what you would like to happen. Goals are an important part of this, and patients come to therapy with many of their own. They may want to "feel better," "get over the past," or "understand" themselves. Some may want other people in their life to be more amenable to their needs and wishes (i.e., they want to change others). Part of the therapist's job is to "translate" the patient's ideas into *specific* psychodynamic goals. This sometimes requires education on the limits of psychotherapy (e.g., patients can change themselves but not necessarily other people). Once goals are identified and the therapist makes a case formulation, specific techniques can be deduced from the latter and used to reach the former. Therefore, identifying good goals is critically important.

Therapists should always try to be *realistic* with goals. It is best to strike a middle ground between those that are too easy or superficial (i.e., we underestimate our patients and enact what Michael Gerson termed "the soft bigotry of low expectations") and those that are not realistically attainable (i.e., we wildly overestimate our patients' capacities for change). If our goals are not located well between these two extremes, feelings of annoyance or disappointment for both patient and therapist will likely result. Relatedly, we should not be naïve in thinking that some goals could ever truly be reached (e.g., see Thomä & Kächele, 1992, p. 320).

Therapists also need to be flexible. Unlike some other human activities (e.g., traveling to a specific location, trying to fix a leaky faucet), therapeutic goals sometimes shift in the process of trying to reach them. Matters that seemed important in the beginning of treatment may recede over time as new concerns enter the spotlight. Therefore, we need to be open to the possibility that some (or all) goals may need to be modified.

Box 3.1.

GOALS OF PSYCHODYNAMIC THERAPY

- Increased ability to love and work
- Increased insight
- Character/personality change
- Acceptance of that which cannot be changed
- Better adaptation
- Symptom relief
- Increased sense of meaning and purpose
- Autonomy from the therapist

Relatedly, it may also be worth noting that goals in any form of therapy, psychodynamic therapy included, are often "fuzzier" than those found in medicine and certain other scientific disciplines. This is not necessarily a bad thing. As Aristotle (1984) noted over 2,300 years ago (and reiterated more recently by the eminent Sigmund Koch (Koch, 1999), it is unreasonable to expect the same degree of precision from wildly different fields. Each discipline has its own objects of inquiry and unique methodological requirements.

Some goals relevant to psychodynamic therapy can be found in Box 3.1. This list is not meant to be exhaustive but may provide a useful starting point. Options for assessing progress toward goals can be found at the ends of each of the following sections. In general, we should synthesize *all* of the available information that we collect (e.g., standardized measures, patient report, therapist observations, "objective" life changes) prior to deciding that a goal has been reached.

SPECIFIC PSYCHODYNAMIC THERAPY GOALS

An Increased Ability to Love and Work

Although insight and making the unconscious conscious (Freud, 1964) were the main goals discussed in the early days of psychoanalysis, Freud himself was supposed to have said that the best indicators of mental health were the capacities to *love* and *work* (*lieben und arbeiten*). I qualify this statement with "supposedly" because the phrase does not appear in any of the 24 volumes of the *Standard Edition of the Complete Psychological Works of Sigmund Freud*. It instead comes to us indirectly via Erik Erikson (Erikson, 1963). Regardless, these goals certainly have an intuitive appeal. They also have a characteristically Freudian flavor: (a) at first glance they appear to be simple but are, in actuality, anything but; (b) they seem to be imbued with clear evolutionary importance; and (c) they are not overly optimistic. "Happiness" in a traditional sense is not a foregone conclusion even if these goals are successfully reached.[1]

LOVE/RELATIONSHIPS

It is important to be clear with Freud's terms. What he seemed to have meant by romantic love was a reality-based interdependence where sexual and affectionate feelings were integrated (Sharpless, 2015). *Ambivalence* was meant to be accepted as well. In other words, Freud believed that strong feelings of love for the other person were inevitably accompanied by strong feelings of dislike or even hate. This may seem counterintuitive, and it is sometimes difficult for patients to grasp this concept, but a closer look at patient–partner interactions will make ambivalence more apparent (e.g., the way patients may bring up the things they "hate" about their beloved during fights). Neither the positive nor the negative feelings are inaccurate, of course, and dynamic therapists believe that both need to be acknowledged for romantic love to flourish. Healthy and satisfying *non*romantic relationships also indicate health. Many patients suffer from profound loneliness, destructive interpersonal patterns, and difficulties connecting with others. This is especially the case in patients who require one of the more supportive therapeutic approaches (see Chapters 5, 14, and 15). As such, forming healthy and nonexploitative friendships could be a very important therapy goal[2] and one that is directly facilitated through the therapeutic relationship. It is well-known that psychodynamic theories presuppose that patients' patterns in the "outside world" will repeat in session. These include maladaptive interpersonal problems as well as those that may be "healthier."

However, the therapeutic relationship can be a double-edged sword. Namely, some of our lonelier patients may find therapy to be so safe and satisfying that it essentially becomes a substitute for "real-world" relationships. This form of resistance to the therapy process can be quite subtle and may only be made apparent through meaningful jokes. For example, when I noted that a male patient had not described any attempts to connect with others for quite some time (a self-identified goal), he laughed and replied, "Oh, well, that's what I've got you for." We then discussed his recurrent pattern of only connecting with one person at a time. This repetition, which minimized the patient's anxiety, also left him in a precarious state such that loneliness was assured when that one special person left.

More generally, a patient's quality of *object relations* is important to note. Although poorer object relations are associated with higher levels of pretherapy symptomatology and can moderate outcome, improvements do tend to happen over the course of treatment. Further, these changes coincide with changes in symptomatology (Barber, Muran, McCarthy, & Keefe, 2013).

WORK

Work, much like love, is part of our identity and our humanness. It may overlap with the goals of meaning and purpose described in the following discussion. So, did Freud believe that people could not be healthy unless they complete a standard 35- to 40-hour work week? I doubt he was that concrete but instead wanted to note that work served many positive functions. Even if the work in question was an unpaid volunteer position—which can be a good goal for our sicker patients—it still allows for the possibility of accomplishment, advancement, a sense of purpose, and a structure/routine. In our healthier patients, jobs and the revenue they generate allow patients to be more independent and take care of the people they love. With a livable salary, they gain the ability to be more fully autonomous and make their own decisions without having to worry about limits imposed by outside agencies.[3] However, moderation is important. The other extreme of being a "workaholic" is not recommended either. A healthy ability to work presupposes the ability to tolerate *not* working and to engage in other aspects of life (Etchegoyen, 2012; Rickman, 1950).

ASSESSMENT

The assessment of a patient's capacities for love and work is usually based upon on-going therapist observations and information gathered at intake (e.g., relationship and employment histories). Therapists need to listen to patient narratives carefully, with empathy, and with a reasonable amount of psychodynamic suspicion (see Chapter 4). This is because many of the issues surrounding relationships and employment are complicated and delicate. For instance, deficits in either of these areas could be associated with powerful feelings of shame. Shame may not only impact a patient's willingness to disclose difficulties but may also make them reluctant to accept needed assistance (e.g., strong pride may make a patient unwilling to use government food stamps). It is also important for therapists to be mindful of any *secondary gain* that may interfere with therapy goals. Examples could include a reluctance to secure employment because of social dependency and/or fear of losing disability benefits (Yeomans, Clarkin, & Kernberg, 2015, pp. 131–133) or not seeking out new friendships for fear of causing jealousy in a current romantic relationship. Care should also be taken in deciding the "endpoints" for reaching the goals of love and work, as patients clearly vary in their capacities.

There are also some more objective means available to assess the nature and quality of patient relationships (see Table 3.1). All of them have some degree of psychometric validation and are good supplements to traditional interviewing.

Increased Insight

One of the shibboleths of classic psychoanalysis would be that *insight* is the primary treatment goal. In fact, Hoffer (1950) listed insight as his first criterion for deciding upon termination. Despite its level of importance, though, insight has not been discussed consistently in the literature (Connolly Gibbons, Crits-Christoph, Barber, & Schamberger, 2007). So what is it? I wish I could provide a precise and universally-acceptable definition, but if you think about it, insight has a vague and wispy, "I know it when I see it" quality that defies easy categorization. Even *how* it occurs is debatable. Is it an abrupt and sudden moment of clarity (Elliott et al., 1994) or something that develops more gradually over time (Jones, Parke, & Pulos, 1992)? More fundamentally, is it a process of making the unconscious conscious (Freud, 1964), connecting past experiences to present behaviors (Strachey, 1934), or even the natural consequence of processing a safe and shared

Table 3.1. SOME MEASURES USED TO ASSESS PSYCHODYNAMIC GOALS

Measures	Description	Source
RELATIONSHIP MEASURES		
Quality of Object Relations Scale	Semi-structured interview assessing lifetime relational patterns with five possible rating levels ranging from "primitive" to "mature"	Azim, Piper, Segal, Nixon, and Duncan (1991)
Inventory of Interpersonal Problems	Self-report measure assessing problems associated with each octant of the interpersonal circumplex (i.e., two orthogonal axes of power and affiliation)	Horowitz, Rosenberg, Baer, Ureno, and Villasenor (1988); Horowitz, Alden, Wiggins, and Pincus (2000)
Psychodynamic Functioning Scales	Broad, clinician-rated measure assessing family relations, friendships, romantic relationships, tolerance for affects, insight, and problem-solving/ adaptive capacity using separate zero-to-100 scales	Hoglend et al. (2000)
INSIGHT MEASURES		
Patient Insight Scale	Seven-item clinician-rated scale	Luborsky et al. (1980)
Self-Awareness Q Sort	Q-sort to assess convergence between patient and independent observer ratings of patient behaviors	Kelman and Parloff (1957)
Rutgers Psychotherapy Progress Scale	Clinician-rated measure of eight aspects of patient progress including insight. Ratings are based upon session material and scores range from zero to 4	Holland, Roberts, and Messer (1998)
PERSONALITY MEASURES		
Structured Clinical Interview for DSM-5 Personality Disorders	Semi-structured clinical interview assessing DSM-5 personality disorders	First, Williams, Benjamin, and Spitzer (2016)
International Personality Disorders Evaluation	Semi-structured clinical interview assessing 11 DSM-IV (or ICD 10) personality disorders	Loranger (1999)

Table 3.1. CONTINUED

Measures	Description	Source
Structural Interview	Semi-structured interview assessing overall levels of personality organization (i.e., neurotic, borderline, or psychotic) via defensive functioning, identity, and reality testing	Kernberg (1984)
SYMPTOM MEASURES		
Anxiety and Related Disorders Interview Schedule for DSM-5	Semi-structured diagnostic interview assessing disorders and individual symptoms on zero-to-8 severity scales. Though primarily focusing on anxiety disorder, other relevant conditions are also assessed.	Brown and Barlow (2014)
Structured Clinical Interview for DSM-5 Disorders	Semi-structured diagnostic interview assessing a broad range of disorders	First, Williams, Karg, and Spitzer (2014)
Outcome Questionnaire–45 (OQ-45)	A repeatable self-report measure consisting of 45 items yielding a total score (0–180) and three subscales rated on five-point scale	Lambert et al. (1996)
Treatment Outcome Package (TOP)	A repeatable self-report measure consisting of 58 items and 11 subscales rated on six-point scales	Krause and Seligman (2005)

Notes: DSM-5 = Diagnostic and Statistical Manual of Mental Disorders, 5th edition (American Psychiatric Association, 2013). DSM-IV = Diagnostic and Statistical Manual of Mental Disorders, 4th edition (American Psychiatric Association, 1994). ICD 10 = International Classification of Disease, 10th edition (World Health Organization, 1990).

relationship with the therapist (Hirsch, 1998)? Could it be all of the above? Karl Menninger (1958) described it quite broadly (and poetically) when he wrote:

> *For what is it that we . . . want of the patient? We want him to see himself. We want him to see that as a result of his being a human being who came into contact (long ago) with other human beings who were not perfect, and as a result of misunderstanding certain things and being misunderstood by certain people, he experienced pain and fright from which he tried to protect himself by devices which he still continues to use not from the present necessity, but from a kind of habit. We want him to see that he persists in the same unprofitable formulae of adaptation. We want him to see that he expects the wrong things from the right*

people and the right things from the wrong people. And, finally, we want him to see that he doesn't want to see it, that he wants to get well—in a way—but is afraid to; that he wants to change, but fights against it. (pp. 135–136)

What is particularly good about his description is the fact that it recognizes the patient's own contributions to their troubles (unconscious or not) while affirming the possibilities for real insight and change (Levy, 1990).

A useful and relatively straightforward definition of insight was proposed by the Rutgers' group (for a review, see Messer & McWilliams, 2007). They defined insight as "the development of new understanding on the part of the patient . . . which is related to the issues he or she is presenting in therapy" (p. 21). The group proposed several specific guideposts. For example, the recognition of patterns/connections and the ability to observe one's own internal processes are both indicative of insight. They also noted that the elimination of pathological beliefs was a positive consequence that accompanied insight gains.

The empirical research on insight was recently reviewed by Barber et al. (2013), and their synthesis provides us with a number us of clinically relevant implications. First, and as would be expected, insight/self-understanding does indeed increase over the course of psychodynamic treatment.[4] Second, gains in insight are associated with symptom reduction. Interestingly, though, pretherapy levels of insight do not appear to be associated with pretreatment symptom levels, and there is mixed evidence for whether low levels of pretherapy insight predict a poorer outcome. Therefore, less insightful patients may still benefit from treatment in much the same way that a physically weaker person may benefit from weight training. In general, though, much about insight remains unknown.

ASSESSMENT

Several assessment options and rating procedures for insight/self-understanding are available, but none are yet considered to be "gold standards." Three are listed in Table 3.1 (see also Connolly Gibbons et al., 2007).

Character/Personality Change

A goal of psychoanalysis and long-term psychodynamic therapy is the alteration of maladaptive personality patterns. This has also been described as "character change" or a large-scale modification of "psychic structure." In classical psychoanalytic parlance, psychic *structure* refers to an organization of experience with a slow rate of change (i.e., it is relatively stable; Rapaport, 1967, p. 701). Therapists infer the existence of psychic structures (e.g., the superego) from a patient's observable behaviors, especially those that seem to be repetitive and problematic (Rockland, 1989).

The form that character change takes can be highly variable. For patients suffering from personality disorders, reductions in psychopathology or, even better, a remission of the actual diagnosis would probably be the clearest evidence that this treatment goal has been reached (Bateman & Fonagy, 2008). Thinking in terms of overall personality *organization* (i.e., normal, neurotic, borderline, and psychotic; Kernberg, 1984; Yeomans et al., 2015) as opposed to more specific personality *disorders*, the goal might be movement toward a healthier level of organization (i.e., borderline to neurotic). Progress could also be indicated via the modification of stable characteristics associated with personality (e.g., move toward a secure attachment style; Levy et al., 2006).

Personality changes are often expected in brief dynamic therapies as well but are usually more limited. For instance, working through conflicts over separation in panic disorder (Busch, Milrod, Singer, & Aronson, 2012) or reducing narcissistic vulnerabilities in depression (Busch, Rudden, & Shapiro, 2016) are reasonable short-term treatment goals.

Fortunately for therapists, a number of good books have been written on personality traits and styles (McWilliams, 2011). These resources can inform treatment goals and are particularly helpful for beginning therapists. When using them, though, it is important not to lose sight of two of the primary strengths of psychodynamic therapy: flexibility and responsiveness to patient needs. If used correctly, psychodynamic principles help clinicians identify extremely subtle personality traits that may not fit neatly into existing categories.

In ending this section, it may be important to note that the line separating "personality traits" and "symptoms" is far from firm. For example, where does social anxiety disorder end and avoidant personality disorder begin (Eikenaes, Hummelen, Abrahamsen, Andrea, & Wilberg, 2013)? The answers to such questions await additional empirical developments.

ASSESSMENT

Many good options for assessing personality disorders are available (see Table 3.1). There is also an interview for personality structure (Kernberg, 1984), and several psychodynamic psychotherapy manuals detail the ways in which more limited forms of personality change can be assessed (Book, 1998; also see the appendix). Projective testing methods are also available (e.g., use of the Rorschach; Huprich, 2015).

Acceptance of That Which Cannot Be Changed

Another goal relates to some of the more disagreeable aspects of the human experience. Namely, we were all born into a world not of our choosing. For instance, none of us had a choice in deciding where or when we were born. It could just as easily have been 20th-century America as 4th-century Egypt. None of us also had any say in selecting the bodies we were given or the parents who bequeathed them to us. We could have been born healthy or sickly to present or absent parents. These and other seemingly arbitrary facts constitute the unshakable parts of our existence. They just *are*. The German philosopher Heidegger described this state of affairs as our "thrownness" (*geworfenheit*; Heidegger, 2010).

Many things in life are like this, and some do not make us happy. For instance, few people relish the thought that they will eventually die. It is similarly difficult to accept a major injury (e.g., amputation of a limb), unalterable life event (e.g., a sexual assault), or loss of a loved one (through death or a romantic breakup). Though these things might not feel good to face, they cannot be changed. Dynamic therapists believe that acknowledging and eventually *accepting* these things is a necessary part of a healthy human life (Gaston, 1995). This holds true for patients and therapists alike.

Clearly, such matters require both accepting and integrating these facts into oneself, as there are no real options for alteration. This has been noted in other orientations as well. Edna Foa and colleagues created a posttraumatic stress disorder analogy that I have always found helpful, but that could just as easily be applied to other losses and injuries. They noted that trauma was sort of like eating spoiled food. Until the bad meal is fully digested and incorporated, the nausea and stomachaches continue (Foa, Hembree, & Rothbaum, 2007, p. 82). In other words, there are negative consequences for avoiding reality, and acceptance may not be a pleasant process. Behavioral and psychodynamic therapies may differ in terms of when and how trauma is best addressed but would agree that traumas do indeed need to be faced and integrated (Sharpless & Barber, 2009a). So how can this goal of acceptance be reached?

Many relevant techniques will be described in Sections II and III, but it may be useful to provide a few brief comments here. First, the *therapist* must be willing to face unpleasant realities. Patients and therapists both have unhealthy capacities for denial (e.g., a therapist giving well-meaning, but unrealistic reassurance to a patient recently diagnosed with terminal cancer), and it will be even harder for patients to accept what their therapists cannot. Second, good timing and clinical judgment are needed to determine how and when the patient needs help in confronting that which they do not want to face (see Chapter 6). Third, hope should be furnished to the patient only if it is *realistic*. Finally, it is important for therapists (and patients) to identify ways that losses/weaknesses can be turned into gains/strengths. Questions such as "What can be learned from this?" or "What can the patient do to make better use of this fact?" should always be in the back of the therapist's mind. Historically, an ability to turn weakness to one's advantage has been associated with health.[5] Even if there are no "objective" benefits to be found—a grim picture, to be sure—patients may learn that they have greater capacities for coping than they realized. This is an important lesson to learn.[6]

ACCEPTANCE OF ONE'S "SHADOW"

A related aspect of acceptance is facing one's "dark side." All of us have one. Just as humans have the potential for great love, beauty, and creativity, they have equal capacities for petty hate, ugliness, and destruction. Freud and other analysts certainly discussed these ideas (Freud, 1961b; Kernberg, 1992; May, 1983) but not quite to the extent of Carl Jung did (Jung, 1969). Though I disagree with several of Jung's core concepts, I find his idea of the "shadow" to be clinically useful and compelling.

At the risk of gross oversimplification, Jung noted that we all have negative aspects of ourselves that are unconscious and not identified with, but are nonetheless real (Jung, 1969). These parts are often seen as "not me" and are usually rejected or ignored. They remain in operation, though, even if they are not accepted. Even worse, these undesirable traits are often *projected onto others* and, in effect, may distort reality. As Jung (1969) noted, "projections change the world into the replica of one's own unknown face" (p. 9). For example, imagine a selfish person who does not recognize this quality in herself but always seems to find (and criticize) it in others.

Jung believed that the shadow (i.e., "shadow aspect") could not truly be ignored but had to be faced and accepted as a real part of the self. If not, it continues to operate outside of awareness. To be clear, an honest confrontation with one's dark side is not easy, but Jung and others believed that it was worth the effort, as a lack of integration could be detrimental to relationships and a good life in general.

"Ego Strength" and Reality-Testing

The psychodynamic phrase for a person's capacity to acknowledge unpleasant realities without utilizing unhealthy defenses is "ego strength" (Bellak, Hurvich, & Gediman, 1973). It is one component of the broader and transtheoretical idea of "reality-testing." Both can certainly improve through treatment and may be the initial steps toward an acceptance of unpleasant facts.

Improving a patient's attunement to consensual reality could be an important general therapy goal (Rockland, 1989). This is especially the case when treating psychotic patients (see Chapters 14 and 15), but higher-functioning individuals may benefit as well. For instance, many patients have difficulties viewing themselves, their behaviors, or the world objectively.[7] Some may ascribe to paranoid beliefs or conspiracy theories that do not coincide with consensual reality (Brotherton & French, 2017). Others hold fast to unrealistic childhood fantasies that keep them from progressing in life. However, it is important to recognize that *any* person can experience temporary deficits in reality testing when the unexpected occurs (i.e., a momentary regression upon hearing bad news), but some people reliably demonstrate trait-like problems (e.g., a borderline patient who continually distorts the intentions of others).

Assessment

I am not aware of any measures designed to assess acceptance of that which cannot be changed. The presence of thought disorder can be assessed via numerous of means (e.g., the *Minnesota Multiphasic Personality Inventory-2*; Butcher et al., 2001). The *Ego Impairment Index* (EII, Perry, & Viglione, 1991) of the Rorschach taps into facets of a patient's ego strength.

General progress with psychotic individuals would be indicated through decreases in hallucinations and delusions, more sustained attention during sessions, and an ability to begin and maintain "appropriate" conversations. Regardless of the level of thought disturbance, there should also an increase in overall cognitive flexibility as indicated by more realistic appraisals of self, others, and real-world events.

Better Adaptation

For some problems, acceptance is not the most appropriate therapeutic goal. Instead of resignation or "overcoming," some problems require *adaptation*. Adaptation is the process of getting needs met and wishes fulfilled within the limitations imposed by the outside world. It can occur through modifying oneself to better fit the environment (i.e., an autoplastic change, possibly through therapy) or altering the environment to better fit oneself (i.e., an alloplastic change; Rado, 1969).

This goal of patient-driven adaptation has been part of psychoanalytic thought for a long time. Freud's writings are suffused with Darwinian influence, but Heinz Hartmann is probably the analytic theorist who emphasized adaptation the most (Hartmann, 1939). Hartmann, the father of ego psychology (with Anna Freud as mother), noted that we are all born with some innate capacities for adaptation but that others appeared later. When raised in what he termed an "average, expectable environment" (p. 24), people inevitably developed the tools they needed to navigate life's many demands. The environment for many of our patients was far from ideal, though, and as a result, certain development achievements were thwarted.

Indeed, many of our patients have profound difficulties getting by in their respective worlds; others may even not want to adapt to the demands placed upon them. The therapist's role in most cases is certainly not to be an agent of social control and decide for them (as that would be a deviation from the psychodynamic "stance" discussed in Chapter 4). Instead, it is our job to help patients understand the relevant psychodynamic factors involved and assist them in deciding whether they even want to adapt. Therapists can also help patients work through the potential ramifications of their decisions.

When thinking about adaptation, it is also important to recognize the fact that patients spend far more time in the outside world than in session. For example, if you meet with a patient for two hours every week, you are together only 1.2% of the time. It goes without saying that many important events transpire outside of the therapy hour. A great amount of detail is needed to adequately understand a patient's actual environment.

Assessment

Assessment of adaptation is generally unstructured and based upon patient report and therapist observation. Patients may note that aspects of their life feel more "seamless" or that they are more successful in their various life roles. They may also experience subjective feelings of success as well as less anxiety and alienation. For more impaired patients, adaptive functioning could be assessed in a more structured form by using the *Vineland Adaptive Behavioral Scales* (Sparo, Cichetti, & Saulnier, 2016).

Symptom Relief

Readers trained in nonpsychodynamic approaches may be surprised that symptom relief was not yet discussed. Though Freud certainly possessed medical model leanings, "symptoms" in the contemporary sense of the term were not emphasized in traditional psychoanalysis as much as they would come to be. Some dynamic therapists remain suspicious (or even dismissive) of current diagnostic trends. This is not a completely unreasonable position to take. For instance, since the third edition of the *Diagnostic and Statistical Manual of Mental Disorders* (DSM; American Psychiatric Association, 1980) was published in 1980, the main diagnostic compendium of the United States has *explicitly* claimed to be "atheoretical" (p. 7). Say what you will of this dubious contention,[8] but some dynamic practitioners view these symptom sets/codes as possessing little clinical relevance.

However, other theorists (Summers & Barber, 2010) argue that use of the DSM or the *International Classifications of Diseases* (ICD; World Health Organization, 2018) is an important and inescapable part of contemporary practice. Even though there are clear weaknesses in the current systems (e.g., lack of sharp boundaries between disorders), they provide several benefits. At the most practical level, if you want to get paid by insurance companies, it is fairly important to utilize accurate diagnostic billing codes. Similarly, if you want to practice independently in the United States, you have to know the DSM categories at least well enough to pass the professional licensure exam (Sharpless & Barber, 2009b).

Fiscal realities aside, there are at least three other important reasons to be a skilled DSM/ICD diagnostician. First, having a good sense of a patient's symptom topography will help flesh out the particular ways in which they are suffering. This is presumably why the assessment of symptomology is a necessary part of Kernberg's (1984) *Structural Interview,* a component of many case formulations (Gabbard, 2014; Summers & Barber, 2010), Axis-5 of the *Operationalized Psychodynamic Diagnosis* (OPD Task Force, 2008), and the S-Axis of the *Psychodynamic Diagnostic Manual-2* (Lingiardi & McWilliams, 2017).

Second, the use of traditional diagnosis facilitates communication with other professionals and may help keep psychodynamic therapy as "part of the mainstream" (Barber & Sharpless, 2015). Regrettably, some theorists continue to mischaracterize dynamic therapy as unscientific or isolationist. These misperceptions can be partially combatted through using our own methods while simultaneously adhering to the broader conventions of psychology and psychiatry (i.e., using DSM or ICD; randomized control trial study designs). Given the fact that almost the entirety of the empirical psychodynamic outcome literature followed these conventions (Leichsenring et al., 2013), proper utilization of therapy manuals presupposes accurate DSM or ICD diagnoses. Relatedly, accurate diagnosis may help *clinicians* more easily engage in joint empirical research (e.g., through practice–research networks; Borkovec, 2002; Castonguay,

Barkham, Lutz, & McAleavey, 2013) and help narrow the ever-widening schism between researchers and practitioners.

Finally, many of our patients think in terms of symptoms and may monitor their treatment progress accordingly. The Internet makes it incredibly easy to access formerly esoteric information (e.g., diagnostic criteria for posttraumatic stress disorder), and patients may present for treatment with their own symptom-based goals. From my perspective, this is not necessarily a bad thing, as they may be more amenable to regular symptom monitoring via questionnaires. Research on session-by-session assessment has shown numerous patient benefits (Lambert, Kahler, Harmon, Shimokawa, & Burlingame, 2011), and this typical cognitive-behavioral strategy is not antithetical to psychodynamic practice. Though some practitioners may fear that regular symptom assessment could interfere with dynamic processes or result in a corruption of the transference, it can also be viewed as an additional source of psychodynamic information. Not only are questionnaires an efficient means for assessing symptom severity without having to barrage patients with questions during every session, but they also serve as another avenue through which patient issues manifest. For example, some patients may disclose information on a self-report measure (e.g., symptom intensification, alliance problems) that they do not report during session, and this interesting pattern could be explored. Some patients use questionnaires to act out their feelings for the therapist (e.g., obstinately and angrily "withholding" material) or as a not-so-subtle form of resistance (i.e., "forgetting" to fill out the form). For some, filling out the measure could be a symptom manifestation in its own right (e.g., obsessively filling it out to such a degree that the purpose and meaning are lost). Any of these reactions serve as windows into the patient's typical conflicts.

ASSESSMENT

Table 3.1 lists some of the more widely used "global" diagnostic instruments as well as two brief, repeatable (i.e., usable session-per-session), and psychometrically valid questionnaires. Multiple resources are available for more specific symptom assessments (Barlow, 2014; also see other therapy manuals).

Increased Sense of Meaning and Purpose

Many patients come to therapy not to remove symptoms or improve relationships but because they feel lost. Something is missing. They may not even know what it is, but they have a troubling and ineffable sense of emptiness. It could be an absence of meaning or purpose or even just a vague and restless sense that they are wasting the limited time they have in life. These feelings are troubling, and many patients try to avoid them by seeking out the many sensations and distractions that contemporary life offers. We know that this can cause problems.

A lack of meaning and purpose can color all experiences and make life feel unbearable. Alternately, these same things, if present, can be powerful buffers. A sense of meaning can allow people to find their way through even terrible events (Frankl, 2006). As Nietzsche (2005) noted, "if you have your 'why?' in life, you can get along with almost any 'how?'" (p. 157).

Many of our patients lack this "why?" They may have lived their lives in such a way that they essentially ignored their needs or foreclosed on their own futures in favor of following the paths chosen for them by others. Alternately, some patients may have actually reached their goals (e.g., a successful career or a family) only to find that they remain unsatisfied. Others realize that their fears kept them so chained to comfortable safety that they missed out on important opportunities (i.e., they did not take enough chances in life). Now, they find themselves overwhelmed by anxious regrets and dread for the future.

Psychodynamic therapy has a lot to offer these patients. Although not often thought of as dealing with "existential issues," it is important to remember that psychoanalysis and existentialism arose from similar cultural contexts (May, 1983). Further, several dynamic suborientations have focused on these concerns to a greater or lesser degree (Binswanger, 1968, 1967; Kohut, 1977; Rank, Taft, & Rank, 1945).

Many "basic skills" and techniques of dynamic therapy can be helpful to patients struggling with these all-too-human issues. There is no manual that I am aware of, but in a very real sense every patient must write their own manual with the help of their therapist. This is facilitated by giving patients enough space (and enough silence) to explore matters they normally avoid (see Chapter 9), helping them alter their life narratives, and casting a light on the many ways that they may avoid important topics (e.g., noting and analyzing defenses). Therapists can also help patients become who they want to be—within reason, of course—through better articulating their nascent wishes, hopes, and values. When combined with a good therapeutic stance, these and other expressive techniques can facilitate the creation or discovery of meaning.

ASSESSMENT

The Meaning in Life Questionnaire (Steger, Frazier, Oishi, & Kaler, 2006) can be used to assess some of these existential concerns. In general, though, when patients make progress in this area they report less feelings of being "lost," less nihilism, less "stuckness," and often fewer symptoms. They report a subjective sense of wholeness and authenticity that feels novel (and hopefully good). Patients with purpose and meaning feel more passionately committed to their families, friends, careers, or even important ideas. They may report more "steadiness" in life.

To be clear, these loftier goals are not incompatible with short-term treatment. For instance, in *Supportive-Expressive Psychotherapy* (Book, 1998), therapists and patients focus on the patient's *core conflictual relationship theme* (CCRT; Luborsky, 1984). The CCRT is a repetitive interpersonal pattern consisting of a patient wish (W), the response of another (RO), and the response of the self (RS). Therapists help patients actualize their healthy, (i.e., nonregressive) Ws through understanding the RO as either a transference distortion or repetition compulsion (Book, 1998). Though not every patient will experience a profound shift in their sense of personal meaning, it is certainly a possibility.

Autonomy from the Therapist

Last, but certainly not least,[9] one of the most important things we can do for our patients is to make ourselves obsolete. Doing good clinical work inevitably entails the loss of a relationship for both parties. This is another inevitable reality that needs to be accepted. However, if you believe in object relations theory and, specifically, the idea that external objects (e.g., other people) can be internalized to become a permanent part of one's own character, then in a real sense you will always be with your patients and they will always be with you. There is a bit of empirical evidence that this may be case. Geller and Farber (1993) found that patients reported internalizing representations of their therapists. Some noted that they used their "internalized therapists" to continue their therapy long past termination. This is consistent with a more general psychodynamic goal to have patients develop increasingly greater capacities for self-analysis and self-reliance (Strupp & Binder, 1984; Thomä & Kächele, 1992).

Assessment

Readiness for termination is usually assessed via mutual agreement that goals have been reached. As termination can be experienced as a profound loss, it is important to take notice of patients for whom separation or dependence may be tender issues. A recrudescence of symptoms or acting out behaviors may occur after the subject of termination is broached. Any unhealthy attempts to maintain the relationship and/or deny therapeutic progress can be handled more skillfully if they are anticipated and discussed before they actually manifest.

NOTES

1. He wrote in an early work with Breuer that "much would be gained if we succeed in transforming your hysterical misery into common unhappiness. With a mental life that has been restored to health, you will be better armed against that unhappiness" (Breuer & Freud, 1955, p. 305). So, for Freud, everyday unhappiness is preferable to misery, but people may have a limited ability to move beyond that. Not all subsequent psychoanalysts have been so pessimistic.
2. For a psychodynamic therapy case in which nonromantic love (i.e., friendship) was a target of treatment, see the case of Fred described in Sharpless (2014).
3. In the United States at least, government assistance agencies often impose limits on how patients can utilize their benefits. Further, many of our intellectually disabled patients have a case worker or family member who oversees their day-to-day finances.
4. Part II details the "classic" techniques thought to increase patient insight.
5. One of Nietzsche's (1967) more memorable quotes is, "I assess the power of a will by how much resistance, pain, torture it endures and knows how to turn to its advantage. . . ." (p. 206)"

6. As Freud noted, "it is something, at any rate, to know that one is thrown upon one's own resources. One learns then to make a proper use of them. . . . And as for the great necessities of Fate, against which there is no help, they will learn to endure them with resignation" (1961a, p. 50).

7. In other words, some patients may need help developing an *observing* as opposed to an *experiencing* ego (i.e., the "good split" discussed in Chapter 8).

8. There are clearly a number of problems with this idea. In general, if you believe that you are being atheoretical, you are likely operating with a theory you are not aware of.

9. This list could obviously go on, as there are many more specific goals. For instance, increasing mentalization, changing maladaptive narratives, or increasing feelings of coherence in the self (Kohut, 2001) could be the main goals for certain patients.

4

The Psychodynamic "Stance"

Stance (noun) is defined as

1. the way in which someone stands, especially when deliberately adopted (as in baseball, golf, and other sports); a person's posture.
2. the attitude of a person or organization toward something; a standpoint.
3. a ledge or foothold on which a belay can be secured (climbing). (Oxford University Press, 2018)

What does it mean to be a psychodynamic therapist? Are psychodynamic therapists, by virtue of being *psychodynamic*, linked together in any real and meaningful way? Do they somehow differ from the practitioners in other modalities? These are all reasonable questions to ask, but answers become complicated fairly quickly (Barber, Muran, McCarthy, & Keefe, 2013; Blagys & Hilsenroth, 2000). Disagreements are also likely depending upon who is asked and which psychodynamic suborientation(s) they adhere to (e.g., self psychology vs. object relations).

One way of addressing a piece of this important puzzle is to articulate what has been variously termed the psychodynamic "stance" (Strupp & Binder, 1984; Summers & Barber, 2010), "attitude" (Fleischer & Lee, 2016; Lemma, Roth, & Pilling, 2008; Summers & Barber, 2010), "way of thinking" (Gabbard, 2014), and "sensibility" (McWilliams, 2004). I usually prefer speaking in terms of a *stance*, as it is one of those interesting words that, as shown in the previously listed definitions, conveys multiple relevant and overlapping meanings.

The psychodynamic stance is a collection of essential values. It contains the "shoulds," the "should nots," and the many taken-for-granted theoretical and philosophical assumptions about people and change processes that dynamic therapists hold dear. A stance supports our clinical practices and influences how we conduct therapy. We develop our stances (as there is clearly not only one "correct" psychodynamic stance) from the books we have read, the supervisors we have had, experiences with patients, and our own idiosyncratic assumptions. Interestingly, our stances are rarely articulated and are usually learned implicitly in the actual "doing" of psychotherapy. Stances also tend to develop over time. As such, beginning therapists often have trouble getting into the rhythm of psychodynamic therapy, especially when it differs from conventional social discourse (e.g., knowing why a psychodynamic therapist would *not* usually provide straightforward advice). This difficulty can become amplified if students were initially trained in approaches with radically different stances.

Trying to articulate a stance is not merely an intellectual exercise or matter of academic debate (though it may be both these things) but also serves at least two important clinical functions. First, when used in conjunction with good theory, stances help guide how, when, and why specific psychodynamic techniques are applied. Second, your stance can help with difficult clinical situations. After all, it is inevitable that therapists will, at least occasionally, find themselves "stuck" in session or blindsided by an unexpected patient communication. During these uncomfortable moments, it is often useful to revisit your stance. In much the same way that a climber looks for a solid ledge of rock to affix a rope to (belay), a good stance can provide therapists with support and a possibility for moving forward. In other words, we can always ask ourselves: "Is what I'm thinking about doing consistent with my stance?" At the very least, a good understanding of your stance should help you know what *not* to do.

Box 4.1 lists what I view as a solid (but somewhat "generic") psychodynamic stance. The individual components will be further explicated in the following discussion. These elements are not exhaustive but seem to cut across the many psychodynamic suborientations and also capture the "human" side of psychodynamic therapy that should not be overlooked. Other sustained discussions of stances can be found in McWilliams (2004) and Strupp and Binder (1984).

COMPONENTS OF THE PSYCHODYNAMIC STANCE

An "Examined Life" Is Important for Patients and Therapists Alike

I surmise that most people do not want to become psychotherapists for the money. There are usually other, more personal motivations that lead to this choice of profession. Psychodynamic therapy, like any other discipline, begins with curiosity. We all have intrinsic motivations to understand other people, our environment, and ourselves. People are fascinating, and attempting to understand how they became who they are—and how best to help them understand *themselves*—could easily occupy several lifetimes of study. To be clear, this curiosity isn't just voyeuristic and/or directed toward the therapist's personal

Box 4.1.

COMPONENTS OF THE PSYCHODYNAMIC STANCE

- An "examined life" is important for patients and therapists alike.
- Human complexity should be acknowledged and respected.
- People are rarely transparent to themselves.
- Personal freedom is gained through the recognition of determinism.
- Human health and happiness are hindered by conflicts and deficits.
- A unique relationship with a therapist can be both curative and informative.
- Therapy is about the patient, not the therapist.
- People have a right to live their lives as they see fit and not suffer indoctrination.
- It is important to acknowledge and recognize common human frailties.
- Psychopathology is always situated in a developmental context.
- Therapists should listen with suspicion.
- Therapists should listen carefully, but not just to words.
- Therapists should be patient and cautious when intervening.

---

titillation (after all, who does not like to know secrets?) but should be genuine and directed toward the complexity of the human condition in all its unadulterated beauty and ugliness.

Depth psychologists, whether psychodynamic or existential, are unanimous in believing that honest introspection (some might characterize it as "brutally honest") and confronting things that are difficult are both requirements for being a fully functioning human being. They believe, as did Socrates at his trial, that "the unexamined life is not worth living for men." (Plato, 1997a, p. 33; see also Lothane, 2002) or, to make this statement a bit more tempered, leading an unexamined life is not a very human way to live.

As discussed in Chapter 3, the acquisition of insight has long been held to be a primary mechanism of change. Collaborative introspection/examination with the therapist is the primary vehicle through which this change is affected. However, psychodynamic therapy is different from the practice of most other disciplines in at least one crucial way. Namely, good psychodynamic therapy presupposes that the experts/practitioners (i.e., therapists) look inward and interrogate *their own* subterranean motivations and experiences with the same level of intensity that they expect of their patients. It is no coincidence that (a) all psychoanalytic training institutes require their trainees to be analyzed and (b) many graduate programs strongly encourage psychotherapy. People uncomfortable with self-observation are unlikely to become good psychodynamic therapists. After all, it would seem a bit strange to ask another person to do something that you are unwilling to do yourself.[1]

Human Complexity Should Be Acknowledged and Respected

Humans are nothing if not confusingly complex, and psychodynamic theory not only respects (and expects) mental complexity but focuses on particular forms. Now, to be clear, no contemporary psychodynamic therapist I have ever met would doubt that people are shaped by biology/genetics, environmental contingencies, culture, time, and learning. Such a denial of our thrownness would be absurd (Heidegger, 2010). Psychodynamic therapists merely recognize additional layers of *mental* complexity that interact with these other factors. Complex mental forces not only help mold our personality but also shape life choices and, in effect, color all our experiences.

The most well-known form of psychodynamic complexity is the belief that *consciousness*, or what one is currently aware of (e.g., the sight of these words on the page or the feel of the chair you are sitting on), is just a surface. It is important, of course, but does not exhaust the full range of mental life. Much goes on below this outward façade. There is a long tradition, going back at least to Freud, of trichotomizing mental life into conscious, preconscious, and unconscious parts (Dewald, 1971; Freud, 1953c). *Preconscious* is the name given to the mental contents and processes that are not currently within conscious awareness, but could be (i.e., they are potentially graspable). For example, most of us are not currently thinking about our 6th grade teacher—in my case, Mr. Mattia—but we can locate this information with little effort. *Unconscious* mental processes are those that are neither currently in awareness nor easily graspable without a good bit of psychological energy. This effort may involve solitary introspection or the process of psychodynamic therapy.

Although this topographical model (Freud, 1953c) might sound strange to people when they first hear of it, it is actually fairly intuitive. If we did not have some sort of unconscious/nonconscious processing in operation, how could we handle complex tasks like driving a car or playing a musical instrument "on autopilot"? If every step was effortful and required conscious attention, daily life would be slow and inefficient. A good bit of empirical data supports the idea that much of the "real action" goes on beneath the surface.[2]

Psychodynamic theorists go further in assuming that there may be important and *meaningful* motivations for our unconscious processes, contents, and patterns. Freud did not "discover" the unconscious.[3] The genius of Freud and his followers consisted of (a) mapping out a language of the unconscious so that it could be potentially understood, (b) describing ways to access it, and (c) describing the techniques required to modify it (see Section II).

Along with the topographical theory, psychodynamic therapists presuppose the complexity of mental life in other ways. The eminent psychoanalyst Robert Wäelder (Wäelder, 2007; see also Sherwood, 1969) described two: overdetermination and the principle of multiple function. *Overdetermination* refers to the belief that every important mental event has many causes. Given that Wäelder was originally trained as a physicist, it is perhaps not surprising that he viewed mental life as causally determined in a multitude of ways. His closely related *principle of multiple function* posited that every attempt by a patient to solve one problem (e.g., a specific symptom, thought, or action) was, at the same time, an attempt to solve other problems. For instance, a man who physically attacks other people when his competence is challenged might do so for all of the following largely unconscious reasons (if not many more):

1. to resolve the uncomfortable power imbalance caused by a person making him feel "less than" (i.e., he does it to beat the other person down to a lower level);
2. by performing an action (i.e., an attack) instead of thinking or understanding what just occurred, he is able to avoid painful feelings that the charges of incompetence may actually be "true"; and
3. acting violently allows him to identify with a powerful, but physically abusive father.

Psychodynamic therapists tune in on these complexities as they explore their patients' lives. They also try not to focus undue attention on any one piece of the puzzle. What makes this particularly tricky is the fact that the many meanings are not always clear to either party.

People Are Rarely Transparent to Themselves

Though not very pleasing to our egos and pretensions toward self-awareness, Freud and other thinkers argued convincingly that we cannot easily know ourselves. Thus, psychodynamic theory is viewed as the most recent blow to our collective human ego. In 1883, the German physiologist Emil du Bois-Reymond noted how two earlier scientists helped rid us of our belief in what could be termed *human exceptionalism* (du Bois-Reymond, 1883). First, Copernicus showed us that the earth was not the center of the universe, but just one planet among many. Further, the sun does not revolve around us, but we around it. Next, Darwin told us that we were just one small part of the long, mindless, and purposeless chain of natural selection and evolution. We may be a bit smarter, have less hair, and operate with poorer senses, but we are animals just like any other. A quarter century later, Freud (1963) added *himself* to the pantheon of "disturbers" and noted that "human megalomania will have suffered its third and most wounding blow from the psychological research of the present time which seeks to prove to the ego that it is not even master in its own house, but must content itself with scanty information of what is going on unconsciously in its mind" (p. 285). Though it is far easier to see how Freud's discussions of sexual and aggressive drives would have appalled straight-laced Victorian mores, I would argue that his claim that we are not transparent to ourselves is a far more difficult pill to swallow.

It is hard to deny that we have an amazing capacity for self-deception, though it is always much easier to recognize this quality in others. We see this in novels and on television shows. For instance, some characters view themselves as better than they are, making rationalizations for the behaviors that they don't like. Others view themselves as worse than they are, self-imposing painful penances they do not objectively deserve and that they would never wish on others. Other people do things that they are neither aware of nor understand but feel compelled to do nonetheless. The variations are essentially endless.

You can even see this lack of awareness in the instinctual behavior of animals. As one small example, anyone who has spent time with dogs has probably noticed how they circle around several times before lying down. It is almost as if the bare floor or shag carpet was long grass that would be uncomfortable to sleep on. Although the ultimate function is unknown, it is seemingly a purposeless, repetitive behavior that the dog "just does" and is not aware of as being unneeded. Some dogs seem unable *not* to do it.[4]

Though in principle not impossible (see Freud's [1958b] discussion of self-analysis), it is much easier to understand a system if you are *outside* of the system. Therefore, it may be easier for an outsider (i.e., a therapist) to see maladaptive patterns in another person, especially if they know what to look for (e.g., discrepancies between the four channels of communication as discussed in Chapter 8). As Freud (1953b) famously wrote, "betrayal oozes out of . . . every pore" (p. 78), and this can be seen by an observant clinician. Having someone else recognize what we cannot easily see in ourselves and, in a sense, make meaningful order out of the confusing chaos of our internal world, is one of the potential benefits of psychodynamic therapy.

Personal Freedom Is Gained Through the Recognition of Determinism

When you look at any subject matter closely, you inevitably run into enormous philosophical problems. Psychodynamic theory is no exception. One that comes up quite a bit in psychology in general is the question of human freedom (Hergenhahn & Henley, 2014). At one extreme is the view that we are totally free agents with absolute responsibility for our actions (e.g., early works of Sartre; Sartre, 2003). In other words, the subjective sense that we are in control of our lives is accurate and true. Another viewpoint is that this feeling of freedom is illusory, that we are instead *fully* determined by the universe, our genetics, our environment, and other factors, and that we have no real ability to make autonomous choices (Hobbes, 1997; La Mettrie, 1912). Clearly, a book on psychodynamic techniques is not an appropriate place to try to answer this question (if it is even definitively answerable), but the question of freedom is a crucial part of the psychodynamic stance.

Although Freud's theories are often described as "deterministic" and "mechanistic," they do seem to imply a middle position between the two extremes (i.e., limited freedom). I would argue that freedom within a psychodynamic world view is certainly not absolute and far less than we imagine. It is instead hard won and only gained through recognizing and understanding all the ways that we are- for lack of a better term- *determined*. Once that recognition is achieved, a *possibility* for freedom emerges. When we are confronted with our negative patterns and are lucky enough to be aware of our patterns *as patterns*, we can choose to say no to our patterns. Thus, we may have the possibility to choose a different ending.

For instance, many people have repetitive relationship problems that essentially make them "unfree." We have all seen these repetitions in patients, friends, or (less likely) ourselves. Consider a person who essentially dates the same partner again and again. Though names and faces change, the same negative pattern is repeatedly lived out (Greenberg & Mitchell, 1983). It is almost as if the soon-to-be-unhappy person was handed a script on their first date and must now act out their fixed role to the inevitable, painful conclusion. Though unhappy, they sincerely do not know how to get "unstuck" or "how this keeps happening". Gabbard (2014) aptly described situations like these as "consciously confused and unconsciously controlled" (p. 12).

Although this situation may seem bleak, it can certainly change. With some effort, the stuck person may begin to notice that they act in ways that reliably lead to rejection from the people they supposedly most want to bring closer. They may even begin to recognize the pathological "pulls" they feel when meeting a potential partner for the first time or the ways in which they are tragically drawn to individuals that seem "strangely familiar" or "safe" in some uncanny way. With insight into the how, the when, and the why, our hypothetical patient could step outside of their system a bit and *observe* themselves as opposed to merely doing what "feels natural" by living out their maladaptive pattern. The hope is that, when they are presented with *another* relationship opportunity that would likely bring them pain, but are in a stronger and more reflective place, they will have the capacity to say "no" to the old pattern and seek out a different kind of experience. In other words, they would gain the possibility for freedom through recognizing the many ways that the pattern enslaves them. Therefore, in this regard, psychodynamic theory could be called an *emancipatory* psychology.

Human Health and Happiness Are Hindered by Conflicts and Deficits

Psychodynamic theorists believe that these negative and repetitive patterns are caused by conflicts and/or deficits. Some of these are an inevitable part of the human condition, but others can be avoided. As many clinical examples of both will be provided in Sections II and III, the two main models will only be briefly mentioned here. Conflict models (e.g., classical psychoanalysis and ego psychology) were developed first and posit that psychopathology arises from competing demands. At a macro level, Freud and others felt that our more primitive animal natures (including our sexual and aggressive drives) were in constant conflict with the demands of a civilized society. To participate in society (and not go to jail), we are all forced to renounce certain desires and delay certain gratification.[5] Freud saw life in a prohibitive society as necessarily leading to frustration, but this was much better than the alternative of living in a brutal, primitive state of nature (Freud, 1961b). Many contemporary dynamic therapists tend to minimize these larger, more evolutionarily driven, societal ideas of conflict and instead focus on smaller forms of intrapsychic and interpersonal conflict (e.g., conflicts between internalized representations of other important people and "society" on a smaller scale).

Deficit models are a more recent theoretical development. Heinz Kohut's self psychology (Kohut, 1971, 1977) is the most obvious example. Kohut emphasized developmental deficits in patients and focused on the curative role of the therapist. Mentalization-based treatment is a more recent model that focuses on remedying fundamental deficits through a specific type of therapist-patient interaction (Bateman & Fonagy, 2016).

A Unique Relationship with a Therapist Can Be Both Curative and Informative

As mentioned in Chapter 1, psychodynamic therapy—or any other face-to face psychotherapy for that matter—enacts changes through a combination of words and a relationship. All of the more distinct dynamic interventions are really just specific manifestations of these two basic tools.

The most distinctive ways that psychodynamic relationships can be curative are both indirect: through analysis of the patient's transference (see Chapter 13) and appropriate use of the therapist's countertransference (see Chapter 8). Two of the more direct[6] routes to change are via the therapeutic alliance and corrective emotional experiences (Barber et al., 2010; Sharpless & Barber, 2012; also see Chapters 7 and 16). Both can obviously occur in nondynamic modalities as well. More generally, though, psychodynamic therapists presuppose that patients are helped by fostering a *real, but unique,* type of human relationship.

It is indeed unique if you think about it. As one supervisor was fond of saying, "This is psychotherapy, not a tea party." It is a good line not only because it is funny, but because it is pregnant with meaning. Namely, psychodynamic therapy should not be limited to platitudes, social conventions, or "just being polite." If it were, it would greatly hamper the power and honesty of the experience. Consider normal social conventions. When patients ask advice from someone else, they usually receive it (and far more cheaply, too). This may not be the case in dynamic therapy where, as noted in Chapter 3, fostering patient autonomy and introspection are goals. Similarly, when a patient becomes visibly uncomfortable during a "normal" conversation, the other person may very well let the matter drop, change the subject, or reassure the patient that "everything will be OK." These would not be typical psychodynamic responses. It would oftentimes be more therapeutically sensible to gently encourage the patient to focus on these uncomfortable thoughts and feelings instead of avoiding them.

In session, patients should also feel free to say things that they would never feel comfortable sharing with friends or family. This includes all the "shameful bits" that are not often acknowledged, let alone faced. Just to give a few examples, I have worked with both men and women who reported rape fantasies (as both perpetrator and victim). I have worked with parents who disclosed that they wished they had never had kids and/or that they legitimately hated their children. I had one patient with severe obsessive-compulsive disorder who felt she was so "dirty" that she washed her genitals with scalding hot water and an abrasive rag. Granted, therapists might feel uncomfortable when confronted with these matters, but from a psychodynamic perspective, it is much better for a patient to *discuss* them rather than to act on them. Words are open to exploration in ways that actions are not, and they obviously carry different types of emotional, moral, and legal consequences. From a practical standpoint, where else can patients discuss these subjects? For all these reasons, there are very few (if any) topics that should be off limits in psychodynamic therapy.

Further, part of the psychodynamic stance involves being neither presumptuous nor prematurely shutting down a patient's dialogue or natural reactions. For instance, if a patient disclosed a loss (e.g., a death in the family) to "any other person" in their life, this disclosure would immediately be followed with an expression of sympathy. A dynamic therapist, on the other hand, would not immediately assume that the patient needed sympathy (or anything else, for that matter). Instead, the therapist would first gently and supportively ask how the event made the patient feel to gain a sense of the complex ways that they might be responding. This implicitly conveys the message that all types of reactions—even those that may not be societally "normal" (e.g., feelings of happiness that someone is dead)—are perfectly acceptable to discuss in session. A reverse situation could also occur where a patient disclosed an important gain (e.g., an unexpected promotion). "Any other person" would immediately congratulate the patient and, as a result, foreclose on the possibility that this might *not* be an unambiguously good event. In fact, it might be associated with deep feelings of dread or personal unworthiness. In both hypothetical examples, maintaining the *uniqueness* of the therapeutic relationship provides the patient with opportunities for self-exploration that may be absent from other interactions.

Another way that psychotherapy is "not a tea party" involves honesty. Other people in the patient's life might not be completely honest with them. Granted, they may have any number of valid reasons why they would withhold their "real" thoughts: they may fear the patient, they may *need* the patient (and desperately fear loss), or they may just not want to hurt the patient and/or spend time dealing with the patient's inevitable negative reactions. As a result, patients do not always get the benefit of honest feedback from others. Psychodynamic therapists may at times say things that the patient does not like, but may need to hear nonetheless.

As one example of this honestly, I can clearly recall working with a patient with a primary diagnosis of bipolar-I disorder (discussed further in Chapter 12). He was very reluctant to look at his actions and instead blamed his problems on "brain chemicals." His current romantic relationship was going downhill, as so many others had. He believed that women could not "handle" his sickness and instead took the "easy way out." After spending some time establishing that his assessment might not be quite accurate, I presented him with another hypothesis. By way of brief summary, I suggested that his overbearing behaviors—well-documented inside and outside of session—and not his psychiatric diagnosis could be driving his partners away and that these might be important to look at. Though he certainly did not like this perspective (and was quite upset with me for saying it), it was needed. This presented him with new insight and a possibility for change. To be clear, though, there is no room in any therapy for cruelty or intentionally trying to overwhelm the patient, even if this is done under the auspices of "being honest." Good timing is everything (see Chapter 6), and patients will not want to work through difficult matters if they do not feel valued or taken seriously.

Therapy Is about the Patient, not the Therapist

One aspect of the uniqueness of the therapeutic relationship merits its own section. Therapy, if it is to be maximally beneficial and psychodynamically appropriate, must be focused on the *patient* and not the therapist. Though this may appear to be an obvious and even unnecessary statement to make, it is not. As anyone who has done a good bit of clinical supervision knows, this patient-centered focus can easily fall prey to drift and move into unhelpful, antitherapeutic places. This is partly due to the unavoidably hierarchical nature of the relationship, but it is also due to the fact that everyone in the relationship is all too human.

Many patients, rightly or wrongly, perceive therapists to be experts in the human condition and "special people" who can cure them of their pain. If present, these beliefs can be quite provocative. Depending on the patient's personality structure, this may result in unhealthy dependency feelings, angry or reactive envy, or anything in between. Especially in cases where patients idealize their therapist, power differentials and patient (mis)perceptions may combine to provide clandestine opportunities for the therapist's own narcissistic gratifications. Several writers have noted the presence of unprocessed narcissistic needs in many therapists (Brightman, 1984; Jones, 1953; Miller, 1981), and the therapeutic setting provides ample opportunities for their expression.

Therapists are human and have natural human needs for connection and validation. These needs can manifest in session and become worse over time. For instance, narcissistically inclined therapists may *strongly* want patients to like them, admire them, and to be in awe of their therapeutic abilities. As a result, they may make "flashy" interpretations that seem intellectually impressive to the patient but lack substance and connection with affect. Others may boast about how busy they are in graduate school, how they are preparing for an important professional conference, or how in demand they are as a supervisor for their junior colleagues.

These tendencies can be even more subtle, though. Instead of noting the patient's idealization and/or analyzing it, the therapist may instead simply accept it and silently crave more. All these behaviors are completely ancillary to the psychodynamic task and only serve to increase the power of the therapist and decrease the autonomy of the patient. In some extreme cases, therapists can foster dependent relationships with long-term clinical consequences.

To be clear, it is not necessarily a bad thing to take a bit of joy and satisfaction for a job well done. However, this should be appropriate to the circumstance and secondary to the needs of the patient. Otherwise, the uniqueness of the therapeutic relationship is destroyed, and this is what the patient needs. After all, where else in the patient's life is attention focused almost exclusively on *them* for 50 minutes at a time? Where else do they have the freedom to look at themselves with the help of another without fear of judgment or retribution? In almost every other relationship they have, patients have to attend to the needs of others. This is a burden.[7]

Strupp and Binder (1984) aptly noted, "Therapy has been said to be a highly personal relationship within a highly impersonal framework" (p. 40). If a patient gets to know the therapist's personal history, values, political beliefs, and so on, they have now transformed the therapist into "just another person" in their life. As a result, the patient now has the unfortunate burden of worrying about the *therapist's* needs (see Chapter 9). They may begin to wonder if they should say what is on their mind (and potentially disagree with or offend the therapist), keep silent about something that is potentially important, or distort their true beliefs to maintain the relationship. In any case, the process of free association has been corrupted, and this resulted from the therapist failing to adhere to this fundamental tenet of the psychodynamic stance.

Just as an aside, when patients ask for personal information, I will usually frame it in terms of this "burden." After exploring a patient's reasons and fantasies for wanting to know personal information about me (and, possibly, determining what they are *really* curious about), I eventually explain how this knowledge will ultimately be limiting and potentially hinder their progress (see also Strupp & Binder, 1984). It is the therapist who is ultimately responsible for protecting the therapy and the unique relationship (Langs, 1973, 1974).

People Have a Right to Live Their Lives as They See Fit and Not Suffer Indoctrination

Power differentials in the therapeutic relationship can have other consequences. Some may be good. For instance, there is a robust literature showing that patients get better if they *believe* that they will get better (i.e., expectancy effects and placebo effects; Tsai, Ogrodniczuk, Sochting, & Mirmiran, 2014; Wampold & Imel, 2015). This is why it is not a bad idea for therapists to let their patients know if (a) psychodynamic therapy is a reasonable treatment choice for their problems and (b) if the therapist feels genuinely confident that they can be helped. If both these beliefs seem accurate, I will inform the patient toward the end of assessment.

However, just as most medicines can also be poisons, there are inherent dangers in power differentials. If therapists are haphazard with their speech, for example, they could inadvertently create a belief that the patient will get *worse* instead of better (i.e., a *nocebo* effect). If they are too leading and/or repetitive in their questions, they could create false memories (Brewin & Andrews, 2017). Although I am fairly certain that no nonpsychopathic therapist ever *intentionally* tried to create false memories, there are a number of cases in the literature that indicate this danger, especially in child therapy (Beck, 2015). In fact, a friend recently told me that her therapist repeatedly asked if she was sexually abused as a child even though she denied this several times. Had she been more suggestible and deferred to the perceived expertise/authority of the therapist, she might have had a very different experience in therapy—and one with potentially deleterious consequences.

It is even easier to indoctrinate patients to see the world as you do than it is to create false memories. We are never "blank slates" in session, and even if we do not directly express our values in words, they come out through silence, a troubled glance, a sigh, or other subtle ways. This is unavoidable (see Chapter 9). The idea of value-free psychotherapy is a chimera, but we should nevertheless aim to avoid indoctrination to the greatest extent possible. We should also try to ensure that the therapeutic focus is never on the therapist's approval or disapproval. This is much easier said than done, though, especially when patients come to us with problems that *we see* as easily solvable or that we feel passionately about. Freud recognized this danger almost a century ago when he noted, "The patient should be educated to liberate and fulfill his own nature, not to resemble ourselves" (Freud, 1955, p. 165).

Therapists, like everyone, have their own values and beliefs that they hold dear. They may feel that they know the "right" things to think or the "right" ways for people to live their lives. Even worse, some therapists may not be aware that these are personal values or beliefs, but instead feel completely certain that they are objectively "correct." Unfortunately, history is rife with examples of well-intentioned people who thought they knew best and, when other people did not listen to their ostensibly good ideas, decided in one way or another to take away the personal autonomy of others "for their own good." This has caused a great deal of damage over the years and is anathema to psychodynamic therapy proper.

In summary, therapists should not be agents of social control (though unfortunate examples of this exist; Chodoff, 2009) but should instead be thought of as agents of patient-driven adaptation. I would argue that, in most cases, psychodynamic therapists should work within the value systems of their patients. If a patient's value system is too discrepant from the therapist's for any potential overlap to occur, the patient should be referred to someone else. As will be seen in Chapters 14 and 15, there are clinical circumstances when suggestion, advice, and even putting limits on a patient's freedom are all clinically warranted, but these techniques should be used sparingly and only when necessary. Further, these interventions should be discussed with the patient afterwards.

Now, the astute reader may find it strange that I am arguing *against* indoctrination of values in a chapter purporting to describe the *essential* values needed to conduct good psychodynamic psychotherapy. This charge is accurate. At the risk of repetition, though, psychodynamic therapy (and every other therapy) is not value neutral, and I am not sure how therapy could be conducted if values were absent. Psychotherapy is value-laden from the moment assessment begins until the therapist and patient say their goodbyes. For example, the act of identifying a "disorder," a "symptom," or a "maladaptive pattern" is a value judgement. How could it be otherwise when you say something is "healthy" or "unhealthy"? Judgments like this might make therapists uncomfortable. The "work around" for any discomfort is the fact that the patient and therapist are usually in agreement about the patient's problems that they want to change. Even if patients are defensive about their problems (e.g., denying negative consequences from alcohol abuse), they inevitably provide information that these issues do indeed cause them harm (e.g., negative responses from others). It is not a therapist's job to "judge" a patient; it is a therapist's job to hold a mirror up to the patient so they can look at themselves more objectively and decide what they would like to do. However, if these attempts fail, and the patient remains resolute in not wanting to change, the therapist must be prepared to let the patient go. Even if it seems to us that the patient is making "a big mistake" and doing something pathological, it is every person's right to live their lives as they see fit.

It is Important to Acknowledge and Recognize Common Human Frailties

Given the right circumstances, we can all become ill. It is an interesting exercise to consider what events would need to transpire to make *you* ill. For instance, what would it take for you to become an agoraphobic? Under what circumstances would you display the traits of borderline personality disorder? What trauma(s) would have to befall you for you to manifest posttraumatic stress disorder? If we are honest with ourselves in following this line of questioning, we are far less different from our patients that we might otherwise believe.

Again, this is another way in which psychodynamic therapy does not present an overly cheery view of human life (see also Messer & Winokur, 1984). It is not a historical coincidence that European existentialism and psychoanalysis arose out of the same cultural context (May, 1983). It is also no coincidence that both disciplines believe that people are fragile and, to a large extent, at the mercy of forces that are beyond their immediate control. As noted in a previous work, "the dynamic sensibility could . . . be characterized by a profound recognition of the human psyche's fragility" (Boswell et al., 2011, p. 100). A positive consequence of facing our own fragility is that it should be easier to have *empathy* for our patients.

Empathy arises from an authentic immersion in the subjective world of another. It is not just an intellectual understanding, but also includes a palpable sense of knowing what something feels like for a particular person at a particular moment. Empathy is the sharing of a real emotional experience. It is also part of our many countertransference reactions.[8] To be clear, the shared emotionality of empathy is not pity. Pity is something quite different. Pity involves a power imbalance and taking a position of superiority over another. It imposes a distance between oneself and the sufferer instead of creating the feeling that "we are all in this together." Pity is not expressed among equals like empathy but is often used as a means of bolstering the position of one person over another.[9] Therefore, if you experience pity for your patient, you are no longer in empathic attunement but in a place of unhelpful superiority, and this will make them feel bad. As noted by the Danish philosopher Kierkegaard (1983), "the proud noble nature can bear everything, but one thing it cannot bear—it cannot bear sympathy [i.e., pity]. In it there is a humiliation that can be inflicted on a person only by a higher power, for he can never become the object of it by himself" (p. 104).

Another clinical component of this idea that "we're all in this together" is the fact that it is acceptable, and sometimes even clinically helpful, to acknowledge our mistakes and limitations to patients (Strupp & Binder, 1984). There is no expectation for perfection in therapy on the part of the patient or the therapist. Given the complexity of the work, both parties have to be tolerate the other's imperfections. Consider a patient with an overly harsh superego and unrealistically high expectations. How meaningful would it be to see their therapist make a mistake and *not* be overly harsh with themselves? As someone who is certainly no stranger to making mistakes in session, I can provide strong anecdotal evidence that this can be an effective clinical intervention in its own right (see Chapter 16). I have always taken comfort from a possibly apocryphal statement attributed to Donald Winnicott. When asked how he decides to intervene with patients, he reputedly said that he intervenes for two reasons: first, to show the patient that he is awake and, second, to show the patient that he can be *wrong*.

Psychopathology Is Always Situated within a Developmental Context

One of the most popular clichés about psychoanalysis found in film is that it exclusively focuses on understanding the past at the expense of the present (e.g., "So, tell me about your mother"). As with a number of stereotypes, this holds a grain of truth. Psychodynamic therapists assume that health and psychopathology should be situated within a broader developmental framework. More specifically, the best way to comprehend a symptom or behavior is to understand its origin, purpose, and development. This was originally called the "genetic approach," not because it bore any relation to the contemporary science of genetics, but because past events were seen as the *genesis*, or origin, of the current symptomatic context.

Humans are blessed and cursed with long memories, whether conscious or not. Therefore, all of the important loves, losses, and intense experiences of the past shaped our present. They will also shape our futures. As noted by Etchegoyen (2012), "we always face a new experience with the baggage of our old habits" (p. 103). On the upside, this means that our reactions to new people and new situations, even if they are terribly confusing, are not random. Instead, they have a "sense" or meaning that can be uncovered. This also implies that our problems are potentially solvable through psychodynamic therapy.

The downside of this developmental framework is that, as much as we would like to believe otherwise, we never come to a new situation or new relationship seeing it "as it really is." We only see these things (at least in some important ways) as we *expect* them to be. Our expectations do not even need to operate at the level of conscious awareness for them to exert a powerful pull. This is a reason why the phenomenon of transference is so important; it serves as a window into our patient's formative developmental experiences.

Freud often used archaeological imagery in his clinical writings (Freud, 1953a). A careless reader might be led to believe that it is the job of a dynamic therapist to "dig up" objective truths just like an archeologist would unearth ancient pottery shards. Therapy does not really work like that. Even if the patient was earnest and strived to be as truthful as possible, their memories would undoubtedly be colored by their *subjective experience* of historical events. If it were possible to go back in the past and watch the patient's early life events unfold in real time, the observer might be left with a very different impression than the one given by the patient. Where the patient saw an invasive and domineering parent, the objective observer may see one who was devoted and attentive. This is the difference between what has been called historical truth and narrative truth (Spence, 1982). We rarely get the former and almost exclusively deal with the latter. This is a thorny but unavoidable feature of clinical work. It is also a reason why it is wise to listen to clinical material with a suspicious ear.

Therapists Should Listen with Suspicion

As previously noted, psychodynamic therapists believe that nothing of *importance* in human life (e.g., a behavior, emotion, or thought) happens at random or is just a coincidence (Dewald, 1971; Freud, 1960). Humans are purposeful, even in their pathology. As succinctly noted by writer Emma Bull, "coincidence is the word we use when we can't see the levers and pulleys" (Bull, 1991, p. 22). Seeing these levers and pulleys is no easy task. Patients are usually just as puzzled by their behaviors as their therapists.

Helping a patient to resolve their puzzles requires a particular type of listening (see Chapter 8). Instead of taking patient communications and meanings at face value, dynamic therapists are *suspicious* of what they hear. They want to find the hidden meanings that lie under the surface of the communication (i.e., the *unconscious* meanings). There is not necessarily an assumption that the patient is lying, but there is also no assumption that the patient is even aware of a behavior, let alone in possession of a good understanding of the reasons behind it. Thus, psychodynamic therapists are members of what Paul Ricoeur (1970) termed the "school of suspicion" (p. 32). He noted, "Beginning with them [i.e., Marx, Nietzsche, and Freud] . . . to seek meaning is no longer to spell out the consciousness of meaning, but to decipher its expressions" (p. 33). Thus, conscious communications are not necessarily to be trusted, but can be deciphered and understood through careful listening (see also Lemma et al., 2008). Members of this school know how easily people can fool themselves; this is especially the case with matters that might not be personally flattering.[10]

The behavioral manifestation of psychodynamic suspicion involves a particular way of responding to patient communications. Take, for example, a patient who repeatedly arrives late to session and always has what appears to be a reasonable excuse. In normal, polite discourse, another person might accept these excuses, secretly think the patient is irresponsible, and leave it at that. Psychodynamic therapists are not as quick to "let things go." Instead, they may encourage the patient (with varying degrees of forcefulness; see Chapter 12) to explore the possibility that other reasons may be in operation that are not consciously acknowledged (e.g., that the patient is displeased with the therapist in some way).

We should also turn a suspicious eye on ourselves. Any time we do or say something unexpected, find ourselves treating one patient differently from others, or even just find ourselves bored in session, it is far more useful to try to understand the reasons for these changes than to just "let them go."

Therapists Should Listen Carefully but Not Just to Words

Though it is important to listen to patient communications with some degree of skepticism, it is even more important to not limit clinical attention to words. Words are only one form of communication, and they can easily be misunderstood. If you think about it, words are not even necessarily needed for fairly complex communications. Animals, even of different classes (e.g., mammals vs. birds), can convey information quite well nonverbally. Though two different animals may never have encountered each other in the wild (e.g., an artic polar bear having a chance encounter with an Australian emu), I surmise that they would pick up a great deal of information from each other. As therapists, we have access not only to (a) what the patient says, but we also have (b) what the patient does not say, (c) the patient's nonverbal behaviors, and (d) our own countertransference reactions. As these will be discussed at length in Chapter 8, I limit discussion here to *affect*, which is a subset of the information gained from channels c and d.

THE IMPORTANCE OF AFFECT

Another stereotype of psychoanalysts—and, presumably, psychodynamic therapists more generally—is that they are cold, distant, and emotionless. When the therapist speaks (which is stereotypically rare), their words have a rational and overly intellectualized "Moses from the mountaintop" quality that seems divorced from the patient's emotional life. This would be *bad* dynamic therapy, as good dynamic therapy takes affect seriously and uses it as a guide for formulations and interventions. As one example, consider *transference-focused psychotherapy*. Practitioners of this approach presuppose the importance of affect from the earliest beginnings of human life. From their perspective, the building blocks of personality are the representations of a self and an other linked by intense affects (Yeomans, Clarkin, & Kernberg, 2015). These object-relational dyads play a key role in development.

At the level of technique, affect serves as a main guidepost for clinical interventions. In dynamic training, having a supervisor tell a student to "follow the affect" is almost as clichéd as a director of the FBI telling agents to "follow the money." However, both are clichés for a reason.

Therapists Should Be Patient and Cautious When Intervening

By long forbearing is a prince persuaded, and a soft tongue breaketh the bone.
—Proverbs 25.15 (King James Version)

Finally, in ending this chapter it is important to note that therapists do not work well when they feel "rushed" to act or under pressure to "do something." To adhere to the stance, take in all the various pieces of patient information, and work effectively, therapists have to be thoughtful and have their wits about them. This can be difficult, especially with patients who demand change as quickly as possible or who may be forceful in their desire for help. However, the best way to help someone is to understand them. Most patients have already described their problems to other people, possibly to other health providers, and have also spent time trying to figure things out for themselves. Presumably these other efforts have been in vain, so it is somewhat unreasonable to assume that a therapist can have everything "figured out" in one session or that the patient's problem is a simple one. However, this strong desire for a quick cure can act like a contagion, with therapists feeling the need as intensely as patients.

Freud warned of this *furor sanandi*, or frenzy to heal, as early as 1915 (Freud, 1958a, p. 171). This warning may be especially salient for beginning therapists. When working with my first patients, I not only felt that I had little to offer them in terms of help, but I also thought that the nominal fee they were charged by the Penn State Psychological Clinic for my services was outrageously overpriced. Thus, I experienced this *furor sanandi* powerfully, and it took time before I became comfortable giving myself "breathing room" in session.

This *furor sanandi* may be part of the reason why many beginning therapists are attracted to formal assessments (e.g., the *Structured Clinical Interview for DSM-5 Disorders*; First, Williams, Karg, & Spitzer, 2016) and cognitive behavioral therapies (CBT). With regard to the former, it can feel very reassuring to have a massive list of questions in front of you and also a clear idea of when the interview is finished (i.e., when all the questions are answered). Regarding the latter, it is almost a CBT tradition to provide patients with at least one coping skill (e.g., diaphragmatic breathing or relaxation training) during the first therapy session (Borkovec & Sharpless, 2004). This results in the therapist having predefined tasks to accomplish and also gives the patient something to go home with. From my perspective, it is much harder to be in a room with someone when you have little sense of where the session will lead and little assurance that the patient will gain anything "concrete."

Regardless, there are at least three good reasons to be cautious about early interventions. First, the patient needs to be socialized into psychodynamic therapy (see Chapter 9); this is not accomplished by the therapist being extremely directive. Second, it is difficult, if not impossible, to effectively intervene without knowing the specifics of the problem. Dynamic therapists require a sophisticated understanding of the patient as well as knowing the reactions that they typically elicits from others. This information forms the foundation for therapy, and this cannot be reached with premature interventions. Third, cautiousness may help avoid unnecessary mistakes. Mistakes will obviously happen in every therapy, but making too many early on in the treatment can reduce patient confidence in the therapist and the therapy.[11] Strupp and Binder (1984) noted a helpful old proverb from Maine: "One can seldom listen his way into trouble" (p. 44). It is far easier to talk or *act* one's way into trouble.

NOTES

1. As will be discussed in Chapter 8, the effective application of psychodynamic techniques requires that therapists be appropriately attuned to their own reactions as well as the reactions of their patients within the jointly constructed interpersonal field.
2. Drew Westen's classic article (Westen, 1999) remains worth reading.
3. This idea can be found in earlier works by Nietzsche (1998), Schopenhauer (1969), and even Plato (1997b).
4. In my more pessimistic moments, I wonder how many similarly meaningless and unconscious behaviors I and other people may engage in on a regular basis.
5. In other words, we must pass "the marshmallow test" (see Mischel, Ebbesen, & Zeiss, 1972).
6. These can also be indirect as discussed in Barber, Khalsa, and Sharpless (2010).
7. This is also the reason why, in psychodynamic therapy, the patient reveals their innermost secrets without therapist reciprocity. This lack of reciprocity, though strange for the patient, is enacted for many good reasons and with specific values in mind (see Chapters 8 and 9).
8. As will be shown in subsequent chapters, empathic attunement is a precondition for the competent application of psychodynamic techniques.
9. Interestingly, theorists as radically different as Kant (2002, p. 150) and Nietzsche (1998) were unanimous in decrying pity.
10. It may be important to note that this process of listening with suspicion is difficult for many beginning therapists. A helpful way to work on this is to carefully watch videotaped therapy sessions with supervisors and have both parties articulate the reasons for their viewpoints.
11. Ways to repair alliance ruptures are described in Chapter 16.

The Supportive–Expressive Continuum

Be as expressive as you can be, and as supportive as you have to be.
—Robert Wallerstein (1989, p. 688)

Be as supportive as you can be so you can be as expressive as you will need to be.
—Paul Wachtel (2011, p. 214)

As noted in Chapter 2, psychodynamic therapy is a very flexible treatment approach.[1] It can be applied to patients who are high functioning (e.g., the "worried well," classic neurotic problems), low-functioning (e.g., treatment-refractory schizophrenia), and just about any level in between. Until relatively recently, though, far more attention and training efforts have been devoted to psychotherapy with higher-functioning patients. From my perspective, the shift toward greater breadth has been positive for the field, as current clinical and economic realities appear to favor those therapists who can effectively respond to an expanded range of clinical problems.

It only makes sense that certain techniques are required for certain clinical problems. A therapist may also need to use the exact same techniques with two different patients, but at different frequencies. So how are these specific techniques selected? Psychodynamic manuals are a good place to start for some of the more well-studied disorders (e.g., see the appendix), but an inevitable bit of interpatient variability will remain unaccounted for. Therefore, determining the most appropriate "mix" is not necessarily intuitive, especially for beginning therapists. It is often helpful to conceptualize your patients on a clinical *continuum*.[2]

Psychodynamic therapies and techniques are often described as occurring along a continuum ranging from *supportive* to *expressive* (Luborsky, 1984). In general, healthier patients require fewer supportive techniques than sicker ones.

It is therefore useful to determine where each patient should be situated along the continuum. A visual representation of this can be found in Figure 5.1. The listed percentages should not be taken too literally, though, as they have varied among theorists (e.g., Rockland, 1989) and are essentially arbitrary. They were primarily included to make the more important point that no therapy is exclusively one or the other (Wallerstein, 1989). The idea of a solely expressive or solely supportive therapy only exists as an abstract ideal and not as a clinical reality. Even in psychoanalysis, which is considered to be the epitome of expressive approaches, supportive elements are nonetheless present. After all, what could be more supportive than meeting with a concerned person who listens to you for three to six hours per week? That structure and human contact is intended to make the difficult expressive work more tolerable.

Further, regardless of a patient's location on the continuum, the basic therapeutic tasks (e.g., generating a good case formulation) and goals (e.g., increasing autonomy, better adaptation) remain essentially unchanged. This makes sense, as we all struggle with similar problems regardless of psychopathology levels (e.g., adapting to a complex environment, finding meaning in life). The ultimate "endpoints" of treatment may look very different, as an appropriate goal for a higher functioning patient (e.g., achieving symptom remission) may be unrealistic for someone who is lower functioning. Even so, the overlap remains considerable.

Despite the overlap, expressive work has historically been viewed as more interesting, challenging, or "sexy" than work with lower-functioning patients. Winston, Rosenthal, and Pinsker (2012) noted, "Supportive psychotherapy is not based on an appealing theory, and it does not offer solutions to intractable clinical problems; the field has no conferences, no stars, and relatively few books" (p. 11). Writing over two decades earlier, Rockland (1989) noted that training

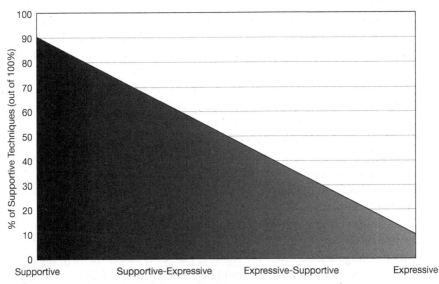

Figure 5.1 The Supportive-Expressive Continuum.

programs were similarly unbalanced in terms of prioritizing expressive work over supportive (pp. 284–285). As such, many students likely spent a good bit more time reading about expressive treatments that were less applicable to their actual caseloads (e.g., externships at community mental health centers or inpatient psychiatry units). An old, and not-too-funny joke I heard during graduate school summed up this situation well: psychotherapists spend most of their time learning to treat patients who are too sick to afford them after graduation. I fear this remains true today, but the situation appears to be improving. Regardless of trends, I have found supportive psychodynamic therapy to be at least as challenging as expressive therapy.[3]

Prior to discussing some ways to determine how supportive a therapy should be, it might be helpful to discuss supportive and expressive work more generally. Specific supportive interventions and their clinical applications will be discussed in Chapters 14 and 15 after the foundational and "classic" psychodynamic techniques are addressed in Chapters 8 through 13.

THE INTENTIONS OF SUPPORTIVE TECHNIQUES

What is meant to be supported by the supportive techniques? In other words, what are the *intentions* behind their use? One primary function is to make psychotherapy possible. Certain supportive techniques help the patient feel comfortable enough to engage the therapy process (e.g., Barber & Sharpless, 2010; Boswell et al., 2011). Opening oneself up to a stranger is no easy task, and therapists must foster a strong alliance with their patients as well as the holding environment described by Winnicott (1989). Many of the "common factors" found in all forms of face-to-face psychotherapy are relevant to this work as well (Crits-Christoph, Gibbons, & Mukherjee, 2013).

Supportive techniques are also intended (a) to maintain patients at their highest level of baseline functioning and (b) to improve their day-to-day internal (i.e., intrapsychic) and external lives whenever possible. The way I usually describe this goal to students is *homeostasis+*. The "homeostasis" piece refers to efforts to maintain a realistic status quo. More specifically, supportive techniques are intended to help patients deal with stressful life events without unhelpfully regressing or resorting to actions that are detrimental to themselves or their therapy. Psychodynamic techniques are helpful here, but extra therapeutic efforts may occasionally be needed (e.g., contacting a case manager, requesting an inpatient hospitalization). In general, though, therapists aim to maximize their patients' chances for remaining at a level of functioning that is appropriate to their actual, realistic capacities.

Instead of uncovering potentially sensitive or troubling material, supportive therapists may actively ignore or choose to "cover over" these topics. For instance, if the treatment goal for a lower-functioning patient is mood stability, the active avoidance of destabilizing material could be accomplished through encouraging the use of suppression (e.g., "I wonder if it might be helpful for us to focus on something else right now?"). Doors that may overwhelm a patient's capacities to cope should only rarely (and always cautiously) be peeked into, let alone fully opened. If they are opened at all, timing and dosage are critical considerations.

In general, the supportive therapies also tend to be active and more closely approximate a "normal" conversation. There is more "give and take" than is usually found in more purely expressive therapies (Winston et al., 2012). This is by design, as therapists want supportive sessions to be experienced as *less* anxiety-provoking for patients than would be the case in expressive work. Therapists never want their patients to be overwhelmed by sessions, but only appropriately challenged.

When patients are overwhelmed by unexpected life events, supportive therapists become even more technically active to help stave off unnecessary anxiety or suffering.[4] Supportive therapists may also use *themselves* in session to support the patient. For instance, when a patient's ego lacks the capacity to fulfill its needed functions (e.g., reality testing, judgment), therapists may temporarily bridge this gap through "lending" their own egos (see Chapters 14 and 15). This is far less common in expressive therapies with less compromised patients. In effect, supportive therapists hope that patients will more directly identify with their relatively healthier egos than would be the case in expressive work.

The "+" part of homeostasis+ refers to efforts to eliminate "real-world" conflicts and increase patient capacities to adapt to their environment. In contrast to expressive techniques, supportive interventions generally focus only on conscious and preconscious issues (Dewald, 1971). Being more "objective," it is easier for both parties to hone in on these issues as opposed to the unconscious issues which are far murkier.[5]

Supportive therapy may also include techniques more commonly associated with other orientations (e.g., cognitive-behavioral therapy) but which have always been a part of the psychodynamic tradition (e.g., "psychoeducation" or "reframing"). So long as they are not inconsistent with psychodynamic principles, goals, and case formulations, supportive therapy is very compatible with an *assimilative* integration of other orientations' techniques (e.g., Stricker, 2010). Thus, behavioral change, environmental manipulations, and symptom reduction are all potentially consistent with supportive work. A more thorough list of supportive therapy intentions can be found in Box 5.1.

THE INTENTIONS OF EXPRESSIVE TECHNIQUES

In contrast to supportive techniques, a primary goal of expressive techniques is to have patients gain a better understanding of *unconscious* patterns and conflicts. The expressive therapist aims to facilitate a deeper exploration of these matters and expand their patient's awareness and insight. This is epitomized by the use of interpretations (and, of course, the broader *process* of interpretation described in Chapter 13). These classic psychodynamic techniques link a patient's confusing symptoms, feelings, or behaviors to the unconscious materials that gives rise to them and, in effect, help these puzzling patterns make more sense. Expressive

---

Box 5.1.

SOME SPECIFIC INTENTIONS OF SUPPORTIVE TECHNIQUES

- Form and maintain a strong therapeutic alliance
- Shore up ego boundaries
- Help the patient adapt to stressors
- Help the patient cope with symptoms
- Help the patient cope with uncomfortable realities
- Help prevent symptomatic relapses
- Decrease or limit patient regression
- Cover over or ignore troubling or potentially overwhelming clinical material
- Encourage the use of adaptive defenses (even if they are not necessarily "higher level")
- Discourage use of primitive, unhelpful defenses
- Maintain the highest realistic level of functioning
- Symptom reduction
- Behavioral change
- Environmental change
- Encourage a healthy identification with the therapist
- Maintain and strengthen ego functions (e.g., reality testing, delay of gratification)

---

therapies often lead to new material and the remembrance of things long forgotten. As such, they are sometimes (and synonymously) termed "uncovering" or "exploratory" therapies (Rockland, 1989).

In contrast to supportive techniques, expressive ones often require a *controlled* patient regression. Patients more appropriate for supportive therapies are often too regressed already, but this is not the case with higher functioning patients. The latter require a limited, in-session regression to better uncover the "deeper" contents of their minds (i.e., unconscious fantasies and motivations). Healthier patients have a stronger ability to return to a nonregressed state at the end of sessions with minimal disruptions to their lives outside of therapy.

Expressive techniques also foster a higher level of independent development. As demonstrated more fully in Chapter 14, supportive therapies directly and indirectly foster more dependence upon the therapist than expressive work. Though this should be minimized to the greatest extent possible, it is essentially unavoidable in more purely supportive treatments. This is less of an ongoing concern in expressive therapies where advice, limit-setting, and other techniques are only used in exceptional circumstances.

The existential goals of psychodynamic therapy (see Chapter 3) may also be facilitated by expressive techniques. For instance, helping a patient to (a) find personal meaning, (b) lead a more fully authentic life, (c) gain more self-fulfillment, and (d) face other aspects of the human experience likely requires a combination of expressive and supportive techniques. Articulating patient values would be difficult without at least some exploratory work.

DETERMINING THE APPROPRIATE AMOUNT OF SUPPORTIVE TECHNIQUES

Determining the best location for your patient on the supportive–expressive continuum is critical. This is partially accomplished through good assessment and close observation. Needless to say, this is not always possible, nor does it always result in a clear conclusion. In questionable cases I recommend erroring on the side of being more expressive than less (for a different viewpoint, see Hellerstein, Pinsker, Rosenthal, & Klee, 1994). This is due primarily to my experience that transitioning to supportive approaches is far easier than transitioning to expressive work.[6]

Several psychodynamic theorists have proposed clinically useful indicators for a more supportive approach. These ideas are summarized in Box 5.2. Though not exhaustive, they will hopefully provide guidance for determining the approximate ratio of supportive to expressive techniques. After considering your patient in terms of the items on this list, it may be useful to first determine whether supportive or expressive techniques should predominate. Next, fine-tune the approximate percentages. All things being equal, the more Box 5.2 items that are relevant for your patient, the more you should prioritize support.

MAKING TRANSITIONS ON THE CONTINUUM

Prior to ending this chapter, mention should be made of patient *transitions*. Specifically, how do you thoughtfully alter your technical mix when you discover that a different ratio is warranted (e.g., you need to increase your use of expressive techniques). I imagine that most therapists have had to make these transitions, but they can be challenging. With the exception or Rockland's (1989, pp. 260–263) classic text, I have found relatively little guidance in the psychodynamic literature.

Transitioning to a More *Supportive* Approach

As previously mentioned, moving to a more supportive approach is usually the easier of the two transitions. Here, the therapist determines that expressive techniques should be deemphasized in favor of more supportive ones. This change is often prompted by unanticipated patient life events (e.g., a diagnosis of Huntington's disease, a sudden death in the family). The patient may be working very well one session and progressing at a fine pace only to abruptly

Box 5.2.

INDICATORS FOR A MORE SUPPORTIVE THERAPY

Indicator
- Failure to establish healthy object relations
- Excessive patient suspiciousness/paranoia
- Unwillingness or inability to accept the reality of their psychological illness
- Mandated, not voluntary referral to treatment
- Family pressure to obtain treatment
- Primary interest in symptom relief (i.e., a limited interest in self-exploration)
- Limited defenses (i.e., more rigid use of fewer, maladaptive defense mechanisms)
- Difficulties with secondary process thought (i.e., the patient needs to think more before speaking)
- Limited ego strength
- Limited impulse control
- Disruptive/chaotic/unstable environment
- Inability to regress and regain control
- Low tolerance for frustration
- Impairments in gross reality testing
- Difficulties sustaining a job
- Difficulties thinking in terms of metaphors or analogies
- Non-reflective responses to trial interpretations
- Patient is an otherwise healthy person experiencing an unexpected life crisis
- Low intelligence
- Multiple failures with expressive therapy
- Chronic substance use/abuse
- Problems in finances
- Problems of geography such that lengthy travel is required and sessions are infrequent
- Active suicidality/suicidal ideation
- Active homicidality/homicidal ideation
- Limited ability to mentalize
- Borderline or psychotic personality organizations
- Somatoform problems
- Overwhelming anxiety related to individuation or separation
- Inability to recognize others as separate from themselves
- Chronic illness

Sources: Dewald, 1971; Gabbard, 2014; Luborsky, 1984; Rockland, 1989; and Winston, Rosenthal, & Pinsker, 2012.

decline after the traumatic event. Some experiences are too disruptive for any person to realistically cope with, and it makes good clinical sense for therapists to respond.

The need for a more supportive approach might also arise from therapist errors in assessment. I clearly remember working with one patient who presented as far more "together" and "healthy" during our initial sessions than he actually was. It was only when I began to make tentative interpretations that the fragility of his ego manifested. Needless to say, I eliminated interpretations from my technical repertoire and quickly scaled up the percentage of supportive interventions.

Transitioning to a More *Expressive* Approach.

Transitions to a more expressive approach are often planned in advance by the therapist. For example, if a patient responds well to a supportive therapy and makes substantial gains (i.e., they indicate that they are open to different types of therapeutic experience), it is perfectly appropriate to increase the use of expressive techniques. This is to be expected as therapy progresses.

Therapist errors might also prompt this transition. For example, patients sometimes present for treatment looking sicker than they really are. Some may do this to more clearly convey their distress whereas others may appear dysregulated due to their ambivalence about treatment. In either case, therapists can easily confuse initial presentations for the status quo. This initial error is compounded if therapists *avoid* expressive techniques. In general, underestimating a patient's true capacity for expressive work only slows down the treatment.

Managing Transitions

Regardless of the direction of the transition (i.e., supportive to expressive or expressive to supportive), changes should not be implemented without discussion. Otherwise, patients become unnecessarily confused and may begin to doubt their own experiences or the therapy (e.g., "Why is my therapist behaving so differently toward me?"). As with most therapy process discussions, this is not a good time for jargon. Clear, experience-near descriptions are preferable.

For example, if a patient is diagnosed with terminal cancer, a more supportive approach would be indicated. The therapist might say,

> That is some very upsetting news, and I can see how deeply it's affecting you. I'm wondering if we might need to shift our focus a bit and try to help you cope with this news as best as you can. You may need me to be here for you in a different way than before. This change may feel different, or even strange at times. If it does, I hope you won't hesitate to let me know so that we can make sure we're on the same page.

For supportive to expressive transitions, a similar discussion would be indicated. If, for example, a patient has made headway in treatment, a therapist might say,

> I was thinking about our work together after last week's session and was really struck by the progress you've made. In earlier sessions, time was mostly spent 'putting out fires' and dealing with those problems you described as your 'chronically chaotic life.' Things feel different now, and I wonder if it might be time to shift our approach. What I propose is that we try to better understand the origins of those other problems, figure out a way to prevent their return, and also try to reach the other goals you've mentioned. In order to do this, you probably need more time to reflect on yourself. I'll be listening very closely and, as you know, I'm not a silent therapist, but I may need to step back a bit so you can look at yourself in new ways.

After explaining the new directions for free association, the therapist continued with,

> I understand that this might feel different than our previous work together, and if it does, I hope you will bring this to my attention so that we can get on the same page.

In closing, a patient's position on the supportive–expressive continuum is not fixed, and modifications—however small—are inevitable. These modifications become more urgent to the degree that patients are getting significantly better or worse. Regardless of the direction of transition, deciding upon a suitable and theoretically defensible mix of techniques for patients not only fosters better responsiveness but also helps determine how to most appropriately challenge your patients during session (i.e., not too much and not too little).

NOTES

1. This move away from a more rigid Freudian orthodoxy and exploration of new treatment avenues was made possible by, among others, Sandor Ferenczi, Otto Rank, and Franz Alexander.
2. A patient's general location on the supportive–expressive continuum, their level of personality organization, and their symptom topography provides a great deal of guidance for choosing techniques.
3. Rockland (1989) contends that the increased level of therapeutic activity makes supportive work *harder* to do.
4. This is part of the challenge of supportive therapy. There are far more chances for therapists to make mistakes.

5. Of course, the therapist should use their hypotheses about the patient's unconscious conflicts and issues to better formulate the case and select appropriate supportive interventions.

6. More systematic empirical data on this point would be helpful, but I am not aware of any.

Characteristics of "Good" Psychodynamic Interventions

*If there is a cardinal law of psychoanalysis, it is to avoid talking nonsense . . .
don't throw out words that have meaning only to the analyst.*
— JACQUES LACAN (1976, p. 34)[1]

An old proverb states, "It's not what you say, but how you say it." In psychodynamic therapy, though, both need to be pretty good. Notice I did not say "perfect," as there is no such thing as the perfect execution of any technique. Certain skills (e.g., phrasing, timing) never stop developing so long as they are continually practiced.

Unfortunately for clinical trainees, there is nothing like a "rule book" that clearly and precisely explains how to make good psychodynamic interventions and when to make them. If there was, it would have certainly made my own graduate training a lot easier. However, this is probably not a reasonable wish given the heterogeneity of patients, the heterogeneity of therapists, and the importance of situational context. Even if this hypothetical rulebook existed, competent therapy sometimes requires knowing when to break the rules.[2]

Therefore, and in lieu of clear guidelines, it might be helpful to summarize some characteristics of "good" interventions that have been discussed in manuals and the broader psychodynamic literatures. Box 6.1 lists eleven of these. Some are intuitive, but others may require a bit of elaboration. Suggestions for crafting *specific* psychodynamic techniques will be reserved for Sections II and III of this book.

LOGICALLY DERIVED FROM A CASE FORMULATION

Psychodynamic formulations[3] are just like any useful theory. They not only tell us what to pay attention to and what might be of lesser clinical importance but also

Box 6.1.

Characteristics of "Good" Psychodynamic Interventions

- Logically derived from a case formulation
- Data-based
- "Risky"
- Tentative (in most cases)
- Concise
- Precise
- Well-timed
- Parsimonious
- Experience-near
- Respectful
- Instantiate the psychodynamic process

help us organize confusing material (i.e., patient communications) into coherent wholes. Most have a hierarchical structure as well such that one main problem is emphasized (e.g., depression), but others (e.g., an eating disorder) are still noted. Without a solid formulation, it is difficult to make any intervention at all, let alone a good one.[4]

Formulations encourage us to be more thoughtful about our techniques and to operate with a long-term time horizon. If we keep our formulations in mind as we listen to patients, we are more likely to maintain focus on our primary clinical goals. This helps to keep us from becoming sidetracked by a patient's "problem of the day" and to instead have sessions build upon one another. When this happens, the clinical power of any one intervention—which is usually quite limited—is augmented by additional interventions until clinical change begins to trickle down to the day-to-day life of the patient. This is often called the process of "working through" (Dewald, 1971).

For example, imagine a therapist whose case formulation focused on dependent personality disorder. The therapist might initially *confront* the patient (see Chapter 12) on dependent behaviors manifested in the transference or in a current romantic relationship. This would be followed by the identification of similar patterns in other relationships, possibly involving earlier developmental epochs. Finally, the therapist helps the patient understand both the origins and functions (e.g., interpersonal and intrapsychic) of their dependency, and the patient gains freedom from the pattern. This entire process of change began with one technique, logically derived from the psychodynamic formulation, which was worked through until the patient improved.

Along with making intuitive sense, there is replicated empirical support for the importance of psychodynamic formulations. Specifically, a number of studies have noted that *accurate* psychodynamic interpretations (i.e., those that correspond to the patients' case formulations) are associated with better patient outcomes and stronger therapeutic alliances (e.g., Andrusyna, Luborsky, Pham, & Tang, 2006; Crits-Christoph, Cooper, & Luborsky, 1988). Several of these studies used patients' *core conflictual relationship themes* (CCRTs), as the basis for the interpretative work (Book, 1998; also see Chapters 3 and 13). With shorter-term psychodynamic therapies (e.g., 16–24 sessions), using a CCRT or similar focus is critical.

DATA-BASED

Good techniques are also based upon good clinical *data*.[5] These data could be anything that the therapist knows that could be clearly communicated *to the patient*. That last part of the sentence is key, though, as it is incredibly easy to confuse patients if techniques miss the mark. Whenever this happens, the therapist's ability to articulate their reasoning may help salvage an intervention even if it was worded poorly. The therapist might reply, "I'm sorry if what I said was confusing. I actually said X because of Y and Z." For this reason, it is safer to base interventions on clinical data than "clinical intuition." Whereas intuition may be useful at times, it is far harder to explain to patients. To quote the late Christopher Hitchens, "What can be asserted without evidence can also be dismissed without evidence" (Hitchens, 2003). It is far better to provide the patient with some evidence.

Clinical data essentially "make the case" for techniques. As such, the ways in which we combine these data are important. As Freud (1964) noted, "[anyone] who does nothing but present the patient with false combinations will neither create a very good impression on him nor carry the treatment very far" (p. 261). Therefore, we should try our best to combine clinical data in a reasonable and logical fashion. However, if we fail and end up saying something inaccurate, patients tend to be fairly forgiving. This is especially the case if they can understand our thinking.

"RISKY"

It goes without saying that any interventions based upon incomplete clinical data are "risky" for therapists to make. However, certain psychodynamic interventions are riskier than others. For instance, confrontations (Chapter 12), interpretations (Chapter 13), upward explanations (Chapter 15), and advice (Chapter 15) all make claims that are, at least in principle, right or wrong (or better or worse).[6] I do not necessarily view this as a bad thing, as good psychodynamic interventions, just like good scientific hypotheses, should be open to external criticism and correction (Popper, 2002).[7] Corrections help move the therapy forward or, at the very least, away from an error. If we do not formulate interventions in this open manner, we run the risk of behaving dogmatically. We could even fall prey to what an early critic of psychoanalysis termed the "famous principle of, 'Head's I win, tails you lose'" (Freud, 1964, p. 257). Namely, if a psychodynamic interpretation is made and the patient accepts it, the therapist is "correct"; if the patient does not accept it, they are "resisting" the truth of the interpretation, and the therapist still remains "correct." This is obviously not an intellectually honest way to do psycho-dynamic therapy.

TENTATIVE (IN MOST CASES)

Given all the previous discussion, I agree with theorists such as Lemma, Roth, and Pilling (2008) who argue that a tentative manner of intervening is prefer-able to one that is more overtly confident.[8] There may be a time and place for forcefulness (see Chapter 12), but if we lack certainty in our interventions, it is safer to present them from a "one down" position. So, instead of saying, "X is the case," the therapist could say, "I wonder if X is the case" or "Could it be that X is the case?" Such phrasings are particularly helpful with unassertive patients who may feel uncomfortable disagreeing with "authority figures," as they explicitly indicate that the therapist could be wrong and implicitly convey an openness to correction.

However, the other extreme of being overly timid with interventions is not good either. After all, if you have no confidence in your intervention, why are you sharing it? Heller (1985) noted,

> Ideally a therapist tries to communicate an air of conviction along with a sense of openness to the client's response and to reasonable doubt. He or she might speak in a clear, firm, and non-trembling voice and evidence comfort in speaking. The therapist conveys knowledge and expertise with forthrightness, but not with the quivering unwillingness of a tentative manner (pp. 133–134).

Therefore, the tonal "sweet spot" falls somewhere between timidity and overconfidence.

CONCISE

Although psychodynamic therapists disagree on a great number of things (Greenberg & Mitchell, 1983), the importance of being concise in interventions is not one of them. In fact, I have yet to meet a dynamic therapist who argued that more words are better than less. I am also unaware of people who epitomized this "less is more" attitude better than the ancient Spartans of Laconia. They were mas-ters of saying a lot with a little. For instance, after Philip II of Macedon invaded southern Greece, he set his sights on Sparta. He wrote them a letter asking if he should come as a friend or as an enemy. The Spartans replied, "Neither" (Plutarch, 1931, p. 403). Perhaps not surprisingly, this one-word response made Philip a bit upset, and he wrote back to say that, if he were to invade Laconia, bad things would happen to them. They simply wrote back, "If" (Plutarch, 1939, p. 510). Given that Freud loved all things that were ancient and Greek, it seems possible that the "Laconic" speech of the Spartans served as a bit of technical inspiration for psychoanalysis.

Even though we are not Spartans, there are good clinical reasons to keep statements short and to the point. First, patients can only absorb so much information. Complex or multicomponent sentences only lead to confusion about what to answer and in what particular order (Luborsky, 1984). A patient's energy is better directed at understanding themselves rather than decoding overly complicated therapist messages. Relatedly, the less a therapist talks, the more time that the patient has to introspect. This is critically important, especially in the expressive psychotherapies. Finally, the act of distilling an intervention down to its simple "essence" is beneficial for *therapists* as well. Crafting an intervention is a cognitively demanding skill that, like any other, becomes easier with repetition (Levy, 1990). The constant practice of formulating our thoughts, justifying assumptions, and determining how best to intervene with a particular patient at a particular moment in time can only make us better clinicians.

PRECISE

Along with concision, psychodynamic therapists also value technical *precision* (Clarkin, Yeomans, & Kernberg, 2006). On the surface, these might seem to be competing values, as increased precision usually leads to longer and *less* concise statements. For example, imagine that a patient with a pattern of tardiness showed up late. The therapist could maximize precision by stating, "I can't help but notice that you were 20 minutes late for our last session and are now 15 minutes late to this one. As this pattern seems to be repeating again, it might be important for us to understand what's going on." Alternately, the therapist could merely say, "So you are late again," thereby maximizing concision. Neither approach is wrong per se, but one may be more clinically appropriate than the other depending upon circumstance.

As a general rule, the precision of an intervention should be dictated by the specific needs of the patient. When crafting the wording you might ask yourself the following question: what does the patient need to know right now for them to fully understand and be helped by this intervention? Anything beyond that level of precision is superfluous and will likely only lead the patient astray. Many therapists have also noted that technical jargon just confuses patients (Strupp & Binder, 1984, p. 167). That kind of precision is more appropriate for conferences and scientific writing than psychotherapy sessions.

Some examples may help. For instance, an intervention related to a "sensitive" topic may require greater therapist precision and more explanation than would be necessary for a "superficial" intervention. This is because the former may require the linkage of several different events to "make the case" (Langs, 1973, 1974). Further, general and abstract statements (e.g., "Losses are hard for you") are usually associated with far less affect than more precise, detail-oriented ones (e.g., "The loss of your father to cancer last year seems to have led to a lot of problems between you and your partner"). Therefore, supportive therapies may emphasize the former while expressive therapies tend to emphasize the latter.[9] Finally, if the alliance is weak, or if the patient is generally suspicious, erroring on the side of more precision is preferred. This leaves less room for patient projection and/or misunderstanding.

WELL-TIMED

Psychodynamic therapists are also unified on the importance of *timing*. Good techniques require good timing and a knowledge of *context*. In this regard, interventions are very similar to jokes. The exact same joke with the exact same wording could either work amazingly well or fall flat depending upon these two interrelated factors.

There are unfortunately no rules for good timing, but some useful advice may still be found. Patience is something that Strupp and Binder (1984) strongly recommended. However, they noted that this virtue is usually in short supply for beginning therapists due to internal pressures to help their patients get better as quickly as possible (i.e., the *furur sanandi* discussed in Chapter 4). This impatience, though certainly understandable, may lead novice therapists to use interventions as soon as they think of them (e.g., blurting out a statement related to the patient's family when they are discussing an unrelated school matter) rather than waiting for a more auspicious time. Poor timing might turn an otherwise powerful intervention into a distracting *non sequitur* with minimal clinical impact.

Session time limits are also important to consider (Yeomans, Clarkin, & Kernberg, 2015). The 50-minute hour is good for scheduling but may occasionally be inadequate. For instance, even if you have a well-formulated intervention that fits the current therapy context, there may simply not be enough time to make good clinical use of it. In these cases, it might be best to save the intervention for a future session. Otherwise, you run a real risk of inadvertently forcing your patient to face these matters alone and without the support of therapy. Patients need time to process their feelings, especially when facing sensitive topics that they normally avoid (e.g., trauma, guilt, shame). It does them a disservice if adequate session time is not provided.[10]

PARSIMONIOUS

Another issue related to the timing of interventions deserves special attention. Menninger (1958) noted that psychodynamic techniques are most effective when carried out according to "the principle of parsimony" (p. 133). In everyday English, parsimony has the negative connotation of being stingy with money, but it possesses a different meaning in psychotherapy. Here it refers to being, at least in a sense, stingy with the amount of assistance that you give patients with your interventions. For Menninger, you are parsimonious if you give "the least necessary quantity of help" (p. 133). Though this may sound strange—Why not give patients all the help that you can?—it is done in the patient's best interests, and actually makes a good bit of clinical sense (Luborsky, 1984, pp. 135–136).

Parsimonious therapists do not just give their patients "the answer" but also help them find it for themselves. If the patient cannot find it, or becomes stuck along the way, the therapist steps in to finish the thought or "connect the dots." Therefore, they only show the patient what they *could* see if they were but a single step ahead. Therapists should never be too far ahead. Freud (1958b) noted with a bit of humor,

> It is not difficult for a skilled analyst to read the patient's secret wishes plainly between the lines of his complaints and the story of his illness; but what a measure of self-complacency and thoughtlessness must be possessed by anyone who can, on the shortest acquaintance, inform a stranger who is entirely ignorant of all the tenets of analysis that he is attached to his mother by incestuous ties, that he harbours wishes for the death of the wife whom he appears to love, that he conceals within himself the intention of betraying his superior, and so on! (p. 140)

This would be a good example of a therapist *not* adhering to the principle of parsimony.

Finally, Menninger (1958) was adamant that, despite the therapist's assistance (limited though it may be), "credit" for the insight nonetheless belonged to the patient. The therapist's personal needs for acknowledgment should never be a component of treatment (see Chapter 4).

EXPERIENCE-NEAR

Many psychodynamic therapists recommend that interventions stay close to the patient's subjective experience. Though clinicians may use all sorts of esoteric knowledge to formulate their techniques, what they ultimately say to the patient should not sound "alien." Therapists can remain experience-near at the *linguistic* level by using their patients' idiosyncratic words (Langs, 1973, 1974). For instance, I once worked with an older woman from the southern United States who reported suffering from "spells." After some clarification, I determined that her spells met the *Diagnostic and Statistical Manual of Mental Disorders* (American Psychiatric Association, 2013) criteria for "panic attacks" (pp. 208–209). However, that was *my* term for the malady, not hers. So, rather than have her expend cognitive effort to "translate" her experience into my (cumbersome) professional language, I simply used hers. The same goes for "swearing" (Fink, 2007). I am perfectly fine using salty language (or the more judgmental-sounding "curse words") in session if that is how the patient normally speaks. Using patients' language is not only good for the alliance but also conveys the message that they will be accepted even if they show their "true" and unfiltered selves.

Interventions can be experience-near at an *emotional* level as well. As discussed further in Sections II and III, some psychodynamic techniques require emotional immediacy. This is not easy for some patients, but evocative language can serve as a stimulus. Thomä and Kächele (1992) noted how Freud's clinical work often included similes, metaphors, and allegories (p. 268). This makes good clinical sense, as these manners of speech may keep patients closer to their affect and away from intellectualizations and abstractions. So, instead of saying, "You've been anxious," a more experience-near phrasing might be, "You've been feeling like you wanted to crawl out of your skin."

Experience-near language may be particularly important for events that happened in the distant past or when referring to people who are long-gone. Patients with early traumas, for instance, may minimize the relevance of a 30-year-old memory or be reluctant to revisit painful times. However, if the trauma is to be overcome, it needs to be processed at emotional and cognitive levels (Gaston, 1995; Summers & Barber, 2010, pp. 149–158). This necessitates a vivid, experience-near return to these painful people and events. For, as Freud (1958a) noted, "when all is said and done, it is impossible to destroy anyone *in absentia* or *in effigie*" (p. 108; emphasis in original). Therapists can help patients overcome trauma (and their traumatizers) by facilitating safe emotional processing.

RESPECTFUL

Psychodynamic work requires a great deal of respect. However, this can have numerous meanings. In psychotherapy, respect indicates a regard for a patient's basic humanity and right to self-determination (see Chapter 4). It may also indicate a deference to the patient's wishes, feelings, and personal traditions. At the level of technique, respect is demonstrated by the therapist's tone and intentions. Respectful interventions come from a place of benevolent curiosity. There is no justification for rudeness, smugness, condescension, or indoctrination (Dewald, 1971). If these qualities are present, they likely indicate an unrecognized enactment or the presence of unresolved countertransference issues.

A patient's true capacities and limitations are also deserving of respect. Therefore, therapists neither overwhelm their patients by using techniques too frequently (e.g., asking so many questions it feels like an "interrogation") nor by intervening too "deeply" (e.g., forcing the patient to explore topics they are not quite ready for). Patients can only take in so much information, especially if it is novel or fosters regression (Thomä & Kächele, 1992).

To be clear, psychodynamic therapists are not always respectful of the patient's *psychopathology*. Though it is obviously a part of the patient, it is the portion that they want removed or minimized. As a result, therapists may actually demonstrate respect for their patient's wishes by disrespecting their pathology. For example, they can help the patient marginalize their pathology by using "part" language.

So, a therapist might say, "Part of you [i.e., the unhealthy, pathological part] wants to do X, even though you said it would be foolish and could hurt you, but another part [i.e., the healthy part] would prefer for you not do that because of A, B, and C." Part language also helps foster "the good split" (see Chapter 9) and increases a patient's observing ego capacities.

INSTANTIATE THE PSYCHODYNAMIC PROCESS

Finally, good interventions aim to reflect the psychodynamic process itself. As noted in Chapter 3, a primary goal of therapy is to have patients no longer need it. This is partially accomplished through their learning psychodynamic procedures and identifying with certain professional aspects of the therapist.[11] The best way to accomplish this is by engaging the treatment (i.e., learning by doing).

This process can start in the very first session. When interacting with patients, therapists implicitly give the message that it is helpful to be curious and to look at oneself. Good therapists also convey a "vibe" that, although human experiences are often confusingly complex, they are potentially understandable with a bit of honest introspection (i.e., quick and easy answers are not always forthcoming). The "honest" piece is key, as we may not always like the things we see. At a more concrete level, therapists can instantiate the psychodynamic process by adhering to good technique. There are better and worse ways of asking questions, for example (see Chapter 10). Good therapist questions (i.e., those which are thoughtful, relevant, and thematically linked) teach patients how to question *themselves*. This applies to the other interventions as well (e.g., interpretation; see Chapter 13). So, in general, every small interaction throughout the entire course of therapy could contribute to its successful resolution.

CONCLUSION

In summary, crafting effective psychodynamic interventions requires a great deal of forethought, responsiveness, and practice. The 11 characteristics discussed in this chapter are not an exhaustive list, but will hopefully serve as useful guides when formulating the techniques described in Sections II and III. Chapter 7 will focus on ways to evaluate the effectiveness (or ineffectiveness) of psychodynamic interventions *after* they are made.

NOTES

1. As translated in Fink (2007, p. 88).
2. For a discussion of the broader issue of adherence versus intervention competence, see Sharpless and Barber (2009).

3. For examples of these, please see McWilliams (1999) and Summers and Barber (2010).

4. Case formulations are widely believed to contribute to our overall therapeutic efficacy (Caspar, 2017).

5. These data need not be limited to what we can learn from the empirical literatures, although this is preferred whenever possible.

6. As the issues of objectivist versus relativist notions of truth and whether psychology is a "science" or a hermeneutic discipline are far too large to discuss in a book on psychodynamic techniques, the reader is encouraged to not interpret my use of truth terms in too literal of a manner. For a more thorough debate on these issues, see Bernstein (1983), Grunbaum (1984), Habermas (1971), Messer, Sass, and Woolfolk (1988), and Spence (1982).

7. Some methods for recognizing the accuracy of interventions are described in Chapter 7.

8. There is ongoing debate in the field on this specific recommendation. For example, Levy (1990) and Yeomans et al. (2015) recommend against tentative interventions.

9. Too much emotion can encourage unhealthy regression in sicker patients.

10. In fact, it is the therapist equivalent of giving the *patient* a *doorknob gift* or *exit line* (Gabbard 2010).

11. See Geller and Farber (1993) for an interesting study of the latter.

How to Assess the Impacts of Interventions

Chapter 6 detailed characteristics of "good" psychodynamic interventions. This chapter will discuss ways to evaluate their clinical impact (or lack thereof). Some caveats are in order, though. First, the bulk of the existing literature has focused on *expressive* techniques. Far less attention has been devoted to evaluating *supportive* interventions. Second, this chapter will limit itself to the proximal[1] indicators of success/corroboration or disconfirmation[2] (i.e., those occurring immediately or shortly after the intervention). As time passes and more techniques are applied, it becomes nearly impossible to disentangle the clinical effects of any one intervention from others. Finally, it is recommended that the clinical signs discussed should not be taken too literally or used too rigidly, but should instead be viewed as *possible* indications of clinical impact. Just like players at a card game, each patient has their own unique set of clinical "tells," and it is incumbent on therapists to learn them. These may differ across patients, across individual sessions with the same patient, or even when using different techniques.

GENERAL PROCEDURE

In general, the three most important things to do after making an intervention are to (a) stop talking, (b) pay attention to the patient's reactions, and (c) look for evidence of corroboration or disconfirmation. That initial step can be hard to do, or at least it was for me. When I made my first few psychodynamic interventions—especially those involving unconscious material—I felt almost obsessively compelled to repeat them, reword them, or add qualifications. These behaviors arose from anxiety and a lack of confidence in my technical ability. Regardless of their origin, though, such reactions only served to confuse the patient and weaken clinical impacts. If needed, therapists can always reword or qualify later.

Steps (b) and (c) of this procedure are a bit more complicated. They require the therapist to carefully consider not just words, but also information coming from all four channels of communication (see Chapter 8). The verbal responses of the patient (e.g., "I agree" or "That's nonsense") are obviously important to consider, but other material might be equally salient, only subtler (e.g., nonverbal clues and an absence of material).[3] Therefore, therapists should listen carefully, with a healthy dose of suspicion, and not only to words. The signs of corroboration most associated with expressive techniques will be discussed first.

SIGNS OF CORROBORATION

Expressive Interventions

Expressive techniques are intended to generate insight and help patients gain freedom from unconscious maladaptive patterns. They often require an exploration of patient material at all three levels of awareness—conscious, preconscious, and unconscious. Perhaps not surprisingly, expressive interventions can result in any number of patient reactions when they "hit home." As shown in Box 7.1, these can range from the picayune and the boring to the meaningful and the dramatic. Several of these will be elaborated upon in the following discussion.

Verbal agreement on the "accuracy" of an intervention is good *preliminary* evidence of corroboration. However, as Freud (1964) noted over a century ago, "a plain 'Yes' from a patient is by no means unambiguous" (p. 262). This suspiciousness, even when getting *positive* feedback from patients, is very much in keeping with the psychoanalytic tradition (Ricoeur, 1970). Though it may sound strange, consider the myriad reasons[4] that a patient might say "yes" when they really mean "no" or "I'm not sure." Some lack assertiveness. Others may fear that any sort of disagreement could push the therapist away. Still others idealize their therapist to such an extent that they end up second-guessing their own judgments. Langs (1973, 1974) noted that certain patients may even agree with their therapists to self-consciously deceive them. Because of these and other reasons, verbal assent can only serve as a starting point, and multiple forms of corroboration are preferable.

Changes in patient affect are also important to consider (Menninger, 1958). The most noticeable of these may be an expression of surprise in the wake of an intervention (e.g., "Wow! I never considered that" or "Oh my God . . ."). Along with words, therapists may get the palpable sense that the patient just had an epiphany

Box 7.1.

POSSIBLE SIGNS OF CORROBORATION FOR EXPRESSIVE INTERVENTIONS

- Assent/verbal agreement
- New clinical material emerges
- "Deeper" clinical material emerges
- The patient expresses surprise
- The patient has an epiphany or "aha" moment
- An insight is now seen as "obvious"
- Emotional release
- Deepening of patient affect
- Increased level of understanding (e.g., for self, others, or situations)
- Increased curiosity
- Stronger therapeutic alliance
- Increased motivation to engage the therapy process
- Temporary shifts in the levels of symptoms or anxiety
- Temporary shifts in the level of regression
- The patient reports relevant fantasies or dreams
- Shifts in the transference
- Decreased defensiveness
- The patient has a corrective emotional experience (CEE)

Note: Patient context is important to consider when interpreting the meaning of these possible signs.

---

or "aha" moment. Patient laughter can also a good sign, especially if it sudden or, from the patient's perspective, unexpected (Dewald, 1971). An example of a less dramatic shift in affect would be increased curiosity about the intervention or the therapeutic process more generally.

Many psychodynamic writers have noted that expressive techniques often *deepen* or *intensify* affect (Frederickson, 1999). For example, a patient describing a topic in abstract terms may become far more emotional after a good intervention. This shift toward affect may be due to a helpful (and controlled) regression or the recognition of formerly disavowed feelings. New insights are often accompanied by an upswell of emotions, and these can be dramatic. Similarly, some patients report catharsis or an emotional release (e.g., after a painful childhood experience is interpreted).

Expressive techniques can also lead to changes in *symptoms*. "Symptom" is meant broadly here (e.g., patient anxiety, somatic complaints, repetitive non-verbal behaviors), and changes in intensity can occur in either direction. Thus, a good intervention may lead to a temporary increase *or* decrease in symptoms depending upon context. Similarly, two people who experience the exact same event might react very differently. Needless to say, these facts make the assessment of interventions potentially confusing. If the therapist is not careful, it could also open them up to the aforementioned charge of "Head's I win, tails you lose" (i.e., the intervention is not falsifiable; see Chapter 6).

To better safeguard against this risk, you can take several precautions. First, try to predict in advance how the patient might respond to the intervention (Dewald, 1971; Maroda, 2010, Chapter 4). If this is difficult, try to at least decide whether the intervention is more likely to "organize" the patient (i.e., steady them and give them relief) or temporarily "disrupt" them (i.e., increase their anxiety or distress). If you are genuinely surprised by the patient's reaction, this may point to difficulties with the current case formulation, problems with the *timing* of the intervention, or other technical factors. Second, when in doubt, try to clarify the patient's response (e.g., "It looks like your leg began shaking after I made that last statement, and then you turned away. Could you help me understand what's going on for you right now?"). Third, pay attention to what happens throughout the remainder of the session. For instance, does the symptom recede as the intervention is more fully "taken in" (e.g., a headache slowly dissipates) or does it worsen over time? Finally, and possibly most important, determine whether the patient generates useful clinical information.

If broad agreement among psychodynamic theorists is any indication, the "best" criterion listed in Box 7.1 would clearly be the emergence of new and "deeper" clinical material (Frederickson, 1999; Isaacs, 1939; Thomä & Kächele, 1992). Along with being popular, this idea also makes clinical sense. Expressive interventions, by their very nature, dramatically alter patients' usual modes of thinking and feeling. For example, a psychodynamic interpretation could explain a patient's mysterious symptom whereas a confrontation might link two events that were formerly seen as separate. Even if the changes wrought from either of these interventions were relatively minor, they may still open new vistas of experience not previously considered. In effect, old habits now possess less power over the patient, who can now view the world differently.

When new perspectives arise, patients tend to generate more clinical material. Therapist help may not even be required. They simply begin to have "deeper" associations, provide more examples, and make novel connections (e.g., "It's funny, but what you just said reminds me of something else that happened at work"). Relevant dreams and fantasies may even be reported in the following weeks (Isaacs, 1939). If any of these signs occur, the intervention was likely well-formed and evocative.

Interestingly, this type of corroboration (i.e., generating new material) can occur whether the patient was temporarily calmed or "disrupted" by the intervention. It can also occur regardless of whether the patient agreed or disagreed with the therapist. The key to determining this can be found in the nature of the new clinical content. Is it truly novel, "deeper," richer, and more complex? If so, this indicates corroboration. When it is stale, superficial, uninspired, and "boring," more work needs to be done.

Supportive Interventions

Supportive techniques have different intentions than expressive ones. These include (a) supporting self-esteem, (b) building knowledge and skills, (c) reducing unhelpful levels of emotion, (d) increasing self-awareness (i.e., of conscious and preconscious material), (e) remedial "parenting," and (f) supporting the therapeutic alliance (see Chapters 5, 14, and 15).[5] Several supportive techniques also make expressive therapies possible. However, as indicated in Box 7.2, there are some differences in the likely signs of corroboration.

As was the case with expressive techniques, patient agreement is a good sign, but no guarantee of success. Additional types of corroboration are preferable, and several of these will be addressed in the following discussion. It may also be important to note that the "reporter" might not be the patient, especially if they are lower functioning. Given the collaborative nature of supportive work, evidence

---

Box 7.2.

POSSIBLE SIGNS OF CORROBORATION FOR SUPPORTIVE INTERVENTIONS

- Assent/verbal agreement
- New clinical material emerges (usually conscious and/or preconscious)
- Return to a heathy emotional "baseline"
- Increased ability to recognize a specific emotion in session
- Recognition of links between feelings, thoughts, and behaviors
- Ability to see an event from different perspectives
- Increased level of understanding (e.g., novel knowledge, a practical matter)
- Shifts in nonverbal behavior that indicate calmness
- Reduced level of regression
- Temporary increase in self-confidence
- The patient takes steps to maintain safety or security
- Improved reality-testing for a specific situation
- Increased curiosity
- Stronger therapeutic alliance
- Increased motivation to engage the therapy process
- The patient puts a feeling into words, not an action
- The patient inhibits an impulsive behavior
- The patient is better able to decide on a course of action
- The patient is better able to take action
- "Softening" of rigid thinking for a particular situation
- The patient has a corrective emotional experience (CEE)

Note: Patient context is important to consider when interpreting the meaning of these possible signs.

---

for the effectiveness of certain interventions (e.g., limit-setting, advice) may very well come from other people (e.g., a social worker, the manager of the patient's group home). This can be very helpful if the sources are reasonably objective.

Many supportive techniques focus on improving emotional function. Though this is usually a long-term goal, intrasession indicators of success can still be found. For instance, both "naming" emotions and helping patients "put feelings into words" may yield small yet noticeable increases in their emotional understanding. In session, this may be indicated by a better ability to identify links between the newly recognized emotions and their corresponding thoughts and behaviors. They may also notice similar affective shifts or, in a subsequent session, report an instance of accurately "reading" another person's emotion.

Supportive interventions can also foster better emotional *control*. Many patients, especially those with borderline or psychotic personality organizations, suffer from overwhelming or "scary" levels of emotion that impede homeostasis (e.g., dramatic "affect storms"; Clarkin, Yeomans, & Kernberg, 2006; see also Carsky, 2013). When therapists "contain" these feelings, reframe them, or even simply reassure the patient that things may not be as dire as they seem, a movement toward baseline indicates success. This shift may be fairly rapid and observable. With less dramatic but nonetheless unhelpful levels of distress (e.g., chronic worry), the success of supportive techniques (e.g., normalizing anxiety) might be indicated by subtler, nonverbal shifts (e.g., less hand-wringing and better attention).

Patients who require supportive therapy frequently have difficulties with behavioral control, and this is a frequent target of intervention (Rockland, 1989; Winston, Rosenthal, & Pinsker, 2012). Interestingly, these difficulties often manifest at the extremes, with some patients making impulsive, even dangerous decisions and others becoming stultified when faced with even minor choices. As with emotional control, corroboration of these techniques (e.g., anticipatory rehearsal, encouragement) is often straightforward and indicated by an alteration to the patient's usual way of doing things. For example, the undercontrolled patient is better able to inhibit behaviors during session, does not "act out" their feelings (e.g., hitting a chair with their fist when angry), and responsibly maintains their personal safety (e.g., by agreeing to a voluntary hospitalization or a therapist limit). The overcontrolled patient may decide upon a needed course of action and carry it to completion prior to the next session.

Certain supportive techniques (e.g., providing information, reframing) also foster clearer, more adaptive thought. When these are successful, patients display more cognitive flexibility and self-control. For instance, if reality testing is successfully applied to a delusion (e.g., "Is it possible that there may be another reason that the officer was looking at you strangely?"), the patient may not only become less agitated but could also generate other appraisals for the event. Their rigid thinking may "soften"—in the situation being discussed, at least—as they entertain the possibility that things may not be as they initially surmised.

A patient's thinking can also be improved by reducing knowledge deficits. As will be discussed in Chapter 14, supportive therapists do this on as "asneeded" basis by providing psychoeducation or other types of instruction. Their effectiveness is shown not only through patient understanding (e.g., alcohol affects sleep patterns) but also by an ability to *apply* the knowledge (e.g., "It might be helpful for me to abstain from alcohol before bed").

Several other indicators of intervention success are shared between the expressive and supportive techniques. For instance, any number of interventions may lead to increased self-confidence and a stronger therapeutic alliance. Even relatively minor successes help patients better tolerate the hard work of therapy and become invested in the process. New patient free associations may emerge, too. Finally, there may also be shifts in the patient's level of regression (Dewald, 1971). The direction is important, though. Whereas an increase may indicate "success" with an expressive technique—at least in certain instances—a reduction in regression is usually the aim of supportive therapies (see Chapter 5).

Corrective Emotional Experiences

Another potential clinical impact is a corrective emotional experience (CEE). CEEs can result from good expressive work, good supportive work, or *neither*. As noted in Chapter 2, there seems to have been a recent resurgence of interest in this construct over the past few years, and not only in psychodynamic circles (Castonguay & Hill, 2012). CEEs are fascinating clinical phenomena, but much about them remains mysterious and unknown (Sharpless & Barber, 2012).

Franz Alexander—who coined the term—defined CEEs as the reexperiencing of an "old, unsettled conflict but with a new ending" (Alexander & French, 1946, p. 338). The emphasis, as the name implies, is on an *experience* for the patient, not an increase in insight or symptom reduction. Patients can still have a true CEE even if they do not consciously recognize it.[6] Interestingly, CEEs do not have to occur in session or even as the result of any intervention at all. Patients may be just as likely to experience CEEs with friends or strangers as with therapists. Further, CEEs may occur after one event or after many repetitions. The components of an "in-session" CEE (i.e., with the therapist) can be found in Box 7.3.

As seen in Box 7.3, CEEs are fairly broad constructs. The "trauma" discussed in component 1 could be major (e.g., criterion A of a posttraumatic stress disorder diagnosis; American Psychiatric Association, 2013, p. 271) or relatively minor (e.g., former criticism of assertiveness). Special mention should be made of the third component, as this has caused some confusion and criticisms of the construct (Sharpless & Barber, 2012). The therapist need not do anything different in terms of their attitude toward the patient. Adopting a good psychodynamic stance (see Chapter 4) should provide ample opportunities for CEEs. There is no need for a therapist to "act" as if they were someone from the patient's past to "set the stage" for a CEE. Given the current state of the CEE literature, though, there is unfortunately very little empirically based guidance on how therapists can best facilitate CEEs.[7]

So what might a CEE look like in psychodynamic practice? I once worked with a patient in her early thirties who suffered from powerful feelings of inadequacy.[8]

Box 7.3.

COMPONENTS OF AN IN-SESSION CORRECTIVE EMOTIONAL EXPERIENCE

1. The patient experienced a traumatic event (construed broadly) in the past that was not successfully/adaptively dealt with.
2. The patient is re-exposed to a similar event or situation in session.
3. The therapist expresses an attitude to the patient that is different from those whom were involved in the original traumatic experience.
4. The patient reacts to this novel situation (i.e., the therapist's nontraumatizing behavior) in a manner different from before (i.e., the experience is incorporated by the patient).
5. The original trauma becomes "corrected" in some manner.[a]
6. The results of the CEE generalize to other situations.

[a]The manner in which this change occurs is not yet known; more empirical work is needed.

Source: Adapted from Sharpless & Barber, 2012.

Though a warm and caring person, she found self-disclosure to be particularly hard. This served to keep her at an emotional distance from others, especially romantic partners. Needless to say, an expressive therapy was quite difficult for her, and supportive elements were introduced early on.

After several months of therapy, she disclosed to me that, for her to be able to discuss herself in any substantive way to me, she had to fantasize that I was not a human being with a real life and emotional reactions, but instead was a "robot" physically confined to the clinic. This intrapsychic compromise allowed her to more fully engage the therapeutic process (at least in the beginning). She was willing to explore this fantasy with me further, and it quickly became apparent that she feared being "humiliated" by me and, presumably, everyone else in her life.

As I listened—robotically, of course—she recounted a long history of feeling "different" from others. This began in childhood, and she associated it with her "nerdy" and "boring" interests (e.g., science fiction, crocheting, Civil War reenactments). Classmates often made fun of her, especially during her teenage years, and gave her a litany of derisive nicknames associated with each of these three topics. Given the sensitive nature of the discussion and the anxious nonverbal behaviors she began to manifest, I thought it best to briefly "pull back" on the intensity of expressive work. I told her that I was unaware of her strong interests in these things and asked her, with genuine curiosity, to describe what she found compelling about them. She immediately looked at me with suspicion, and I had the strong sense that she feared I was going to make fun of her as well. I did not comment on this but continued to look at her with earnest expectation. She then hesitantly began to discuss her fascination with Civil War food preparation methods and other topics I had little knowledge of. As she continued, her passion was evident. She found herself enjoying the conversation and, especially, my follow-up questions, which attempted to link these interests and experiences to her pervasive social anxiety.

I essentially viewed this interchange as a supportive intervention that, at best, may have minimally strengthened the bond component of our therapeutic alliance. I did not expect it to have any real clinical impact. During our next session, however, she expressed excitement about an upcoming outing with a new friend. She apparently had a good conversation with a co-worker who also liked science fiction. This colleague invited her to a local comic book store that carried a lot of movie memorabilia. I soon learned that my patient was the instigator of the initial conversation and disclosed her own sci fi interests first (to be fair, this other person was wearing a t-shirt of the 1986 movie *Aliens*, but I was nonetheless impressed by my patient's bravery). Thus, she appeared to have met all six of the in-session CEE criteria detailed in Box 7.3. Interestingly, and as previously indicated, this CEE was neither planned in advance nor expected. In fact, it could have easily occurred outside of session with someone else. Regardless, CEEs are potentially important signs of corroboration to consider.

SIGNS OF DISCONFIRMATION

Effective and meaningful interventions are what we all prefer, but it is inevitable that mistakes will be made. Therapists are often required to make uncertain judgements based upon incomplete information and within narrow time constraints. This is not a great recipe for clinical success. However, it is just as important to recognize the signs of disconfirmation as those of corroboration. When errors are made, patients may have any number of reactions ranging from the barely perceptible (e.g., blank looks and mild confusion) to the painfully apparent (e.g., alliance ruptures or the patient "storming" out of session).[9] A sampling of other signs of disconfirmation can be found in Box 7.4. Many of these are the opposite of corroborative signs. However, at the risk of repetition, it is important to reiterate the importance of *context* when interpreting the meaning of these signs. Some (e.g., increased defenses or resistance) may actually indicate that the therapist and patient are approaching an important clinical matter.

Although therapeutic missteps can obviously be disheartening, they point to a need for additional reflection on technique-crafting and case formulation. It is more helpful to discover this earlier in treatment rather than later. On the upside, these errors also serve as good opportunities to model appropriate self-evaluation to the patient (e.g., openly acknowledging the error and attempting to understand it or correct it without resorting to unhealthy levels of self-criticism or defensiveness; see Chapter 16).

Before ending this section, it is important to discuss disconfirmation and negative therapeutic reactions more generally. In almost all cases, therapists should allow *patients* to be the final arbiter of an intervention's effectiveness or

Box 7.4.

INDICATIONS OF DISCONFIRMATION

- Rejection/verbal disagreement
- Confusion after the intervention
- No change in the patient
- Stalled free association
- Stalled session progress
- Unexpected increase in symptom or anxiety levels that do not abate
- Disruptive regression
- The patient reports feeling misunderstood
- The patient displaces their feelings toward the therapist (e.g., they make mention of a person in their life who does not understand them)
- Lack of new material or presentation of stale, repetitive material
- Increased resistance to treatment
- Increased use of defenses
- Acting out of negative emotions
- The patient begins to ruminate
- The patient emotionally disconnects from the therapist and/or the session topic
- Alliance rupture
- Intensification of negative transference
- Disruptions to the treatment routine (e.g., patient misses the next session or arrives late)

Note: Patient context is important to consider when interpreting the meaning of these possible signs.

"correctness" and not argue with them. Whenever patients disagree with an intervention, it is *rarely* due to obstinacy or defensiveness (Langs, 1973, 1974). It is far more likely due to an error on our part. Unfortunately, it is a common human failing to become too invested in one's own theories and thoughts (Popper, 2002), and this is rarely helpful in clinical settings. Even if the technique was logically deduced from the formulation, elegantly worded, and otherwise thoughtful, it might simply not have been a good time to use it.

NOTES

1. Some suggestions for evaluating overall progress toward goals were detailed in Chapter 3.
2. See Chapter 13 for a lengthier discussion of "support" and "disconfirmation."

3. This is another reason that trainees should record and review their therapy sessions.
4. Many of these are based on patient transferences.
5. Examples of several techniques from each category and suggestions for their use will be provided throughout Chapters 14 and 15.
6. You can even witness CEEs happen in the animal world. There is a YouTube video of a horribly abused dog being petted for the first time. It wailed and cried whenever a human came near. With repetition and patience from a kind human, he was able to "take it in" and eventually became a friendly, loving dog that enjoyed affection. Clearly, no interpretations (or even words) were needed, and no conscious insight may have been generated, yet something was "repaired" nonetheless.
7. Several hypothesized therapist and patient factors that may either facilitate or discourage CEEs can be found in Sharpless and Barber (2012).
8. She met diagnostic criteria for both social anxiety disorder and generalized anxiety disorder.
9. For an interesting review of how negative therapeutic reactions have been viewed across the history of psychoanalysis, see Etchegoyen (2012, pp. 737–761).

The "Classic" Psychodynamic Therapy Techniques in Contemporary Practice

Foundational Techniques Part I

Before discussing the "classic" psychodynamic techniques (i.e., questions, clarifications, confrontations, and interpretations), it is important to cover what could be termed *foundational techniques* (see Box 8.1). These skills not only foster psychodynamic processes but also help therapists maintain appropriate boundaries. Admittedly, they are not as dramatic or "sexy" as interpretations, for instance, but are nonetheless crucial, as they form the soil out of which more sophisticated interventions grow. Several of these (e.g., evenly-hovering attention, therapist anonymity) will be situated in a historical context, as they have undergone significant theoretical modifications over the past hundred years and remain matters of academic debate.

This chapter specifically focuses on therapist silence, patient free association, and ways to listen in a psychodynamic manner. Though these may seem to be straightforward, or even elementary techniques, it would likely require several book length treatises to fully address each. Instead, I hope to present them in a broad, yet clinically useful and not oversimplified manner.

THERAPIST SILENCE

Silence may be the most misunderstood and confusing intervention in the psychodynamic armamentarium. Some readers might even be surprised to see silence described as a technique, but it is a powerful one. It is also not without risk and requires practice to apply it effectively. Silence is risky because it always conveys *meaning*, and these meanings are often idiosyncratic. As an illustration of this, please take a moment and think about the last time someone was silent

---

Box 8.1.

FOUNDATIONAL PSYCHODYNAMIC TECHNIQUES

- The appropriate use of therapist silence
- How to foster patient free association
- How to listen in a psychodynamic manner (e.g., evenly-hovering attention; the four channels of communication)
- How to behave in a psychodynamic manner (e.g. ambiguity, abstinence, technical neutrality, modeling of adaptive behaviors)
- Ways to start psychodynamic therapy (e.g., contracting; forming and enhancing the therapeutic alliance, fostering the "good split")

---

with you. How did you interpret it? In all likelihood, your appraisal of the silence was not only context-dependent (i.e., specific to a particular person and situation) but also colored by your own developmental history (i.e., prior experiences with silence). Therefore, you might have been correct in some situations, incorrect in others, or more generally inclined to interpret silence in one particular manner (i.e., a specific bias). Our patients respond to silences in a similar fashion. Table 8.1 lists possible interpretations written from hypothetical patient perspectives. As is apparent, some are positive whereas others are extremely negative.

The Purposes of Silence

Given silence's lack of clarity and danger for misinterpretation, why use it at all? The answer is that, despite the risks, it serves at least three important functions for patients and two for therapists. First and foremost, silence provides patients with the much-needed "space" required to look inward. It creates the *possibility* for patient free association (McWilliams, 2004). If you think about it, silence is a rare commodity in nontherapy interactions. Most conversations in "real life" are not as unidirectional, and a lopsided silence from one half of the dyad would violate many social norms. An unfortunate consequence of these norms is that patients rarely get an opportunity to focus solely on themselves when in the presence of a concerned and fully attentive other. This is one of the more unique aspects of dynamic therapy.

Silence is also intended to exert a subtle form of "pressure" on the patient so they can better examine the mysterious processes of their inner world (Langs, 1973, 1974, p. 374). This pressure encourages patient regression, a state that facilitates the freer expression of conscious and unconscious contents (Menninger, 1958). When doing psychodynamic therapy, especially the expressive variants, a controlled regression provides access to much of the information needed to unlock

Table 8.1. SOME OF THE POTENTIAL PATIENT INTERPRETATIONS
OF THERAPIST SILENCE

You approve of my behavior.	You disapprove of my behavior.
You are in sync with me.	You want me to "stew" in my feelings.
You will not criticize me.	You are withholding something from me.
You view me as an adult who can handle this.	You are angry at me.
I make you anxious.	You want to frustrate me.
You feel close to me.	You are depriving me of feeling close to you.
You accept me.	You reject me.
You are taking me seriously.	You feel embarrassed by/for me.
You are thinking about what I just said.	You can tolerate my feelings.
You are lost in your own thoughts.	You want to tease me.
You are not interested in me.	You don't understand me.
You are unavailable to me.	I intrigue you.
You are more powerful than me.	You feel awkward.
You appreciate what I am saying and want me to continue.	I am doing quite well on my own and do not need your help.

the meanings, purposes, and origins of maladaptive patterns and symptoms.[1] The overall intention of silence is to foster the *process* of psychodynamic therapy.

Finally, silence is meant to increase patient autonomy. With less input from the therapist, the patient becomes far more responsible for what is said and done in session (Langs, 1973, 1974). Thus, patients learn how to better rely upon *their own* capacities for growth and self-care. This is thought to improve ego functions in general and help patients reach the goal of autonomy.

There are also therapist-centered reasons to utilize silence. First, therapists, like patients, also require "space" to work effectively. Silence reduces cognitive demands so that therapists can *listen* in a psychodynamic manner (see the following discussion). This is not an easy task and requires attention to multiple, and often simultaneous, channels of patient communication. Without silence and this special type of listening, the therapist would be unable to understand the patient in a nuanced fashion or purposefully intervene on their behalf.

Lastly, silence allows therapists to convey nonverbal messages. It is important that these be thoughtful communications and not inadvertently negative ones (e.g., Table 8.1). Therapists should convey interest, safety, openness, synchrony, and earnestness with their silence.[2] If they discern negative patient reactions, it is wise to break silence and intervene.

When to Break Silence

Although it clearly has benefits, few patients would return to see a silent therapist. So the question now becomes "How much silence is enough for psychodynamic processes to occur, yet not so much that it becomes intolerable for the patient?" The answer to this is, perhaps not surprisingly: "it depends." Silence differs in expressive and supportive therapies and even varies within sessions when seeing the same patient. Therefore, it may be imprudent to provide firm rules, but several rough guidelines for breaking silence are listed in Table 8.2. Some writers have provided more stringent recommendations (e.g., Langs, 1973, 1974, pp. 374–375), but I would argue that the sheer range of patient problems addressed in current psychodynamic therapies necessitates a flexible therapeutic approach.

In general, there is no need to break silence if patient material is flowing well. In these cases, it is usually best to stay out of the patient's way and keep listening. However, I agree with Levy (1990, p. 22) that it would be very peculiar for a therapist to be completely silent for an entire session. In fact, I cannot imagine any situation where this would be advisable. Patients, especially if they are new to therapy, usually require a modicum of reassurance that they are "doing it right." Although we all know there is not one correct way to be a psychodynamic patient, we also do not want to introduce needless anxiety to the process. Therefore, using good nonverbal behaviors (e.g., an open body posture, attentiveness, nods) and a sensible number of "mm hmms" (i.e., conveying a message such as "Keep going" or "That's interesting") lets the patient know that they are proceeding well and

Table 8.2. SOME REASONS TO BREAK THERAPIST SILENCE

Free association is being used defensively.	More information is needed *at this moment.*
Free association stalls altogether/ excessive patient silence is present.	The session/topic feels "stale", superficial, or repetitive.
The patient requires temporary support.	The therapist is ready to intervene.
Important defenses emerge.	The patient is acting out/acting in.
An important theme emerges which requires attention.	The patient makes a potentially important parapraxis (i.e., slip of the tongue).
The patient violates an aspect of the treatment contract.	The patient has an intense emotional experience that requires discussion.
The patient appears to be concealing material.	The patient is not being truthful.
The patient regresses too much.	Threats to self or other emerge.
A rupture in the alliance has taken place.	The patient reacts negatively to an intervention.

that you are indeed not asleep. These are some of the least intrusive ways to break silence.

However, many authors (e.g., Nichols, 1986) have noted that beginning therapists are rarely, if ever, too silent. This is consistent with my anecdotal experience as well. They are instead far more likely to be too chatty. This tendency may stem from discomfort with the less structured nature of psychodynamic work (i.e., "Anything could happen") or possibly from a mistaken belief that they always have to "do something" during session. As demonstrated in the following discussion, listening, if done properly, actually does quite a bit for the patient.

Continually assessing the impact of therapist communications may also guard against chattiness. If you think about it, each time the therapist talks, the process of free association is interrupted. Whenever the patient's thoughts are disturbed, it may take some time for them to get "back on track." Now, to be clear, if the material is important, it will likely be repeated many times, possibly even within the same session. Therapists should nonetheless try to be careful when deciding whether to speak or be silent.

A few of the markers in Table 8.2 require special mention. When *patients* fall silent, it is usually a good idea to check in. This should happen sooner rather than later for lower functioning patients, but in general I would not allow more than two minutes or so go by unless this silence has been discussed in advance. For example, you might say to a patient, "It seems like you're experiencing a lot right now and may be having problems even knowing where to begin. Just to let you know, I am perfectly fine just sitting here with you as you collect your thoughts if that would be helpful." In this instance, any subsequent silence would convey acceptance of the patient and an understanding that they are struggling with difficult material. In general, every therapy has its unique "rhythm," and what might be unbearable silence for one patient would be beneficial for another. In many cases, stalled free association can be helped by asking a simple question (e.g., "What's going on for you right now?").

The other extreme (i.e., a dearth of patient silence) could also prompt therapist action. Some patients will *pseudo-free associate*, speaking as if they are doing the hard work of psychodynamic introspection but are, in actuality, repeating material or focusing on trite themes. They are not really "digging," and their verbosity may actually be a means to control session content and/or limit the therapist's involvement. In these cases, it is wise to check in, too.

Therapists sometimes need additional information, and this is an eminently good reason to break silence. As will be discussed further in Chapter 10, though, it is important to keep these requests on a "need to know *now*" basis. If information is not necessary at a particular moment in time, it is often better for the therapist to make a mental note of the question and retain it for future use. Again, this will help minimize disruptions.

Finally, therapists occasionally have agenda items that need to be addressed. For example, a patient may have missed an appointment without notification. All things being equal, I would want the patient to start the next session as usual. This not only maintains standard therapeutic operating procedures, but also allows me the opportunity to see whether the patient brings the matter up on their own without prompting. Regardless of whether they do or not, their decision provides clinically useful information that would be lost were I to begin the session. If 5 to 10 minutes passed and they had still not brought up the no-show, I would raise the matter (e.g., via a "spotlight" confrontation as described in Chapter 12) so that there is ample time for discussion.

The Different Uses of Silence in Expressive and Supportive Therapies

The majority of suggestions provided are most appropriate for *expressive* psychotherapies. Patients who are suitable for these approaches can better tolerate the ambiguity of silence as well as the demands for free association described in the following discussion. Therefore, when working with neurotic or higher-level borderline patients, I am quiet as soon as I take my seat and convey a warm, open, and expectant demeanor. Some patients may make "small talk" on the way to the office door or when in the process of sitting down, but I try to become silent when we are both "therapeutically situated." This arrangement acts almost like a "switch" prompting the patient to therapeutically regress and begin to free associate. Higher-functioning patients are often able to regress relatively easily and also "switch back" at the end of session so as to go about their day with a minimal amount of therapy-induced interference.[3]

Lower-functioning patients require a modified approach. Though I try my best to approximate expressive procedures to the extent that is possible and appropriate, I am more than willing to be as active and verbal as needed. At minimum, patients should be given enough space to decide what they want to focus on in session. However, lengthy therapist silences are contraindicated. This is because silence can become either a vehicle for patient projection or a painful reminder of previous relationships (e.g., a caregiver reacting to the patient's paranoid fears with silent bemusement). It may be difficult to temper strong negative transferences in session, especially if the patient does not yet trust the therapist. In this case, it would be more prudent to *not* be silent. Winston, Rosenthal, and Pinsker (2012) captured this difference in application well when they noted, "Faced with a long pause, the expressive therapist thinks, 'is there an indication for me to speak?' In contrast, the supportive therapist thinks, 'Is there a reason for me *not* to speak?'" (p. 18).

HOW TO FOSTER FREE ASSOCIATION

Therapist silence facilitates free association. Freud valued this method of gaining clinical material so highly that he essentially formulated it into a patient *duty*. He communicated his "fundamental rule" as follows:

One more thing before you start. What you tell me must differ in one respect from an ordinary conversation. Ordinarily you rightly try to keep a connecting thread running through your remarks and you exclude any intrusive ideas that may occur to you and any side-issues, so as not to wander too far from the point. But in this case you must proceed differently. You will notice that as you relate things various thoughts will occur to you which you would like to put aside on the ground of certain criticisms and objections. You will be tempted to say to yourself that this or that is irrelevant here, or is quite unimportant, or nonsensical, so that there is no need to say it. You must never give in to these criticisms, but must say it in spite of them – indeed, you must say it precisely because you feel an aversion to doing so. Later on you will find out and learn to understand the reason for this injunction, which is really the only one you have to follow. So say whatever goes through your mind. Act as though, for instance, you were a traveler sitting next to the window of a railway carriage and describing to someone inside the carriage the changing views which you see outside. Finally, never forget that you have promised to be absolutely honest, and never leave anything out because, for some reason or other, it is unpleasant to tell it. (Freud, 1958a, pp. 134–135)

As with so much of Freud's thought, free association has been interpreted and applied in different ways (e.g., see Glover, 1955; Schafer, 1976; Spence, 1982)[4] ranging from an idealized "You *must* say everything" to "You *may* say everything" (Thomä & Kächele, 1992, p. 227). I am more inclined to convey the latter meaning to patients, as it has the softer suggestion that they possess the freedom to say whatever they like in session regardless of social anxiety or shame and irrespective of what they believe to be the normal boundaries of social decorum. In effect, they are not disappointing the therapist if they do not free associate but are instead missing out on an opportunity to better understand themselves.

Many have noted that free association in the classic Freudian sense is an ideal that, even if the patient wished to fully comply, cannot be reached in practice (Langs, 1973, 1974).[5] Consider the degree of patient health and insight that would be required to fully engage in it (e.g., deep knowledge of personal defensive processes, acceptance of competing personal motivations). It may be the case that patients only really get *close* to idealized free association as they are near termination (Etchegoyen, 2012). In fact, the ability to better engage in free association may be a sign that clinical progress occurred.

Purposes of Free Association

Free association provides the majority of clinical content used in session. By way of an artistic analogy, the therapy could be considered a stretched canvas, the therapist's silence and psychodynamic stance are the palette, brushes are various dynamic techniques, and free association provides the bulk of the paint.

Therapists provide paint as well in the form of countertransference reactions, theory, and so on. The therapist and patient then sort the different colors on the palette—occasionally blending/adding texture to them—before finally choosing which ones to place on the brush and apply to the canvas.

Free association, along with therapist silence, also encourages regression (e.g., Loewald, 1960; Mitchell & Black, 1995) and a better access to the less obvious aspects of the patient's inner life (i.e., unconscious contents). When free associating, the patient attempts to disconnect themselves from their normally censorious thought patterns, moving from secondary process thought (i.e., our usual manner of "adult" thinking) to primary process thought (i.e., the language of the unconscious; see Dewald, 1971). This allows them to enter into a different sort of mental state and access other types of memory and information. There are actually some data supporting this that were derived from positron emission topography (PET) research. Andreasen et al. (1995) identified interesting differences in random (i.e., akin to free association) versus more focused episodic memory tasks, with the former eliciting large activations in association centers of the brain (Gabbard, 2014).

Free association is also clinically useful because there are inevitably *obstructions* to the process. For instance, if a patient suddenly became silent when discussing an ostensibly important topic, this may indicate potential conflict and/or defensive operations. Rapid shifts away from a particular subject matter could be similarly noteworthy. Of course, patients may just hit a nonmeaningful wall or "run out of steam," so it is incumbent upon the therapist to have a good enough sense of their patient to determine whether the obstruction is truly an important event or just some random clinical "noise." In general, though, psychodynamic theory presupposes that thoughts are nonrandomly linked and that the *succession* and *order* of thoughts may be just as meaningful as the individual thoughts themselves.[6]

Ways to Foster Free Association

It may already be obvious at this point, but free association is not easy to do. Most patients have trouble with it, as they want to sound coherent to the therapist and fear being so "naked" and vulnerable in front of another. As such, patients need to be socialized into treatment. Though some writers have noted that it acceptable to leave the fundamental rule unstated (Racker, 1968), I see no benefit in *not* explaining the process, even during the very first therapy session. I will say something like the following to a "standard" long-term psychotherapy patient:

We've talked about a number of important things today. As you can see, I'm not a silent therapist, and as I get the chance to know you better, I will have a number of things to say. Since you know yourself better than I do, and we only have limited time together, it's important that you start our sessions. You can begin wherever you like. In general, you should not only keep me informed of the important happenings in your life and the things we've talked about today, but also do your best to let your thoughts go where they may. If you feel that you shouldn't say something, either because it seems trivial, silly, or even embarrassing, I encourage you to say it. The smallest things may lead us to important places. If you ever find yourself struggling, try to let your thoughts go and say the first thing that comes into your mind. If you find yourself having reactions to me or to something that I've said, I encourage you to bring these things to my attention as well.

This initial description is not enough for most patients. They usually require reminders and clarifications as their first silences occur. When a patient meets one of the previously discussed obstructions, the therapist can apply the techniques described in Chapters 11 to 13, but if the therapist is unsure of the context, it may be easiest to ask a good, simple question (see Chapter 10). It could be as straightforward as "What is making it difficult for you to talk right now?"

There are several potential pitfalls to free association. At the risk of excessive repetition, it is important to be patient with your patients' free association. Like therapist silence, it is clearly at variance with normal interpersonal expectations. It would also be a shame if patients inadvertently received the message that "silence is bad" in psychotherapy (Levy, 1990); silences are *inevitable*. Further, it is advisable to consider how a patient's particular form of character pathology interacts with free association. As noted by Etchegoyen (2012), "whereas the obsessive will have doubts about what he has to communicate and how he should do it, the depressive will feel he faces a problem of conscience when hurtful things occur to him, and the psychopath will believe we have given him free reign to insult us" (p. 556). Every unique reaction provides valuable information.

The Different Applications of Free Association in Expressive and Supportive Therapies

The use of free association, just like therapist silence, should be adapted to the patient's position on the supportive–expressive continuum. Dewald (1971) framed this concisely when he noted that patients in insight-oriented therapy should "speak first and think later," whereas those in supportive therapy should "think first and then speak" (pp. 172–173). The former encourages regression and primary process thinking whereas the latter encourages secondary process thinking and a "good split" between observing and experiencing egos (Greenson, 1967; also see Chapter 9). There is little need to encourage regression in the more purely supportive therapies, as these patients are likely already regressed. They instead require ego *strengthening.*

Free Association in Long- and Short-Term Therapies

Regarding the mode of therapy, free association in the "freest" sense is primarily reserved for longer-term therapies. If you only have 10 to 20 sessions with a patient, traditional free association is likely not the most efficient vehicle for change. Therefore, in short- to medium-term therapies—for example, *panic-focused psychodynamic psychotherapy* (Busch, Milrod, Singer, & Aronson, 2012) and *transference-focused psychotherapy* (Yeomans, Clarkin, & Kernberg, 2015)—free association is modified. Patients are usually encouraged to limit their free association to presenting problems and/or the foci of treatment (e.g., panic attacks; interpersonal tumult).

HOW TO LISTEN IN A PSYCHODYNAMIC MANNER

Silence and free association are prerequisites for psychodynamic listening. Though it may seem patently obvious, the single most important thing that a therapist can do is listen; everything else is secondary. Without an ability to listen carefully and in a particular way, you will be unable to understand patients. Further, without good and empathic listening skills, not only will your therapeutic alliance suffer, but you will not know how or when to intervene or even be able to judge the effectiveness of your interventions (see Chapter 7).

Unfortunately, the way that people normally listen to others is incompatible with good psychodynamic therapy. "Normal" listening has a good amount of self-focus. Some have described it in stronger terms as "highly narcissistic and self-centered" (Fink, 2007, p. 4). In normal listening, we usually engage in a continual process of relating what we hear from others *to ourselves*. Our thoughts tend to drift to our concerns, our experiences, and our typical judgments of good and bad/right and wrong. Making matters more complicated, we also have what could be called "folk psychological theories." These are idiosyncratic beliefs that we use to explain how and why people think and behave in the interesting ways that they do (Frederickson, 1999). Some of our theories may be accurate, but many are not, as they derive from *our* lives and not from the information we gather from patients.

Along with the psychodynamic stance discussed in Chapter 4 (especially healthy suspiciousness), there are several other common dynamic principles that are helpful for listening. Fortunately, these skills are much easier to practice than other dynamic techniques, as there are multiple opportunities to listen every day. Psychodynamic listening can even be practiced when home alone and watching the news (Fink, 2007).[7] In much the same way that patients in behavioral therapies need to regularly practice relaxation to reach their goal of a more relaxed lifestyle (e.g., Bernstein, Borkovec, & Hazlett-Stevens, 2000), psychodynamic therapists need to be similarly diligent when learning how to listen.

Freud's Ideal of "Evenly-Hovering Attention" and Theoretical Alternatives

Freud had strong opinions on how to listen to patients. His idea went by several different names (e.g., evenly suspended attention, free-floating attention), but for consistency's sake I will refer to it as "evenly-hovering attention" (i.e., *gleichschwebend*; Freud, 1958b). He wrote:

> *The technique . . . is a very simple one. It consists simply in not directing one's notice to anything in particular. . . . For as soon as anyone deliberately concentrates his attention to a certain degree, he begins to select from the material before him . . . in making these selections he will be following his expectations and inclinations. This, however, is precisely what must not be done. In making the selection . . . he is in danger of never finding anything but what he already knows; and if he follows his inclinations he will certainly falsify what he may perceive. He should simply listen, and not bother about whether he is keeping anything in mind.* (Freud, 1958b, pp. 111–112)

In this passage, Freud seems to encourage us to listen without prejudice (in the sense of prejudging) and instead to give ourselves over to the many possibilities in the conscious and unconscious minds of both our patients and ourselves. This could even be thought of as the therapist's equivalent to patient free association.

For Freud, listening was a *passive* process in which the analyst tried to avoid imposing theoretical ideas or preconceptions onto the patient. Instead, the therapist tried to listen with what could be termed *fresh ears*, letting nothing unduly influence their attention. After enough material is generated, evenly-hovering attention is no longer needed (for the time being at least), and the therapist *acts* by making an intervention based on session material.

Evenly-hovering attention is a fascinating concept that was developed further by people such as Reik (1948; see also Safran, 2011). However, this idea has been sharply criticized (Spence, 1982, pp. 113–114), not on the grounds of whether it was clever or not, but because this ideal may not actually be possible. Spence and others influenced by hermeneutic philosophers (Bernstein, 1983; Gadamer, 1975) believed that listening was a more *active* process that necessarily involved both selective attention and prejudgments. Could it really be otherwise? Perform a quick thought experiment: could you listen to your patient for any reasonable length of time without having theories and your own personal experiences subtly intrude into your thoughts? Probably not, but the next question we might ask ourselves is whether this is necessarily a bad thing.

Therapists, just like their patients (see Chapter 3), can gain freedom through recognizing the many ways that they are determined. With regard to the *theories* that are held, it is important to not view them as absolute "truths" but rather as useful tools that allow us to see people and the world in particular ways. Even though I love psychodynamic theories, I also recognize that they, like all theories (e.g., behaviorism, special relativity) are necessarily incomplete. This is due to the unavoidable fact that, just as a theory tells us which phenomena are important to pay attention to (e.g., defense mechanisms, transference), they also tell us what is less important and even *unimportant*. So long as we recognize this fact and do not reify our theories (i.e., treat them as if they were "real things"), they are useful constructs.

Similarly, patient material might affect us in different ways depending upon our personal life histories. As one example, a female patient may come to session and report a great deal of pain and vague gastrointestinal symptoms. Suppose this patient is being seen by a male therapist whose mother tended to somaticize her distress and often complained about her own symptoms. When listening to the patient, the therapist may not only start searching for evidence of somatization (or even "faking it") but might also experience the patient as annoying. If the therapist is unaware of these personal biases, it could lead them to miss important information or even alienate the patient. If, on the other hand, the therapist is aware of these biases, they could entertain somatization as just one of *several* possibilities (e.g., medication side effects) and avoid prematurely prioritizing one hypothesis over others. This latter situation is obviously preferable to having "blind" prejudgments/ biases in operation (Bernstein, 1983).[8] Awareness of prejudgments may be particularly important when dealing with people who are different from you—whether in terms of age, culture, race, symptomatology, or socioeconomic background—and may help minimize the innumerable possibilities for misunderstanding.

Due to all these reasons, listening without expectation is likely not possible. Instead of trying to reach this unattainable goal of evenly-hovering attention, it might be more prudent to (a) self-consciously recognize our theories as helpful, but limited tools and (b) try to become more aware of our pre-existing personal biases. With awareness of these two sources of prejudgment, we can try to listen with more openness and flexibility.

Empathic Attention to the Four Channels of Communication

It would make our jobs much easier if we only needed to pay attention to *words*. We are not so lucky, as words are only one very limited form of communication. To gain a good enough understanding of our patients, we have to take in several other different streams of information. The type and number of "channels" vary according to psychodynamic author (e.g., three in Yeomans et al., 2015; seven in Cabaniss, Cherry, Douglas, & Schwartz, 2011), but I usually focus on the four listed in Box 8.2. Each of these channels not only provides information on its own, but becomes even more useful when discrepancies arise (e.g., angry nonverbal behaviors juxtaposed with verbal denials of anger). These discrepancies, just like breaks in free association, may point to unresolved issues or potential conflicts.

Box 8.2.

THE FOUR CHANNELS OF COMMUNICATION

- What is said
- What is *not* said
- Nonverbal behaviors
- The therapist's countertransference reactions

CHANNEL 1: WHAT IS SAID

When we engage in what Frederickson (1999) termed "natural" listening, we primarily pay attention to speech *content* (pp. 5–9). This makes sense, as words are important starting points. They are quick and efficient means of conveying information and signifying important life events and reactions. Words themselves have individual meanings (e.g., "afraid," "regrets"), and the patient's idiosyncratic *combinations* of words generate even greater meanings (e.g., "I am afraid that I am going to die with regrets"). Along with syntax and semantics, words also convey information through the volume, tone, and speed with which they are articulated.

When listening psychodynamically, as opposed to naturally, words do not only convey surface-level information. They are also believed to point toward unconscious themes which preoccupy the patient. For example, when listening to a patient's initial free associations, the therapist may identify an emerging topic that serves as a link between the seemingly disparate communications (e.g., a theme of anxiety over abandonment).

Words may also point to unconscious reactions and conflicts. For example, "off-the-cuff" remarks (Cabaniss et al., 2011) said to the therapist (e.g., "You look like a priest today") may indicate transference phenomena (i.e., "I am experiencing you as judgmental, just like my father"). Similarly, comments directed toward others may in actuality be intended for the therapist (i.e., displacements). Further, *parapraxes* in their many forms (i.e., slips of the tongue, pen, or action) may also indicate unconscious processes. If, for instance, a patient was discussing their upcoming wedding ceremony and accidentally replaced the word "wedding" with "funeral," the listener would not even need to have dynamic training to hypothesize that premarital anxiety may be present.

It is important to also keep in mind that verbal disclosures are not solely influenced by patient factors. What a patient says in session is largely dependent upon their overall comfort level. Without appropriate therapist empathy and a good alliance, it is unlikely that patients will feel relaxed enough to provide good information through this channel.

CHANNEL 2: WHAT IS *NOT* SAID

Just as the old cliché states that "silences can be deafening," verbal absences can sometimes be apocalyptically meaningful. This is because a lack of communication is itself a communication. Absences are often judged *as absences* based on the therapist's experience of what is "normal" or "expected." We and our patients fortunately share in the human experience and have interacted with many people over the course of our respective lives. As a result, we can always ask ourselves the question: "all things being equal, what should also be here that is not?"

Some clinical examples may help. For instance, if a patient described in great detail how they cruelly harmed their romantic partner but disclosed no feelings of remorse, the absence of guilt may be telling. It may indicate anything from defensiveness, poor empathy, or even psychopathic traits. As another example, if a patient spent 40 minutes discussing their family and never once mentioned their father, this could point to important clinical material (i.e., the omission of paternal conflict).

Brief mention should also be made of lies. Lies of omission or commission are more common in psychotherapy than many clinicians realize (Blanchard & Farber, 2015). Though there are many patient motivations for dishonesty and the withholding of information, lies can create serious problems in session and ultimately corrupt the treatment.[9] Therefore, they should be addressed as soon as possible.

CHANNEL 3: NONVERBAL BEHAVIORS

Both a picture and a nonverbal behavior can be worth a thousand words. Gestures, facial expressions, and actions all convey massive amounts of information in a recognizable but nonlinguistic manner. Some of these behaviors are obvious, as when we witness a phobic patient's pupils dilate upon seeing a large spider. Some can be more ambiguous, as when we observe a slight tremor on a patient's hands. Is this shaking due to fear, anxiety, a neurological condition, or a medication side effect? This example points to the major difficulty with Channel 2. Namely, although nonverbal communications are informative, they are notoriously difficult to interpret. This is especially the case with patients who may not be able to communicate with Channel 1 at all (e.g., severely intellectually disabled people or those suffering from mutism).

This decoding problem is not unique to nonverbals, though, as most words have multiple definitions as well (e.g., gravity means "seriousness" and a physical force). However, there are no dictionaries for the many meanings of actions. As just one example, consider tears. When a patient's eyes well up after their therapist asks what is was like for them to put their beloved dog to sleep, the meaning may be readily apparent. In other situations, the meaning could be far murkier. We have all heard of tears of joy (i.e., happiness), "hot tears" (i.e., anger), and even tears of frustration. These are all *emotional* or *psychic tears*, but there are also *reflex tears* (i.e., caused by noxious fumes) and *basal tears*, which keep the eyes moist. Tears can also be self-consciously produced to elicit sympathy or pity (i.e., the tears of the crocodilian).

Both "acting in" (behaviors within session) and "acting out" (behaviors outside of session) are also considered to be nonverbal communications. In both variants, emotions or conflicts are discharged in *action* instead of being explored and expressed with words. Examples range from the subtle (e.g., a patient upset with their therapist leaves their soiled paper towel on the floor of the office bathroom) to the extreme (a patient with an eroticized transference begins to undress during session).[10]

Though often ambiguous, Channel 2 data are valuable. After introducing myself to a new assessment patient, his first action upon entering my office was not to take the seat I offered, but to instead sit on the heating unit. This was in a corner, next to the window and was, strategically, the point in the office that was farthest away from both my chair and the door. Please think for a moment of the many possible messages—ranging from the reasonable to the preposterous—that the patient could be communicating through his action. Could he be confused, scared, or hearing impaired? Moving toward the more preposterous, could he be really cold, have a heater fetish, or maybe just need direct sunlight? When I situated his behavior in the context of other Channel 2 communications (e.g., the fact that he was somewhat malodorous, appeared disheveled, and his eyes were darting to and fro), I considered paranoia and/or schizophrenia to be the most likely explanation. This hypothesis was subsequently supported through information gained from Channels 1 and 4.

CHANNEL 4: THERAPIST COUNTERTRANSFERENCE

Countertransference information deserves special mention. Indeed, it is hard to imagine contemporary psychodynamic therapy without heavily relying upon this channel. Confusion in terminology may occur, however, as this term has undergone heavy theoretical and technical modification over the past century (Sharpless & Barber, 2015).

Freud's original concept was quite narrow: a therapist's transference onto the patient. This was not a desirable state of affairs and was seen as dangerous for the treatment. Later, the scope of countertransference was broadened to include "the total emotional reaction of the psychoanalyst to the patient in the treatment situation" (Kernberg, 1965, p. 38).

This *totalistic* conception of countertransference profoundly influenced the moment-to-moment practice of psychodynamic therapy, as therapists began to more systematically use their reactions to patients to guide interventions. Therefore, a therapist's subjective feelings of boredom, annoyance, anger, or any subtle "pulls" to act in a particular way (i.e., an enactment) could convey **valuable clinical information** (e.g., **Cabaniss, Cherry, Douglas, & Schwartz, 2011**). To be clear, though, countertransference reactions are most useful when therapists have a good understanding of themselves. It is crucial to be able to differentiate between an idiosyncratic, *unique* reaction to the patient (e.g., the therapist previously described and his somaticizing patient) versus a reaction that *almost anyone* in their patient's inner circle would have.[11] Similarly, it is very important to pay attention to any feelings of threat that may be emanating from the patient.

These "gut-level" reactions are evolutionarily adaptive and, presumably, there for a reason (i.e., to help you avoid bodily harm).

Proper psychodynamic listening presupposes that the therapist can be an emotionally engaged *participant* in their patient's internal world as well as a keen *observer* of all their many subtle and nuanced communications. Some have seen the participant and the observer stance as a false dichotomy because a shared interpersonal space is thought to be created during session that is both/neither of the two (Sullivan, 1953; see also Stolorow, Brandschaft, & Atwood, 1995). I have no reason to view this as inaccurate. Regardless, even if the two constructs cannot truly be decoupled, they may nonetheless be useful abstractions to consider. At the very least, there are shifts in emphasis over the course of any given session that are noteworthy (e.g., being emotionally engaged in one moment and finding oneself being preoccupied with an unusual speech mannerism of the patient at another).

NOTES

1. Silence, in a sense, fans the transferential flame.
2. Silence should not be used as a means for the therapist to act out nontherapeutic reactions. For instance, we are all familiar with receiving "the silent treatment" from someone. This passive expression of anger has no place in psychotherapy. Similarly, silence can also be used as a means of conveying superiority or power over the patient (Heller, 1985).
3. This may not be the case with some borderline patients. In these instances, it is prudent to allow more time to transition from session to the "outside world" by not opening up new material too close to the end of session or, alternately, by closing off distressing chains of association.
4. In fact, Strachey's translation of Freud added to this confusion. Freud used the German terms *Einfall,* or literally, "irruption" as well as *Assoziation,* which indicates connection. As noted by Thomä and Kächele (1992), *Einfall* implies a spontaneously occurring idea (which has a creative quality) as opposed to mere connection. These have been collapsed in our English translations, but one can see the utility of considering "free association" in this broader sense.
5. Thomä and Kächele (1992) wisely noted that patient instructions to free associate do not remove conscious resistances, let alone unconscious ones.
6. This is also in keeping with psychic determinism and overdetermination (see Chapter 4).
7. I recommend that my students *not* practice psychodynamic listening on their friends or relatives. Along with the very real possibility that they might create awkward moments, a pre-existing relationship inhibits the ability to be appropriately abstinent and neutral (see Chapter 9).
8. Gadamer (1975) and Bernstein, (1983), among others, would argue that, far from being a bad thing, prejudices/prejudgments are actually gateways to shared understanding. However, this is only if we are not *blind* to them but instead use them as windows into the world of others who might not share the same prejudgments.

Through interacting together, an enlarged space of shared understanding (i.e., a "fusion of horizons") is created. In this sense, prejudgments enable us to not only gain more knowledge about our patients but also increase empathy.

9. Several confrontations (see Chapter 12) can be useful for dealing with patient dishonesty.

10. For additional discussions of acting out, see McWilliams (2011) and Yeomans et al. (2015).

11. It is often useful for the therapist to recall patient reports of other people having similar reactions and to bring these to the patient's attention. This helps circumvent excessive therapist self-disclosure of countertransference reactions.

9

Foundational Techniques Part II

The previous chapter addressed the important foundational techniques of therapist silence, patient free association, and ways to listen in a psychodynamic manner. In this chapter, we will focus on therapist behaviors which help (a) establish the "frame" of psychodynamic therapy and (b) help socialize the patient into treatment.

HOW TO BEHAVE IN A PSYCHODYNAMIC MANNER

How should a therapist "act" when conducting psychodynamic psychotherapy? When I started treating my initial patients during the summer of my first year of graduate school, I was very preoccupied with this question. I had done a good bit of reading about technical neutrality, abstinence, and so on, so I felt that I had a theoretical handle on *what not to do*. A bigger problem when I entered session was that I did not exactly know what *to do*. Sadly for my patients, I believe that I unwittingly adopted the caricatured presentation of a movie psychoanalyst. As I reviewed video of these first sessions with both my classmates and my psychodynamic supervisor (shown on a large monitor in an embarrassing therapist–patient split screen, no less), I barely recognized myself; my usual expressions and personality traits were noticeably absent. Though I feared that *too many* of my reactions were coming across to patients, it was painfully apparent to me that the exact opposite was true.[1] Fortunately, both my supervisor and my patients were very understanding as I learned to better think and feel my way into being a therapist.

Looking back, I mistakenly viewed some of the concepts detailed in the following discussion as "rules" to be followed instead of helpful guidelines/regulative ideals. These concepts are not meant to squeeze the humanity out of therapists, but are there to help maintain session focus (i.e., on the patient), establish good boundaries, and allow the psychodynamic process to unfold. The application of these skills necessarily varies according to the needs of each patient (see Chapter 5). Further, this manner of acting need not be "acting" in the sense of "faking" a role. There are ways to adhere to good psychodynamic techniques without being robotic or inauthentic.

Patient-Appropriate Psychodynamic Ambiguity

Psychodynamic therapists self-consciously impose boundaries between themselves and patients. The nature and extent of these boundaries vary according to which therapist is asked, and they also appear to have shifted over time. For instance, some of my older psychoanalyst supervisors told me that, during the heyday of *American ego psychology*, it was not uncommon for analysts to remove wedding rings before session. This was done so patients had no idea if they were married or not. Though this may sound extreme to our contemporary ears, it is nonetheless reflective of a general reluctance to have too much of the therapist bleed into session. This reluctance is captured by the terms *ambiguity* and *abstinence*. Though they do share some conceptual overlap and are sometimes collapsed under one umbrella term (i.e., "abstinence"), they can be considered separately according to their different *intentions*.

The presumption behind anonymity was that too much patient knowledge of the therapist, whether in terms of history, values, beliefs, and so on, interfered with the therapeutic process. Not only would this personal information shift attention away from the patient's internal world and toward the therapist, but it also burdened the patient (see Chapters 4 and 10).

Freud's (1958) famous analogy for anonymity or *analytic reserve* was: "The doctor should be opaque to his patients and, like a mirror, should show them nothing but what is shown to him" (p. 118). Much like the ideal of evenly-hovering attention (Chapter 8), this idea has been incisively critiqued, and most therapists today believe that behaving like a "mirror" or "blank screen" is an impossibility. Think about how much you can tell about a person just from their accent, their word choices, the clothes they wear, the books they own, and the way they decorate their office. All these behaviors convey information. Therefore, no one is, or ever could be, a totally blank screen to any other person. This inadvertent flow of information from the therapist to the patient does not imply that "anything goes" or that therapists should *intend* to be transparent; in most cases this would be unhelpful. These limitations on ambiguity should instead serve a cautionary function and remind us of our potential influence on patients.

Individual therapists differ in the information they are comfortable disclosing. The reader is encouraged to find their own boundaries but, speaking only for myself, I impose numerous limits. I will certainly respond to questions about my professional background (e.g., education, therapeutic approaches taken, experience with their particular problem) and, at times, my knowledge of certain cultural commonplaces (e.g., whether I saw a particular movie or read a particular book). However, I see no benefit resulting from a patient knowing about my personal history, family background, social or political beliefs, sexual behaviors, or personal dreams and wishes.[2] Not only are the answers to these questions potentially burdensome for the patient, but they are also truly beside the point. Straightforward disclosures often do not even answer the patient's "real" questions. For instance, when working with patients who are older than you, it is fairly common to be asked about your age. A dynamic therapist would likely not respond to this question directly, not only because it is irrelevant to the therapy process but also because the words do not convey the patient's true intentions. The patient is better served by responding to the *underlying* question and not the surface words (e.g., "I wonder if you are concerned I might not have enough experience to help you with your problem"). Many patient requests for disclosure are like this (see Chapter 10). Granted, some disclosures could easily serve as "short-cuts" to forming the bond part of the alliance (e.g., "See how similar we are?"; see also Henretty & Levitt, 2010), but would move the relationship toward friendship. One can be both relatively anonymous and a warm, caring therapist (McWilliams, 2011).

Reasonable levels of ambiguity may be harder to maintain due to current technological advances and social media. Many therapists today have a "digital footprint" consisting of social media pictures, blogs, news articles, and online comments. All of these are potentially searchable, and therapists would be naïve to think their patients do not do this (Kolmes & Taube, 2016). For instance, one of my patients brought up the fact that I received an award from the Penn State University Library for working 1,000 hours during undergrad. Though a small and relatively impersonal matter, I am certain this information was never disclosed during session, and I later found it online.

Patient Appropriate Psychodynamic Abstinence

As opposed to anonymity, which seeks to focus session attention on the patient and minimize the impact of the therapist's viewpoints, abstinence protects against patients gaining unhealthy *gratifications*. These are desired by the patient but ultimately counterproductive. Patients come to therapy with any number of unmet needs and subterranean wishes; these only intensify as the patient safely regresses during session. Some patients may display dependent needs (e.g., "Please tell me what to do"), some have a desire for specialness (e.g., "Please treat me differently than others"; "If you care, the normal rules don't apply to me"), and others wish to transgress normal boundaries and express primitive needs (e.g., sexual, aggressive, or otherwise).

Patient desires often manifest as transference. Transference has been defined in many ways over the past hundred years (Sharpless & Barber, 2015) but can be usefully thought of as the patient's attempts to organize and assimilate their relationship with the therapist into pre-existing relational histories and psychic structures (Stolorow, Brandschaft, & Atwood, 1995). Transference wishes, like any other need, feel natural and eminently reasonable to the person experiencing them. From Freud (1958a) onward, however, there has been relative unanimity that some needs should not be directly gratified by the therapist; they should instead be analyzed and understood.[3]

Maintaining patient-appropriate levels of abstinence is challenging and often violates the conventions of normal human behavior. For instance, when normal people ask for advice, normal people usually respond with advice. Therapists should not always be normal. This is especially the case in the more expressive approaches (Chapter 15 discusses advice in the context of supportive therapies). Advice undermines the goal of patient autonomy, as patients may passively follow guidance instead of learning how to better rely on *their own* capacities (Etchegoyen, 2012). Behavior therapists are not the only ones who believe in positive reinforcement, and giving advice once will only result in additional requests.

As previously noted, patients may want to be treated as if they were "special," and an appropriate application of abstinence is useful in these cases. For example, several of my patients have attempted to violate terms of the therapeutic contract without consequence (i.e., repeatedly arriving late to session and attempting to stay late past the end time). If I merely gratified these needs, not only would their behavior likely get worse and their maladaptive needs remain unexplored, but I would also begin to feel resentful of their lackadaisical attitude toward treatment and their seeming indifference to my schedule. Therefore, not only would therapeutic progress falter, but I would also have negative countertransference reactions. If I instead remained appropriately abstinent and focused on the task of *understanding* their needs—as opposed to fulfilling them—progress would be more likely to occur.[4]

In general, it is perfectly acceptable for patients to have certain needs frustrated in therapy. Though sessions should feel safe and devoid of overt judgment, therapy cannot always be satisfying or comfortable. As previously noted, the goal of autonomy requires patients to recognize their role in getting their own needs met. In other words, patients increasingly learn to rely upon *themselves,* not the therapist. Freud believed that the experience of frustration served as a motivating force in therapy (see Ainslie, 1986), and this makes sense. If therapy satisfied all needs and eliminated responsibility, what would be the patient's impetus for change?

It is important to note that abstinence should be applied to *therapists'* needs just as consistently as to patients'. Abstinence should serve to limit unhealthy therapist motivations—narcissistic or otherwise—from leaking out in session. In a parallel fashion to patients, some therapists feel a need to have their specialness acknowledged, and this is rarely therapeutic.

For example, I discovered that a supervisee working exclusively with adults structured his initial patient meetings in what I judged to be a nonanonymous and nonabstinent manner. Prior to session, he placed a multicolored stuffed animal (a member of the supernatural bestiary) on the patient's chair. When patients entered the office they necessarily had to deal with the toy in some fashion. As the patient would confusedly (and very reasonably, from my perspective) inquire into why it was on the chair and what they should do with it, the therapist would note its "name" and say that it "was there for them if they needed it." The therapist's desk also displayed a number of personal items (e.g., photos of his children), and the walls were adorned with large cut-outs of phrases and sayings that he found inspirational. After gently inquiring into the potential impacts that these nonabstinent behaviors and personal disclosures could have on his patients, I encouraged him to explore his own motivations. They seemed to be more therapist-centered. In general, any distractions away from patient concerns should be assiduously avoided.

In ending this section, it is important to note that partial gratifications of transference wishes are inevitable in therapy, and that this is not necessarily a bad thing. Partial gratifications include innocuous therapist behaviors such as laughing at patient jokes, empathically listening, tearing up during sad stories, and so on (Gabbard, 2014). These authentic human reactions help inject warmth and support into an admittedly difficult process. Further, therapists can themselves use humor during session so long as it is done for therapeutic purposes and not to aggrandize themselves in the eyes of their patients. Humor not only lightens the heaviness of therapeutic exploration but also facilitates multiple perspective-taking and fosters a movement away from rigid patterns of understanding and meaning-making (Borkovec & Sharpless, 2004).

Technical Neutrality

Technical neutrality is often confused with therapeutic abstinence, but they refer to different prohibitions. Neutrality also has slightly different meanings depending on the patient's level of personality organization (i.e., neurotic, borderline, or psychotic). However, it essentially consists of not taking sides in conflicts or making unnecessary judgments.

Interestingly, neither Sigmund nor Anna Freud coined the phrase "technical neutrality," but Anna defined it. In 1936 she wrote that "when he [the analyst] sets about the work of enlightenment, he takes his stand at a point equidistant from the id, the ego, and the superego" (Freud, 1966, p. 28).

She felt that it was not the therapist's job to side with any of these psychic structures (e.g., superego over id) but to instead help the patient understand their structural *conflicts* to meet psychodynamic goals, especially insight. Thus, the therapist should remain between the conflicting forces (i.e., away from both) but close to the "observing ego." Many contemporary dynamic therapists would view this conception of neutrality as most applicable to *neurotically organized* individuals.

Therapists working with *borderline-organized* patients utilize a different conception of neutrality. Since borderlines often lack the clear psychic structures of neurotics (Yeomans, Clarkin, & Kernberg, 2015), therapists instead adopt a neutral position based on the patient's object relations. Specifically, therapists try to occupy a space between the patient's conflicted representations of self and other as well as between split-off object relational dyads. As one example, the therapist would side neither with a patient's internal representation of a weak, abused self nor the representation of a strong, abusive other.

Neutrality with psychotic patients has not yet been well-defined but would include a similarly nonjudgmental stance and a therapist partnership with the observing ego. The brittleness of the psychotic ego, combined with its tenuous linkage to consensual reality, usually necessitates frequent deviations from neutrality. This is in keeping with the less abstinent and more "real" interactions found in supportive treatments (see Chapters 5, 14, and 15)

Like some other psychodynamic constructs, neutrality is an ideal that likely cannot be reached in practice. For the good of our patients, though, we should approximate neutrality to the greatest extent that is possible. What does this mean? Clearly, therapists are also human beings, and we can all be unhelpfully judgmental by holding strong personal opinions about how our patients should live their lives. We often think—but hopefully do not say—that "they should do what I would do if I was in their situation." However, as noted several times already, psychodynamic therapists should not be agents of social control or vehicles for patient indoctrination. We have a duty to keep our personal judgments to ourselves and not allow them to manifest *even indirectly* in session (e.g., a disapproving eyebrow raise). Technical neutrality helps ensure that patients find their own way in life.

There are several situations where neutrality is contraindicated. We cannot withhold judgment on dangerous behaviors (i.e., threats to self or others; antisocial activities) or threats to treatment (e.g., violating terms of the treatment contract). Fortunately, in these situations we do not even necessarily need to bring up our *personal* predilections or judgments, as they are clearly documented elsewhere (e.g., the therapy contract described in the following discussion; state/provincial/national laws that govern what to do with threats). Regardless of the particular way in which we "judge," though, we clearly cannot stay neutral in these circumstances.

. Whenever deviations from neutrality occur, and especially in those cases where there are direct therapist suggestions for action, it is usually a good idea to discuss these deviations with patients. This is often most helpful *after* the fact and when the patient is closer to their baseline functioning (Yeomans et al., 2015). Such discussions may help foster the patient's observing ego and capacity to mentalize. For example, a therapist might state: "You may remember last week I suggested that you not continue calling your ex-girlfriend due to your restraining order. As you know, this is not what I usually do in sessions with you, so it might be worthwhile for you and me to discuss how this came about. Do you have any thoughts about this to get us started?"

Modeling of Adaptive Behavior

Through all their words and deeds, therapists convey a particular way of being in the world (Heller, 1985). Further, no psychotherapy is ever value-neutral, nor

Table 9.1. SOME BEHAVIORS AND VALUES TO MODEL FOR PATIENTS.

Asking good questions	Behaving in an ethical manner
Postponing gratifications	Thoughtfully exploring confusing experiences
Self-respect	Self-awareness
Self-reliance	Self-protection (e.g., emotional)
Treatment of others in a noncoercive and nonexploitative manner	Appropriately acknowledging errors and limitations
Honesty	Nonperfectionism
Right to privacy	Ego strength
Reliability (e.g., punctuality)	Good judgment

could it be. Therefore, psychodynamic therapists strive to act in such a way that they model *adaptive* ways of living and being for their patients. Some of these are listed in Table 9.1. The astute reader may notice some overlap with "good parenting" behaviors. Given that no two children or patients are exactly alike, the application of these values and behaviors could be more or less challenging.

Several examples may help. If, for instance, a patient had a particularly harsh superego and was very self-critical of any perceived errors, the therapist would do well to directly own up to their own mistakes in session. This would not be done to needlessly self-punish but to instead convey the message that "it is perfectly acceptable to occasionally make mistakes."[5] Similarly, therapists should strive to be reliable in their dealings with all patients, but most assiduously with their least responsible ones. Sessions should start and end on time, and it should be apparent to the patient that the therapist is working hard on their behalf.

Special mention should be made of ethical and honest behavior. Patients may ask therapists to take unethical actions, usually under the guise of "helping" them in some way. This may be more common with patients who have a history of unethical/criminal behaviors. For example, they may ask their therapist to lie for them or engage in some type of insurance fraud (e.g., listing less "severe" diagnoses on insurance forms). Therapists need to be especially careful of these situations and stand their ethical ground. This diligence may result in tense situations and even patient anger, but the alternatives are unacceptable and antitherapeutic.

HOW TO START PSYCHODYNAMIC PSYCHOTHERAPY

For psychodynamic techniques to be effectively applied, patients need to be socialized into therapy. There are too many different types of therapies and therapists for a patient to reasonably know what to expect and what is expected. This can be a problem for them. Further, psychodynamic therapists may, at times, defy the patient's expectations (e.g., with therapist silence and anonymity). Therefore, patients need to have some idea of what they should do. Therapy is hard enough, and I see no purpose in troubling patients with excessive ambiguity.[6] Along with clearly explaining the need for unfiltered free associations (see Chapter 8), a treatment contract helps clarify the process.

Frame-Setting/Contracting

Most professional relationships use some form of contract, and psychodynamic therapy is no exception. The function of the contract is to define each party's respective roles and responsibilities. As shown in Table 9.2, some roles are shared, some are complimentary, and others are unique to each party. Some responsibilities are implicitly learned in the process of doing psychotherapy (e.g., allowing the therapist time or space to be thoughtful) whereas others should be directly broached during the first session (e.g., therapist limits of confidentiality, trainee status). Therapy contracts are usually done orally and informally but, if needed, could easily be written down to make them more "official."

In general, I like the *transference-focused psychotherapy* (TFP) approach to contracting (for more details, see Yeomans et al., 2015; Yeomans, Selzer, & Clarkin, 1992). Though formulated for borderline patients, the principles can be applied across the four levels of personality organization (i.e., normal, neurotic, borderline, and psychotic). TFP views the contract as a joint creation of the therapist and the patient. It is not a one-sided procedure, but rather results from a dialogue. Though some parts of the contract may be "deal breakers" (e.g., a patient not accepting a plan to deal with suicidality), others are certainly more negotiable (e.g., fees). Further, contracts are not viewed as "finalized" and can always be scaled up or down according to the emergence of new clinical material and, of course, patient–therapist agreement.

TFP encourages the *least restrictive* contract necessary for treatment. As contracts are intended to serve the patient's and therapist's best interests, they need to be restrictive enough to be helpful (i.e., do they allow real therapy to take place?) but not so constraining that they are unreasonable for either party. Not only does this idea of "least restrictive" imply that you need to know your patient fairly well (e.g., level of judgment, suicidal risk, etc.), but you also need to know your own comfort levels. One way of conceptualizing contracts is to think of them as a method to ensure that the therapist has time and space to think clearly (Yeomans et al., 2015, p. 100). This could vary according to patient. When treating a relatively healthy neurotic patient, for example, the contract may only require the contents of Table 9.2. If, however, you are working with a more labile borderline patient with a history of suicide attempts and regular cutting behaviors, a more sophisticated contract would be advisable (e.g., explicit procedures on what to do when the patient feels suicidal; limits to patient phone calls). In the former case, the process of contracting may only take a few minutes, but in the latter it may take several sessions.

Table 9.2. SOME GENERAL RESPONSIBILITIES IN PSYCHODYNAMIC THERAPY

Therapist Responsibilities	Patient Responsibilities
Patient-focused attentiveness	Free association
Honesty (appropriate to the patient)	Honesty
Offer regular sessions and give notice of absences	Attend sessions regularly and give notice of absences
Provide a safe, open environment for the patient to explore themselves (i.e., "space")	Tolerate occasional therapist silence
Help identify patient's problems	Help identify their own problems
Establish reasonable wishes and expectations for therapy	Establish reasonable wishes and expectations for therapy
Assist the patient in self-exploration	Take an *active* role in the treatment
Attempt to gain a sophisticated understanding of the patient's internal and external worlds	Attempt to reflect on the therapist's comments or interactions, even if they are uncomfortable
Frank discussion of patient commitments and the limits of therapist involvement (attendance, fees, time limits, etc.)	Adherence to terms of the contract and willingness to discuss deviations (preferably in advance)
Help focus sessions on important matters (at least during certain times)	Self-exploration even in the face of uncertainty or confusion
Follow ethical and legal guidelines	Disclose potential threats to self or other
Disclose professional information (e.g., credentials, graduate student/trainee status)	Candidly discuss feelings toward the therapist and the therapy (especially desires to end treatment)
Provide contact info and emergency instructions	Willingness to maintain treatment, at least for a while, even if things get "tough"
Protect patient confidentiality	Allow the therapist time/space to be thoughtful
Maintain professional boundaries	
Protect and maintain the treatment	

Needless to say, contracts should be individualized for each patient and easily understandable. There is no role for jargon or long-winded statements during contracting, as these inevitably only lead to patient confusion. It is also a good idea to periodically check in with patients to make sure they understand the individual elements of the contract and can provide informed consent.

Contracting may help the therapist circumvent future threats to treatment. Along with the more dramatic examples (e.g., suicidal and homicidal behaviors), there are any number of subtler threats that can be preemptively dealt with. For instance, if your patient has a history of sudden and one-sided terminations, the contract could include a requirement for prior discussion with the therapist.

Forming and Enhancing the Therapeutic Alliance

The therapeutic/working alliance has three components: agreement on goals, agreement on tasks, and the bond between patient and therapist (Bordin, 1979; Horvath & Greenberg, 1989). Of all the "common factor" variables in psycho-therapy research, there is likely no construct as well-studied as the alliance (Muran & Barber, 2010). The alliance is reliably associated with outcome in all therapies, dynamic therapy included (Barber, Muran, McCarthy, & Keefe, 2013), but the precise nature of this association is complex and somewhat contested (Zilcha-Mano, 2017). Regardless, once there is consensus on the spe-cific goals for treatment as well as agreement on who exactly is going to do what (i.e., clarity on patient and therapist *roles*), you are well on your way to having an alliance.

Given limited space, only some of the *therapist* factors associated with the alli-ance will be noted here (for more details, see Barber et al., 2013; Sharpless, Muran, & Barber, 2010). In general, professionalism, attachment style (secure is better), flexibility, good use of techniques (including silence), and certain personality traits (e.g., agreeableness, conscientiousness) are all thought to help form a strong alliance. More bond-specific qualities include empathy, attentiveness, interested-ness, the capacity to tolerate strong affect, responsiveness, and sensitivity. In sum-mary, patients need to like us and trust us enough for them to be able to tolerate intense self-examination.

Fostering the "Good Split"

One of the most important things that a therapist can do when starting work with their patients is to help them foster what I will term the "good split." Typically, the idea of having any sort of split is seen by psychologists/psychiatrists as bad (e.g., the defense mechanism of splitting so common in borderline patients), but this is not always the case. It is extremely desirable for patients to have a split between the *experiencing* and *observing* parts of their egos (Greenson, 1967). All patients, even the most impaired, have this capacity to a greater or lesser degree. If they are in the latter group, the impact of psychodynamic therapy will be profoundly lim-ited until this deficit is remedied.

We are all familiar with an *experiencing ego*. For instance, you may sometimes feel sad and cry without reflection. In this case, you are aware of your sadness but are "in the moment" and totally engrossed in the experience. If you were instead to look at yourself (almost like you would observe another person), study your feelings, and reflect on your sadness and what—if anything—you should do about it, you are engaging your *observing ego* capacities.

It might be useful to think of the distinction between the experiencing and observing egos as different ways of listening to music. In the former, you become absorbed in a song. You are moved by it, and as you listen the rest of your environment recedes into the background. Alternately, you could think about the song in a different way. You could instead try to figure out the time signature or key of the music or begin to wonder how the guitar player was able to get that particular tone out of their amplifier. Both ways of listening can be useful depending upon the goals and attendant circumstances.[7]

Given the high value that psychodynamic therapists place on self-examination for both themselves and their patients, the utility of having an observing ego is apparent. How could an exploratory therapy take place if this capacity was not engaged? How could a patient even identity their problems *as problems* unless they could observe them? To be clear, though, I am not arguing that the observing ego is "good" for therapy and the experiencing one is "bad." The matter is far more complicated and nuanced, as dynamic therapy requires that patients utilize both at different times. Even in psychoanalysis, the epitome of expressive therapy, the experiencing ego is purposefully engaged by design. This is the reason why free association and the chaise/couch are used: both encourage a controlled regression so that the patient can experience thoughts and emotions as they happen in the moment and without the observing ego's interference. There is certainly a role for observation in psychodynamic therapy, but intense experiences are also required. Good therapy presupposes both.

Psychodynamic therapists have many means available to encourage a good split. First, and most important, therapists can ask thoughtful questions and make helpful clarifications (see Chapters 10 and 11). Self-monitoring is not limited to cognitive and behavioral approaches, and psychodynamic patients require it as well. They may not be assigned the task of maintaining daily diaries but need to begin noticing when and where they have their troubling symptoms, reactions, or emotions. Therapists can assist them by asking questions such as, "Where were you during your last panic attack? What were you feeling at the time? What do you make of the fact that you were at your parent's house during that episode?"

Second, therapists need to engage their patient's curiosity. For most patients, this is not a terribly challenging task. If they were not at least mildly curious about themselves they would probably not have started therapy in the first place. Therapists can help by shining a spotlight on the patient's personal mysteries. For example, if you were treating a graduate student in epidemiology with self-destructive tendencies toward procrastination, you might say something like this (e.g., a connective confrontation; see Chapter 12),

From what you've told me, you love your work and are enjoying classes. In fact, you told me you've never felt so full of purpose. Yet, you just gave me another example of waiting until the last minute to turn in an important assignment. How do you understand this discrepancy? What I mean by that is, on the one hand, you noted that you've never felt more passionate in your life, and it would be terrible for you to fail out of school, yet on the other hand you are acting in such a way that you, yourself, are actually making this feared outcome more likely to occur by not doing your best work. I don't know about you, but I am very puzzled by this and hope we can begin to understand it better.

A therapist's tone, body language, and authentic curiosity carry a lot of weight in generating patient interest. If these are all present, the therapist will be less likely to be perceived as unhelpfully judgmental.

Third, and related to the previous point, it is important for therapists to help engage patients' *intrinsic motivations* for change. These can be extremely powerful and help the patient become more amenable to the hard work of self-observation. As noted in Chapter 3, once patients know *why* they are doing something (i.e., intrinsic motivations), the *how* (i.e., engaging in the process of dynamic therapy) becomes more tolerable. Using the previous case of procrastination, the therapist could reflect back to the patient all the many reasons they gave for wanting to succeed in graduate school (e.g., an interesting career, the ability to travel the world, a chance to make a difference in public health). Notice than none of these motivations need to (or should) come from the therapist. In much of psychodynamic therapy, the therapist's job is merely to listen carefully and allow the patient to hear their own words coming from *without*.

NOTES

1. If anything, I looked very similar to the fantasized "robot" that the patient in Chapter 7 had imagined me to be.
2. For a more thorough discussion of self-disclosures in therapy, see Farber (2006).
3. In certain applications of psychodynamic therapy, limited gratifications can take place (e.g., supportive therapies and certain aspects of self psychology as applied to narcissistic patients).
4. For an excellent demonstration of maintaining abstinence in response to an erotic transference, see the vignette of "Brenda" in Gabbard (2010).
5. Minor technical mistakes are inevitable in any therapy, so there is no need for therapists to "fake" mistakes to convey this message.
6. For an excellent example of how to socialize patients into dynamic therapy, see Luborsky (1984, pp. 192–199).
7. A therapist's alternation between participation and observation may work in a parallel fashion.

10

The Process of Questioning

INTRODUCTION TO THE PROCESS OF QUESTIONING

Questions can be powerful. They not only drive us to look closely at ourselves and the outside world but also prompt us to take action. We are all familiar with "existential" questions such as "Who am I?" "Why am I here?" "What does it mean to live a good life?" Asking these is part and parcel of being human. These queries also likely prompted the development of much of philosophy, religion, and the natural and human sciences. As such, questions have served as some of the most fundamental motivators for human behavior.

If you listen closely, almost all patients come to psychotherapy because they have unanswered questions. It is often a good clinical exercise for therapists to try to identify these, as they are usually only tacitly conveyed. Patients may be troubled by questions such as "Why am I always so sad?" "Why do I keep losing friends?" "Why do I keep sabotaging myself?" The process of dynamic therapy can help patients find answers.

THERAPIST QUESTIONS IN PSYCHODYNAMIC THERAPY

I know that it almost painfully cliché for a therapist to respond to a patient's question with *more* questions, but this is indeed an accurate description of an important part of the psychodynamic process. Could it really be otherwise? What I mean by this is that the only way to ultimately help the patient answer their questions is through the therapist asking their own questions, and in a particular way. As with therapist silence (Chapter 8), the proper use of questions

Box 10.1.

WHAT ARE THERAPIST QUESTIONS?

- *Therapist Questions* are statements meant to generate patient information that is unknown to the therapist but potentially needed for the treatment. Questions may be used to facilitate free association or to gain more specific information about the patient, their problems, and the unique ways that they think, feel, behave, and respond to the therapeutic process.

in therapy is surprisingly complex and, at least in some ways, counterintuitive (Langs, 1973, 1974).

Before proceeding to the therapeutic use of questions, it is important to first define them within a psychodynamic framework (see Box 10.1). As the definition of many canonical psychodynamic terms has shifted over time and according to author, techniques have been separated according to their therapeutic *intentions* and *functions*. As such, the primary function of questions is to *generate information*. This information is typically conscious or preconscious (Dewald, 1971)[1], and therefore readily accessible to the patient. Some questions may help foster free association whereas others focus on specific types of information. Regardless of the type of question, they are intended to produce novel and important clinical data. Thus, questioning is a process that does not really cease until therapy ends.

DIFFERENT TYPES OF QUESTIONS

Questions can be broadly divided into those intended to stimulate patient exploration and those intended to provide the therapist with specific pieces of information. Both are necessary for the process of psychodynamic psychotherapy to unfold.

Type I: Questions Intended to Stimulate Exploration

This first type of question is fairly vague and *open-ended*. It is meant to essentially serve as a stimulus for patient disclosure and free association. When asking these questions (see Box 10.2), the therapist does not have firm expectations or a clear agenda, but instead wants the patient to look inward and begin generating clinical data. Given that the patient largely directs the nature and extent of their disclosures with Type I questions,[2] the material is likely to be unexpected and presented in idiosyncratic ways. Therefore, the therapist not only unearths new information but also gains a window into the patient's thought processes. As will be discussed further, Type I questions have an important role in *all* the dynamic

---

Box 10.2.

EXAMPLES OF TWO TYPES OF THERAPIST QUESTIONS

Type I: Questions intended to stimulate patient exploration

- What seems to be troubling you?
- How do you understand his reaction to you?
- Could you tell me how affection was typically expressed in your family?

Type II: Questions intended to provide specific information

- When was the last time you made a suicide attempt?
- How old were you when your brother died?
- Did any of your other family members suffer from schizophrenia?

---

psychotherapies and are used in many psychodynamic assessment instruments.[3] Open-ended material is a prerequisite for generating the hypotheses needed for case formulation and/or treatment planning.

Type II: Questions Intended to Provide Specific Information

These types of questions are more *close-ended*. As a result, they limit the patient's freedom of response to a greater degree than the former type (see Box 10.2). In other words, they are direct questions with an expectation for direct answers.[4] To be clear, though, this does not imply that Type II questions should be "leading" or put words in the patient's mouth (e.g., "That really hurt you, right?") but are oriented toward gaining specific bits of therapy-relevant detail. As is probably apparent, there is always a specific therapist agenda behind these queries (e.g., assessing the level of threat).

ON THE WORDING OF QUESTIONS

One of the trickiest things about questions is their wording. It is always a good idea to be mindful of this. As was the case in previous chapters, the "normal" way of asking questions is somewhat at odds with dynamic therapy. For instance, in normal discourse questions are often preceded with "why" (e.g., "Why do you feel that way?"). Many dynamic therapists (e.g., Cabaniss, Cherry, Douglas, & Schwartz, 2011) caution against this practice on several grounds. Specifically, the use of "why" questions may elicit defensiveness and/or a feeling that the patient is not really being queried for information, but being asked to justify themselves. The word "why" may also harken back to earlier periods of development when parents used similar wordings (e.g., "Why did you do that?!?"). "Why" also conveys the impression that there is indeed a simple, straightforward answer that should already be known to the patient. Given the complex and often exploratory nature of psychodynamic therapy, this would be a dubious assumption at best. Instead, I usually phrase questions using: "How do you understand X?" "Do you have any thoughts about X?" "What do you believe was responsible for X?" Wordings like these tend to avoid defensive reactions and access similar patient material.

It is also helpful to ask questions using the patients' idiosyncratic wordings (see Chapter 6). So long as you are both in agreement on definitions (e.g., once you have established that a patient's "up times" are indeed manic episodes), this approach only strengthens the therapeutic alliance. Further, when using their own words, patients need to devote less cognitive attention to the question (i.e., they will not have to translate their experiences into unfamiliar psychiatric categories) and can instead devote more energy to their own thoughts.

Questions should only be as specific and structured as they need to be. If you have a fairly nonspecific agenda (e.g., you want to learn about the patient's love life), keep the questions as vague as possible, yet still able to stimulate patient discourse (e.g., "Could you tell me about your romantic relationships?"). If, on the other hand, you want Type II information, the wording should be more directive (e.g., "When did you have your last medication check?"). Aiming for the minimally needed level of structure also helps guard against therapist verbosity. Many of us error on the side of *too many* words as opposed to too few, and asking overly complicated questions only serves to confuse patients.

Mention should also be made of emotion-inducing words. It is often difficult for people to simultaneously think and feel. Usually one overpowers the other. However, proper dynamic therapy presupposes that patients access their emotions as well as their thoughts. This is not easy for many patients (e.g., those with obsessive character traits; Summers & Barber, 2010). In such cases, it is often wise to sprinkle emotional words or evocative imagery throughout questions. If, for instance, you wanted to understand a patient's reactions to depression, you might ask "How did you cope with depression?" Alternately, if you wanted to evoke more affect, you could ask, "How did you get by when you were in that dark place?"

THE FREQUENCY AND RELEVANCE OF QUESTIONS

It is very easy to turn therapy into an interrogation. Given the limited time that we have with patients (i.e., often only 50–100 minutes per week) and the unavoidable facts that (a) their lives are complicated, (b) their problems are complicated, (c) some patients are less than reliable historians, (d) patients see the world and themselves differently than we do, and (e) we really want to help them feel better, it is understandable that we may be inclined to deluge them with questions. However, we would still have a lot to ask even if we spent 24 hours a day with them. Therefore, barring the development of telepathy, there is always going to be more to learn about our patients, and people are inevitably surprising. So, how do we determine when we are doing too much questioning or not using questions in the right way?

Once assessment is finished, the Type I, more open-ended kinds of questions are often used to either identify or help focus central patient themes. Thus, asking too many questions, or asking questions haphazardly in order to "do something" in session, will likely only derail the patient's chain of associations and further scatter their thoughts (Langs, 1973, 1974). In most cases, listening carefully is the preferred approach. If no theme emerges at the beginning of session (e.g., within 10–15 minutes), clarifications (Chapter 11) or confrontations (Chapter 12) may be warranted.

A lack of theme or "something to work on" may make some therapists anxious. I have worked with supervisees who became extremely uncomfortable in these situations. Due to their own anxiety, they often made suggestions or subtly forced the patient onto a topic via leading questions like, "I seem to remember that you were upset about the family reunion last week. I wonder if you have any thoughts about that today?" The family reunion could indeed be important to the patient, but other clinical matters may be more pressing, only a bit more inchoate in their mind and/or troubling to discuss.

Regarding Type II questions, we are faced with a clearer and, in some ways, easier clinical decision. When considering use of one of these techniques, I recommend asking yourself if you really "need to know it *now*," or if the question could instead wait until a more appropriate time.[5] Most therapists can easily generate a litany of questions when listening to patient narratives, but not all of them are relevant at that moment. Therefore, if you suddenly realize that you have no idea whether the patient has a sibling or not, consider asking them the next time they discuss their family as opposed to interrupting the current flow of associations. This same principle applies to therapist *clarifications* (see Chapter 11). In most situations it does not really matter if a patient is describing a maternal *or* paternal uncle or if an event happened in their junior or senior year of high school. Some details are unnecessary for the therapeutic process.

In essence, there are potential costs and benefits for each question that is asked. Without good questions, therapy would be a fruitless patient monologue. With too many questions, the patient becomes the unwitting subject of a therapist-sponsored inquisition and will be unable to engage in the subtle and demanding process of psychodynamic introspection. Therapist questions are best when they model good *self*-questioning (i.e., questions that the patient could ask themselves) and help promote both thoughtfulness and the "good split."

Finally, it is important to consider the many ways that a patient may experience therapist questions and their frequency. Obviously, questions are just like any other intervention: they can elicit numerous patient reactions. Some of these might be consistent with existing transference phenomena, but others may be a result of actual technical errors on the part of the therapist. Too few questions may convey the message that the therapist lacks interest; too many might lead to an impression that the therapist feels the patient is not working hard enough. Thus, it is always a good idea to pay attention to patients' reactions to questions. Indications that you are questioning patients too much or too little include alliance ruptures (e.g., the patient withdrawals) or displacements of the transference (e.g., after multiple questions the patient notes how their boss keeps giving them "the third degree" at work). In general, the "sweet spot" for question frequency is patient-specific, but it is usually advisable to error on the side of *underquestioning* in the more expressive dynamic therapies.

USE OF QUESTIONS IN DIAGNOSTIC ASSESSMENT

As any assessor knows, diagnostic interviews are riddled with questions. Regardless of whether they are structured or semi-structured interviews, the questions are primarily of the Type II variety. The appeal is easy to see: they are an expedient means of gaining the information needed to establish whether or not symptom thresholds are met. Although this approach is efficient, it presupposes a cooperative, truthful, and minimally insightful patient. This is not always a good assumption, especially when working with patients who are very troubled. Given space limitations, I will only focus on the use of questions to assess for psychosis.

The assessment of *florid* psychosis is fairly easy. Even a layperson with no training can discern when patients respond to internal stimuli (e.g., hallucinations), openly discuss their delusions, or otherwise "act crazy." However, many psychotic patients, especially the relatively healthier ones with some degree of cognitive control, have learned that disclosure of their psychotic experiences results in severe punishment from the world (e.g., ridicule from others, unwanted hospitalizations). They may feel this to be especially the case when dealing with mental health professionals. Even if a part of them truly wants help (i.e., they voluntarily sought out treatment), they may still "test" the therapist a bit before letting them know the extent of their problems. With these patients, the therapist may have a difficult time detecting the actual magnitude of deficits in reality-testing. This may be especially the case when administering semi-structured clinical diagnostic interviews. Many psychotic patients can "hold it together" if only asked face-valid Type II questions with a corresponding expectation for direct answers.

One way to generate information helpful for these differential diagnostic assessments is to remove some of the structure from questions and carefully listen to the patient's responses. The move from Type II to Type I questions requires the patient to organize their internal world for the therapist instead of just responding to specific and direct stimuli. When doing this, psychotic thought processes become more apparent.

An example may help. Suppose a patient presented for treatment, and the therapist detected possible paranoia (e.g., the patient stated, "My neighbor is watching me"). This would be an appropriate time to ask a more open-ended, Type I question (e.g., "Could you tell me about your neighbor? What led you to that conclusion?" "Do you believe that there is something specific about you that might have drawn this unwanted attention?").[6] It is important that such queries come from a place of *concerned confusion* on the part of the therapist rather than judgmental disbelief. If the patient feels comfortable enough to be honest, the therapist will have a better sense of whether the neighborly observation was (a) a real event, (b) a normative distortion of experience (i.e., suspicious but not paranoid thinking), or (c) paranoid thinking in the pathological sense of the term (i.e., "I am being surveilled").

WHAT TO DO WHEN THE QUESTIONER BECOMES THE QUESTIONED

In ending this chapter, mention should also be made of what to do when the tables are turned. At one point or another, patients ask questions instead of following the "normal" session protocol. This is to be expected and certainly not unreasonable behavior on the part of the patient. The theoretical justification for *not* generally answering personal questions was detailed in Chapters 4 and 9, but here I provide some specific technical recommendations.

The easiest (but not necessarily best) approach is to *always* answer patients' questions (e.g., "Are you married?") by posing another question (e.g., "What led you to ask that?"). This counterquestion rule, originally discussed by Ferenczi (1950, p. 92), has been passed down from supervisor to supervisee for generations (for a thoughtful review, see Thomä & Kächele, 1992). One can see the appeal of a rigid adherence to this rule, as it provides clear guidance to clinicians and abrogates some of the enormous complexity of clinical work. However, competent practice likely requires not just knowing the rules but also knowing when they should be broken (Sharpless & Barber, 2009a). Further, if we are honest with ourselves, we would be a bit annoyed if our own therapists stubbornly adhered to the counterquestion rule. There are better and more nuanced ways to navigate one's way through patient questions. As noted by one of my former supervisors, "It is of course a matter of analytic judgment whether an answer, explanation, or acknowledgment of the patient's question about the analyst is in the best interests of the analytic process" (Curtis, 1979, p. 174).

In certain situations, it might be eminently reasonable to answer questions with a counterquestion, and at other times it might be useful to answer just "like anyone else." When the therapist has an inkling that the question has a clinically relevant subtext or if they are genuinely surprised by the content, counterquestions may be in order. When answering, however, the *manner* in which you do so is decisive. It will do little good to appear evasive or dismissive. Earnest curiosity is much more effective and disarming. Cabaniss et al. (2011, p. 95) noted some excellent wordings for counterquestions (e.g., "What brought that to mind right now?"), and therapist tone is similarly important.

In other cases, it is fine to be "normal" and answer. If a patient asks if you are sick, and anyone who is minimally observant would have had the same thought, it is probably best to just say, "Yes, I am feeling a bit under the weather today" instead of seeking out a panoply of transference associations.

Many questions are not so straightforward, though, and leave the therapist to wonder about the "right thing" to do. This is where an understanding of the goals of psychodynamic therapy and the psychodynamic stance can be useful guideposts. In general, when struggling with how or if to answer a question, it is important to be thoughtful, as it is the therapist's job to preserve the therapy and maintain boundaries. As such, therapists do not have to succumb to the patient's pressure to respond. It might be best to let the patient know, "I'd like to take a bit of time to think about how my answering your question might affect the treatment. Let's discuss this more next week." This not only gives some "breathing room" for the therapist, but also models thoughtful, forward-thinking behavior for the patient.

NOTES

1. As will be discussed in Chapter, 13, only interpretations directly address unconscious material.
2. The majority of these types of therapist questions fall within the 1–2 octant of Benjamin's *Structural Analysis of Social Behavior* (SASB) coding system (Benjamin & Gushing, 2000). Thus, they pull for a 2–2 patient response (i.e., "disclosing and expressing").
3. For example, many questions in Kernberg's (1984) *Structural Interview* are in this category.
4. Most of these questions correspond to a SASB code of 1–4 and pull for a patient response of 2–4 (i.e., "trusting and relying").
5. See Chapter 8 as well.
6. These questions can be followed with clarifications or confrontations (see Chapters 11 and 12).

11

The Process of Clarification

INTRODUCTION

Listening to patients (Chapter 8) and asking good questions (Chapter 10) results in a lot of information. With verbose patients, the amount could be enormous. Our theories and case formulations help guide and direct our focus, but it is inevitable that we will sometimes be confused. Regardless of best intentions, words are imprecise, and patients often struggle to articulate painful and perplexing experiences that may never have been previously described. As a result, both patients and therapists are left to sort through, refine, and eventually understand these words, feelings, and actions. This is the *process of clarification*. However, prior to formally defining this, it may be helpful to place clarifications in an historical context.

A BRIEF HISTORY OF CLARIFICATIONS IN PSYCHODYNAMIC THERAPY

When compared to interpretations, clarifications are newcomers to the stockpile of psychodynamic techniques (Brown, 1986). This does not mean that they were absent from even the earliest days of psychoanalysis, but the term did not acquire a technical meaning until half a century later. Freud appears to have only used "clarification" in the common, colloquial sense (Brown, 1986), but I have little doubt he did a great deal of clarification in his practice.

"Clarification" was brought into the psychotherapy lexicon by a *non-*psychodynamic therapist (Bibring, 1954). Specifically, Carl Rogers systematized the term during the early development of *client-centered psychotherapy* (Rogers, 1942). Although very familiar with Freudian theories,[1] Rogers eschewed many traditional elements of psychoanalysis (e.g., interpretation; therapeutic abstinence; emphasis on the unconscious). He instead wanted to activate what he surmised to be innate capacities for patient self-growth and healing through the therapist's facilitation of specific interpersonal and intrapersonal conditions (e.g., unconditional positive regard). It might be easy to caricature Rogerian therapy as an overly optimistic and almost robotic regurgitation of patient material, but this would obscure its true subtlety (e.g., see Rogers, 1995). Clarifications in the Rogerian sense were not just reflections or empathic validations, but were intended to extend the patients' described experiences and foster greater emotional understanding (Rogers, 1942). Edward Bibring recognized the importance of clarification and subsequently adopted it into the family of psychodynamic techniques (Bibring, 1954). "Clarifications" have been with us ever since.

An unfortunate (but likely inevitable) consequence of our field's long history is that the meanings of certain terms have shifted. "Clarification" is one of these, and it appears to have been defined inconsistently over time and across authors. For instance, where Bibring (1954) or Brown (1986) might see a clarification, Dewald (1971) and Langs (1973, 1974) would instead see a confrontation. Further, what Fink (2007) might term a question would be considered a clarification by Rockland (1989). As with the preceding chapters, my compromise for these semantic differences is to distinguish techniques according to their therapeutic intentions. However, given that many clarifications are made in the form of a question (Adler & Myerson, 1973), there will inevitably be overlap, with certain clarifications blurring into questions, and vice versa (i.e., they do "double duty" by generating and clarifying information).

CLARIFICATIONS IN PSYCHODYNAMIC THERAPY

Clarifications are defined in Box 11.1. At the risk of stating the obvious, clarifications require something to be clarified (i.e., muddled material that is readily available). Thus, the process of clarification always begins with *conscious*

Box 11.1.

WHAT ARE CLARIFICATIONS?

- *Clarifications* are statements intended to expand upon and/or clarify readily available patient/therapist information. The process of clarification may involve the patient or therapist describing, elaborating upon, reordering, or restating material to the other party. All of these are done to facilitate mutual understanding.

---

contents known to the patient or therapist. The starting point could be a statement (e.g., "I wonder if I'm going crazy?"), behavior (e.g., a patient begins repeatedly picking at his face), emotion (e.g., "I feel so disgusted right now"), historical fact (e.g., "I was raised in a puritanical household"), or similar clinical communication. If the communication is unclear, yet deemed potentially important, the therapist (or patient) then attempts to remedy this situation.

In contrast to questions, which may lack a specific motive, clarifications are always purposeful. They are intended to resolve ambiguities, get the therapist and patient "on the same page," and cast fuzzy material into sharper relief. Some of the more important clarifications in psychodynamic therapy also promote a holistic understanding of events. They illuminate not only "facts" but also the accompanying emotional reactions and cognitive appraisals. As such, clarifications help set the stage for other dynamic interventions (e.g., interpretations).

They also set the stage for additional clarifications, as the process rarely ends after only one attempt. In many cases, clarifications often result in a need for more clarification and new questions. The even more thorny matter of deciding that a "good enough" clarification has been reached ultimately rests on the clinical judgment of the therapist and the needs of the patient.

Clinical judgment is also needed when deciding *what* to clarify. It would obviously be an inefficient use of session time to give attention to every ambiguous statement. Fortunately, therapists who listen carefully to their patients and their theories will usually have at least a tacit sense that a particular bit of confusing material warrants clarification (Dewald, 1971). In certain cases—especially when the patient is well-known—the therapist may even be a step or two ahead (i.e., the therapist possesses a clearer or richer understanding than their patient). At these moments, the therapist might use clarifications to either help the patient "catch up" or to gently nudge them in that direction. However, given that we are all fallible humans, it is usually a good idea to "check in" and ensure that we are indeed accurate in our assumptions.

Fortunately, the process of clarification is interesting and often enjoyable. All things being equal, clarifications are perceived to be much less stressful than interpretations because they lack direct involvement with the patient's unconscious (Bibring, 1954). This is one reason why this technique plays such a pivotal role in the early phases of treatment. Clarifications not only sharpen clinical data and demonstrate that the therapist is sincerely interested but also foster patient insight in a more tempered fashion than usually occurs with confrontations or interpretations.

DIFFERENT TYPES OF CLARIFICATIONS

As with questions (see Chapter 10), the process of clarification is highly individualized. An infinite number of specific clarifications could be part of that process. However, for didactic purposes, I have tried to distill clarifications down to three types, each reflecting slightly different intentions and clinical situations.

Clarification of *Patient* Communications

THE THERAPIST INVITES THE PATIENT TO CLARIFY

This first approach involves the therapist directly inviting the patient to clarify an unclear communication. Here, the onus is on the patient to make sense of things, not the therapist. This is most consistent with expressive approaches but can also be found in supportive therapy.

Therapists can encourage clarification in any number of ways. Probably the simplest is to just say "Huh?" after the confusing statement is uttered. A slightly more elegant way to clarify would be to repeat the patient's words, almost verbatim, but with a slight change in emphasis (Langs, 1973, 1974). So, if a patient said, "I was lost back then," the therapist could reply, "You were *lost* back then," with the implication being that the patient should elaborate upon the emphasized "lost." Another variation of this would be to repeat a phrase back to the patient but essentially substitute a comma for the period. Again, the therapist's intention is to convey the message that the patient should say more until clarity is reached.[2]

Therapists can also ask for specific examples (e.g., "I'm a bit confused by that; could you tell me about the last time that happened?"). It is very easy to become puzzled when patients—or therapists, for that matter—make broad, sweeping generalizations or rely upon intellectual abstractions. These may lead therapists to overestimate the extent to which they understand their patients.[3] For example, a female patient with borderline personality organization once said to me, "When I get upset, it lasts *forever*. The pain just goes on and on and on." I assumed this to mean that she had extremely protracted episodes, possibly lasting for days. When I asked about her last few instances, though, it soon became apparent that none lasted longer than an hour. This clarification not only gave me additional insight into how subjectively distressing these episodes were for her, but also into the accuracy of her self-observations.

Examples also help patients better access their authentic feelings. It is far easier to avoid affect when speaking in generalities (e.g., "I always get rejected by the people I love") than when divulging a specific instance (e.g., "Alex broke up with me over email a week after we moved in together"). The latter are clearly more visceral, experience-near, and liable to elicit strong sentiments. As many psychodynamic interventions work best when conducted with affective immediacy (e.g., interpretations; Strachey, 1934), this form of clarification can be critical.

A third variation is to ask patients to clarify the *sequence* of events. This may involve the patient reordering individual parts of their narrative or explicitly spelling out the important intervening steps (i.e., what I describe to patients as "connecting the dots"). As an example of the former, the previously described borderline patient would often mix recent and past events without noting which was which. These stories were so affectively charged for her—often involving profound abuse and humiliation—that I rarely knew whether an incident occurred yesterday or 20 years ago. Whenever this knowledge was critical for my understanding, I would interrupt her flow of associations and ask her to parse out a rough historical timeline.

As an example of "connecting the dots," this same patient would regularly gloss over important details. This was common when events were painful to discuss or, from her perspective, shameful (especially her sexual abuse history). Interestingly, both psychodynamic (Gaston, 1995) and cognitive behavioral (Foa, Keane, Terence, Friedman, & Cohen, 2008) therapists agree that avoiding traumatic events inhibits the successful processing of these events.[4] There are many ways for patients to avoid, and one of her recurring strategies was to speed through painful stories and then quickly move on to other topics. My technical response to this pattern was to gently encourage her to fill in the details (e.g., people involved, reactions).[5]

The Therapist (Tentatively) Clarifies the Patient's Communications

A second broad approach is for the therapist to take a more active role by making a tentative clarification of the patient's material *to the patient*. There are at least three reasons to do this. First, it is often useful for the therapist to "check in" and gauge their level of understanding. Second, therapists may want to show that they are being attentive and observant. It feels good to be understood, and both behaviors strengthen the therapeutic alliance (e.g., Sharpless, Muran, & Barber, 2010). Finally, there are situations where it is more practical for therapists to take the lead. If, for instance, a specific clarification is necessary (i.e., it is a "need-to-know-now" clarification), but asking the patient to do so runs the risk of sidetracking them from a more important therapy process, it might be more expedient for the therapist to succinctly clarify *for* the patient (e.g., "So if I'm understanding you, this happened before your graduation ceremony, right?"). At the risk of belaboring the point, however, it is important to never forcefully put words in the patient's mouth. Tentative therapist clarifications are almost always preferable to presumptuous, forceful ones.

Terminological clarifications are sometimes needed. After all, many words have multiple or even radically different meanings (e.g., "egregious" can mean remarkably good *or* remarkably bad). The patient's manner of speaking, volume of speech, or accent might lead to confusion as well. It is also easy for words to be misheard by the therapist or used idiosyncratically by the patient. For instance, a new patient once told me that his best friend was "a dog." I was unable to tell from his tone if he was referring to an actual dog (i.e., man's best friend) or if he meant that his friend was a "dog" in the colloquial sense (i.e., a human male who would say or do whatever was needed to sleep with a woman). You could imagine the possibilities for therapist embarrassment by assuming the wrong meaning. So I decided to clarify and asked, "Do you mean that your friend is a "dog" to women, or something else?"

Oftentimes a therapist can clarify material by filling in gaps or more fully forming the patient's own nascent ideas. If applied with finesse, these can be powerful interventions. For instance, imagine that a patient struggling with depression said, "I don't know what to do. I just lay in bed all day and see my life slipping away." The therapist could encourage the patient to elaborate, but in this situation, it might be more effective to offer a Rogerian-influenced empathic elaboration such as, "I hear you, and I get the sense that you feel so bad and hopeless at times that part of you wants to say, 'Fuck it,' and just give up. Is that accurate?" This remains close to the patient's communication but extends it a bit by articulating feelings of hopelessness. It also "checks in" at the end to make sure the therapist is not distorting the patient's experience. When correct, clarifications like these help patients feel understood and encourage introspection (Dewald, 1971). If inaccurate, patients may feel more comfortable correcting the therapist than they would if the clarification was put forth in a less tentative manner.

Clarification of *Therapist* Communications

Finally, mention should be made of therapists clarifying *their own* communications. If you are anything like me, you will often confuse your patients. Unfortunately, some of them may be too nice to mention this directly or too inhibited to assert themselves. Therefore, it is incumbent upon us to listen for confusion in the other channels of communication (Chapter 8) and try to rectify the situation.

Some of the ways we clarify our own words parallel what we do with patients' words. We might rephrase something (e.g., "I just realized that might have been confusing. What I really meant to say was . . .") or define a particular term for the patient (e.g., anxiety, fantasy, emotional dysregulation). We can also "connect the dots" for the patient or provide examples (e.g., "When I noted that you often feel guilty, I was specifically thinking about those times at work where you beat up on yourself for making even minor mistakes").

Reminders could also be considered a form of therapist clarification. As one example, many patients are not aware of the differences between assessment and psychotherapy.[6] In situations where these roles are distinct, it is important to clarify the limits of the relationship and remain firm. For instance, if you are a diagnostician in a psychodynamic therapy outcome trial, your patient might be confused and/or want to blur boundaries by discussing therapy material instead of answering diagnostic questions. In this case, it would be appropriate to clarify the situation for them (e.g., "What you said sounds really important and something you may want to discuss with your therapist. Since our task for today is to get an idea of the symptoms you've been having lately, we can't really do that matter justice").

When we receive patient requests for clarification, we should usually respond. If a patient is unsure of when the therapist will be out of town, a direct clarification is in order. If a patient seems confused about an aspect of the treatment contract, this should be addressed. Similarly, if a patient wants to know what they can expect from treatment, it is a good idea to be honest and forthright to the best of your ability. A situation like this came up during the first session with an older, narcissistic gentleman. He was very reluctant to enter treatment and had a history of abruptly terminating with several providers who "pissed" him off. He told me frankly that the only reason he made the appointment was because his partner gave him an "ultimatum." Perhaps not surprisingly, he presented in a very defensive and hostile manner. In the middle of session, he asked me, using a very condescending tone, how I knew that therapy with me was going to "cure" him. This was an important matter to clarify, and I had to pause and try my best to sort through the information I was receiving from the other channels of communication (especially my own countertransference). Given what little I knew about his history and defensive operations, I had a sense that the merest hint of what he perceived to be "more therapist bullshit" would turn him off to treatment. I also knew from working with other narcissists that he was likely projecting his own inadequate sense of self onto me (McWilliams, 2011). This type of transference can lead therapists to either shut down or defensively compensate by "puffing themselves up" (e.g., becoming hostile with the patient or letting the patient know how good they really are—strategies that will not likely end well). I decided to be straightforward in my clarification and said, "I actually have no idea if I can help you or not. It depends not just on what I do, but also upon you and whether there are things you'd like to understand about yourself. I only know that nothing positive will happen if we're not working together and both looking closely at you."[7] As he was expecting me to lie and, in effect, make a promise I could not keep (which I found out later was very much in keeping with his relational expectations), my honest answer "passed the test" and reassured him enough to continue treatment.

HOW TO PRESENT CLARIFICATIONS TO THE PATIENT

Many of the suggestions for the wording of questions (see Chapter 10) are the same for clarifications. Further, it is hopefully apparent from the examples that the therapist's *tone* is extremely important. The implicit "vibe" behind the process of clarification should be something along the lines of, "Even though you and I are different people, I really want to understand you and your experiences at a deep level. We will both occasionally misunderstand each other, but that is OK, is to be expected, and can be resolved." Thus, clarifications should always arise from a place of supportive curiosity, humility, and collaboration.

This is especially the case with patients who come from different backgrounds or who have different levels of education or language fluency. In these cases, the need for clarification could be far more substantial. Patients will be cognizant of these differences as well and may have any number of reactions. They might feel embarrassed by their limited vocabulary or be hesitant to ask the therapist for clarifications. Further, the process of free association might become inhibited if they are less able to "let their thoughts go." Honest discussions about these issues are usually warranted, and it is helpful to directly encourage the patient to seek clarification as needed. Mild humor works well here. When a Brazilian patient apologized to me when I did not understand one of his statements, I laughed and said, "Well, your English is much better than my Portuguese, so no worries."

SOME SPECIFIC EXAMPLES OF USING CLARIFICATIONS

In general, clarifications are flexible interventions that can applied to any number of specific clinical situations. To elaborate on this process, four specific ways of using clarifications in session will be described in the following sections.

Clarifications and the "Slow, Not So Bright Therapist" Approach

The process of clarification can help patients slow down and become more reflective. For instance, a male patient with difficulties controlling anger and a limited ability to mentalize once came to session and said, "So I went to the bar, just like any other Friday, and the next thing you know I'm in a fight with some guy, and the cops got called on me." At first glance, it appeared that he was quite surprised by this chain of events, but beyond that, few details were provided. One of my favorite ways to clarify situations such as these and work with patients who might be impressionistic—or generally prone to externalize responsibility—is to adopt the "slow, not too bright therapist" approach (Levy, 1990, p. 24; for a similar method, see Bateman & Fonagy, 2006, pp. 124–125). My understanding of this phrase is to act puzzled, try to slow the patient down, and also ask a number of sequential questions and clarifications.[8] In this case, the purpose was to help the patient work *backwards*, moving from the conclusion of the story to the very beginning. This helped the patient unearth the moment-to-moment decisions and trigger points until a complete and coherent story arc emerged. An example of this process using this particular fight-prone patient can be found in Table 11.1.

This "slow, not too bright therapist" approach, working backwards toward the beginning, not only helps illuminate the patient's choices and roles in complicated events but also helps modulate strong affects and strengthen observing ego capacities. It may also broaden narratives and make them more nuanced (Summers & Barber, 2010). Further, the somewhat befuddled, yet curious manner of the therapist is nonthreatening, and often circumvents patient defensiveness.

Clarifications and Mentalization

Clarifications can also be used to assess and stimulate mentalization[9] in *mentalization-based therapy* (MBT; Bateman & Fonagy, 2016) and other modalities. Although formal assessments of mentalization exist,[10] clarifications can also be used. By inviting the patient to explicate and expand upon the motives behind their own actions and feelings, the therapist can gain a window into the magnitude of any mentalization deficits. In these situations, it is usually preferable for the therapist to clarify *for* the patient as little as possible but to instead encourage them to struggle with the process. This will enhance their own capacities.

Table 11.1. An Example of the Process of Clarification

Therapist Statement	Type of Intervention
You seem surprised that you were arrested. Is that accurate?	Clarification
What do you mean by "completely justified"?	Clarification
How did the fight actually end?	Question
Ok, but I'm a bit confused how the police got involved . . .	Question
So you're saying that the other guy threw the first punch?	Clarification
He was *messing* with you . . .	Clarification
What did it feel like when he said that?	Question/ Clarification
So he was the only one making hostile remarks at the bar?	Question
Can you give me an example of what you mean?	Clarification
What do you think led him to take notice of you in the first place?	Question
It sounds like a really upsetting experience for you, and my intention with these questions is not to place blame on you or him, though I can understand why you might be feeling that way. I'm actually hoping we can make some more sense of how this came about by looking at the situation more closely together.	Clarification in response to a mild alliance rupture

MBT also includes an interesting variant of clarification. Specifically, MBT therapists encourage their patients to clarify and reconstruct the *therapist's* motives. This is thought to be a particularly good way to practice mentalization, as the therapist's mental states are readily available, in the present moment, and "alive" in the room. Although this technique does not appear to be common outside of MBT, I have found it clinically useful with certain patients.

Clarification of Psychosis

Clarifications can also be used to assess reality testing. As noted in Chapter 10, open-ended (i.e., Type I) questions can help discern psychotic thought processes. However, the material that is generated may still be unclear. So, if I asked the patient a question such as, "Do you believe that there is something about you that might have led your neighbor to start watching you?" and they responded, "He thinks I'm special," I would not have enough information to rule out a psychotic disorder, but would certainly be intrigued by this answer. An additional clarification such as "Can you help me understand what you mean by 'special'?" or "I'm a bit confused; how would your being special result in her wanting to watch you?" might result in more useful diagnostic information.

If a patient is indeed psychotic, clarifications are relatively safe techniques to use. Clarifications only involve conscious and preconscious material and are therefore far less likely to encourage regression than interpretations (see Chapter 13). However, they can still help increase understanding and make the patient more transparent to themselves. Further, by inviting the patient to clarify their experiences for the therapist, the therapist implicitly gives the message that people's thoughts are their own and that they are not, in fact, transparent to others.[11] The poor ego boundaries of psychotic patients (e.g., as manifested by a belief that thoughts can be inserted or removed from others) may be partially helped through a judicious application of clarifications and questions.[12]

Clarification of Mental Status

Finally, clarifications, when used tactfully, can help assess general mental status. For example, imagine that I met with a new patient. Over the course of the first session I asked a Type I question such as "Could you tell me about an important person in your life?" and the patient responded with a lengthy harangue on the environment and global warming. This response would be very puzzling to me and would raise a number of clinical possibilities. Is the patient trying to avoid the topic of important others? Is it possible that they did not hear my question correctly? Do they have "organic" difficulties with attention or memory? Might they be generally prone to tangentiality? To begin the process of clarification, I would first gently ask, "Could you help me understand how that relates to my question?" and listen to their response. Regardless of the content, it would provide me with an invaluable insight into their current mental status. Additional clarifications would likely follow.

POTENTIAL DANGERS IN THE PROCESS OF CLARIFICATION

As is hopefully apparent, clarifications are very important for psychodynamic therapy. They are flexible interventions that are appropriate for any level of patient personality organization (i.e., normal to psychotic). They are also essential, as they facilitate patient–therapist understanding and help lay the groundwork for subsequent interventions. However, as is the case with every therapeutic intervention, there are some attendant dangers.

Overuse of Clarifications

Clarifications can be disruptive if overused. For instance, too many invitations for patient clarification are distracting and impede the process of free association. They can also be damaging to the alliance if the patient feels that they are not sufficiently understood (i.e., "If you understood me, you wouldn't need to ask me to explain myself so often"). Overreliance on clarification may indicate that (a) the patient has significant problems with clarity or (b) the therapist may be "bogged down" or obsessively stuck on unnecessary details.

Too many *therapist* clarifications of the patient are also problematic. Though they may help the patient feel more understood than in the previous example, excessive therapist clarification may send the unhelpful message that the patient is incapable of clarifying for themselves. This message is wildly inconsistent with psychodynamic goals (see Chapter 3). It is far better for therapists to allow their patients an opportunity to augment their own clarificatory capacities. Therapist "scaffolding" and modeling of the process of clarification may be beneficial—especially in supportive therapies—but should never become overbearing or reduce patient autonomy. One wants to be helpfully facilitative but not overly responsible for the patient's own clarity.

Finally, excessive therapist clarification of the *therapist's own communications* is not good either (Langs, 1973, 1974). This pattern could point to at least three different problems. First, it may indicate that the therapist misjudged the patient's degree of psychological mindedness or vocabulary level. In essence, the therapist continually "talks over the patient," leading to confusion. Second, this pattern could suggest that the therapist has a more general problem lucidly communicating ideas. If the need for excessive clarification occurs across multiple patients, this possibility becomes more likely. Additional supervision, role playing with peers, and video recording of sessions may help improve therapist clarity and concision (see Chapter 6). A final possibility is that the patient may be using therapist clarifications defensively. Instead of focusing on the more challenging aspects of therapy (e.g., introspection and facing difficult experiences), the patient avoids these tasks through repetitively asking the therapist for explanations. In effect, clarification becomes a convenient distraction from doing "real" psychodynamic psychotherapy.

Regardless of subtype, clarifications can clearly be overused. When this pattern emerges, therapists should quickly identify the reasons behind it as well as any potential clinical implications (e.g., alliance ruptures). More generally, Robert Langs warned against becoming a "clarificationist" who neglected other psychodynamic techniques (Langs, 1973, 1974, p. 414). He surmised that these therapists were uncomfortable working with unconscious contents, preferring instead to remain closer to the surface (i.e., conscious and preconscious materials). However, all things being equal, if patients can tolerate and potentially benefit from the more expressive techniques (e.g., confrontations and interpretations), these should also be used. If not, the pace of therapy may become unnecessarily sluggish.

Underuse of Clarifications

Clarifications can also be *underused* in therapy. As previously noted, they are necessary interventions, and no therapy should be without them. They help ensure that the patient and therapist understand each other. Therefore, if you find yourself using only very few clarifications, introspection is again in order.

Too little clarification may indicate that that therapist is overconfident in their perceived ability to understand the patient. I have wondered if this overconfidence increases with the length of the treatment (i.e., the therapist starts taking understanding for granted). Regardless, even if we have worked with a patient for years, we should periodically check in to find out if we are wrong.

Therapists can also be conditioned (i.e., punished) out of using clarifications. Some patients, especially those experiencing twinship transferences (Kohut, 2001) and/or certain borderline personality structures, may have strong reactions to clarifications. They may expect, or even haughtily demand, that the therapist display an exquisite—bordering on telepathic—understanding of their experiences (Yeomans et al., 2015, pp. 155–156). When this unrealistic expectation is violated, they may become exceedingly critical of their "inadequate" (i.e., devalued) therapist. As a result, some therapists may choose discretion to be the better part of valor, and quickly phase this technique out of their repertoires. However, intense patient reactions like these indicate a need for *more* clarification, not less.

NOTES

1. For example, Rogers and other humanistic psychologists were heavily influenced by the pioneering works of Otto Rank and Sandor Ferenczi (de Carvalho, 1999; Kramer, 1995).
2. Fink (2007) and other Lacanians often term this strategy "punctuation."
3. This is because a therapist's fantasy of what the patient means (which often defaults to personal experiences of what "normal" is) may be wildly discrepant from the patient's actual meaning.
4. However, there are clear differences in the timing and manner in which the events are processed (Sharpless & Barber, 2009, p. 50).
5. With this particular patient, clarification was often preceded by a confrontation of her avoidance strategy.
6. Many patients are similarly confused by the distinction between psychologists and psychiatrists, especially in terms of prescription privileges.
7. This clarification was followed by a confrontation. I next said, "You've had several unsuccessfully therapies in the past, so part of our job will be to figure out how to have it go differently this time. What are your thoughts on why they didn't work out?"
8. I have also heard a variant of this called the "Columbo" approach.
9. This is the capacity to understand the behavior of oneself and others in terms of internal mental states (Bateman & Fonagy, 2016).

10. The *Reflective Functioning Interview* (Fonagy, Target, Steele, & Steele, 1998), derived from the *Adult Attachment Interview* (George, Kaplan, & Main, 1996), is one such measure.

11. With borderline patients, clarifications allow the patient to realize that the therapist is not omniscient (Yeomans, Clarkin, & Kernberg, 2015, p. 156).

12. To be clear, though, it is rarely advisable for therapists to directly challenge delusions or hallucinations. It is often better to be supportive by encouraging more engagement with consensual reality (see Chapters 14 and 15).

12

The Process of Confrontation

INTRODUCTION TO CONFRONTATION

When you see the word "confrontation," what comes to mind? Do you imagine two fighters squaring off in a ring, an aggressive lawyer dramatically pointing out inconsistencies to a floundering witness, or possibly two drunk people at a pub slurringly swearing at each other? If so, this is because confrontations are usually thought to involve some sort or conflict. In common parlance, they imply a moment of intense antagonism between two or more people (Weisman, 1973). If we used this definition, confrontation would seem to have little to no role in the psychotherapeutic process. However, this would be a gross misunderstanding of confrontation as a *technique*.

As noted previously, the long history of psychodynamic thought has given us—some might say saddled us with—a great deal of terminological baggage. Many of our classic ideas are confusing to learn (e.g., object, abstinence) because their meanings in the psychodynamic world diverge so much from "common" usage. The subject of this chapter is another example of this trend, and as will be demonstrated below, confrontations are seldom "confrontational" in the colloquial sense of the word. At times, though, they can be direct, directive, or even forceful.

A BRIEF HISTORY OF CONFRONTATIONS IN PSYCHODYNAMIC THERAPY

"Confrontation" is not found in the index to the *Standard Edition of the Complete Psychological Works of Sigmund Freud* (Freud, 1974). As was the case with *clarifications* (Chapter 11), Freud neither named nor defined confrontations, and instead used several other terms and phrases interchangeably (Corwin, 1973). He seemed far more interested in outlining the psychoanalytic *process* rather than codifying it into a lexicon of specific techniques. However, Freud no doubt used confrontations liberally in his own clinical work. In fact, Karpf (1986) argued that Freud's early psychoanalytic practice consisted primarily of confrontation, catharsis, and reconstruction of the patient's past. Following 1910 and the further development of his theory of repression, *interpretation* assumed a more central therapeutic role (Karpf, 1986, pp. 188–189).

To be clear, though, the technique of confrontation was never truly absent from psychodynamic thought even if it was de-emphasized far more than it would come to be in contemporary practice. For instance, "confrontation" was also not mentioned in Bibring's (1954) canonical list of early psychoanalytic interventions (i.e., suggestion, abreaction, manipulation, clarification, and interpretation). However, its presence in that list was nonetheless implicit.[1]

Interestingly, when "confrontation" began to appear more frequently in the literature, it was defined inconsistently across theorists. Thus, one person's confrontation might be another's clarification (Devereaux, 1951; cf. Langs, 1973, 1974) or even interpretation. This problem led a number of respected psychodynamic scholars to convene a conference at Tufts University with the hope of reaching a better consensus on this important technique (Adler & Myerson, 1973). The conference resulted in a published book and a number of interesting ideas, but the overall conclusions were somewhat disheartening. Adler and Myerson (1973) summarized:

> *Though some of the authors have attempted to approach the topic from a broad and some from an in-depth perspective, none would claim to have arrived at an ultimate conceptualization of the issue. Furthermore, the contributions are too disparate in approach and, in fact, sometimes too contradictory in their formulation for the editors to be able to present an integrated overview that will be satisfactory to the various authors. . . . The symposium brought out the fact that there was less disagreement among the panelists about when they use confrontation than about what they mean by it.* (pp. 9–10)

In my reading of the subsequent literature, these conclusions reached in the early 1970s remain essentially unchanged today. Therefore, lacking a clear consensus from the field, I will maintain the approach of previous chapters and focus on the functions and purposes of confrontation.[2]

CONFRONTATIONS IN PSYCHODYNAMIC THERAPY

As defined in Box 12.1, confrontations direct a patient's attention to clinical content that the therapist feels is important. It might be helpful to think of the process as a therapist pointing their finger at something and saying "Let's take a look at

Box 12.1.

What Are Therapist Confrontations?

- **_Confrontations_** are efforts to direct attention (at varying levels of forcefulness) to important but overlooked/denied/incongruous patient communications. Confrontations may be used to (a) encourage the patient to resolve inconsistencies between different channels of communication and/or conscious and preconscious materials, (b) note denial or acting out behaviors, (c) help the patient face an uncomfortable reality, or (d) indicate that clinical material has psychodynamic importance.

that." However, patients are rarely confronted on physical objects and are far more likely to be confronted on their words, feelings, and actions.

Confrontations often direct patients to face things that they might not want to face and to struggle with complex material (e.g., trying to resolve an inconsistency). Needless to say, bringing a patient's inconsistencies or avoidance to light may result in any number of reactions, and some of these may be defensive and negative. It is therefore prudent for therapists to pay close attention to the therapeutic alliance when they confront. To be clear, though, all patients need to occasionally go outside of their comfort zones and wrestle with difficult matters if they hope to reach their treatment goals. It is the therapist's responsibility to keep the amount of stress at a reasonable, productive, and manageable level. Insight is not helpful if the patient is too uncomfortable to stay in session.

As will be described, confrontations often generate far more insight than questions or clarifications; in this way they are similar to interpretations (see Chapter 13). However, there are at least two important differences between the two techniques. First, confrontations only focus on conscious and preconscious elements (Dewald, 1971). In other words, confrontations are always based on material that is evident (or at least potentially evident) to both the patient and the therapist. In contrast, the use of unconscious material is the defining feature of interpretations. Confrontations—like clarifications and questions—remain far closer to observable clinical data (i.e., what has already been discussed at some point in session). However, it is common for patients to begin noticing unconscious feelings, thoughts, and patterns as they work through a confrontation. This is why confrontations are usually thought of as preparatory techniques for expressive work (Greenson, 1967).

Confrontations also differ from interpretations in the typical responses that they elicit. When an accurate _interpretation_ is made, it helps resolve a patient's conflict, answer a question, or reduce uncertainty.[3] Thus, accurate interpretations often serve an _organizing_ function for the patient. They may help the patient better understand themselves, even if they might not like what they come to understand. In contrast, confrontations tend to draw attention to a problem or raise questions without offering a clear resolution. They often create helpful confusion and generate some measure of anxiety. If done well, confrontations motivate the patient to try to understand this newly realized material.

As such, confrontations are powerful and flexible interventions capable of meeting many treatment goals. Several scholars (e.g., Langs, 1973, 1974) have gone so far as to say that they are the most important interventions that omit the direct use of unconscious material. Therefore, when working with patients who require a more supportive approach, confrontations may be the primary conduits of self-understanding (see Chapter 5).

What Do Therapists Usually Confront?

Psychodynamic therapy presupposes that people are not always transparent to themselves. Everyone can benefit from recognizing and understanding things in their life that (a) they do not understand, (b) are not in their best interests, or (c) are inconsistent with their self-image, values, or stated wishes. A recognition of these patterns is an important first step toward change. The unique relationship between patient and therapist and the judicious use of confrontations make this process of change possible. However, it can be difficult at times to figure out where to focus a confrontation.

Box 12.2 lists patient situations that a therapist might want to confront. Some are intuitive (e.g., patient avoidance or denial), but others might require a bit of explanation. For instance, "acting out" and "acting in" behaviors should almost always be confronted. Given that they consist of putting feelings into *actions* instead of words, they are antithetical to the psychodynamic process. They also often lead to destructive consequences (i.e., to self and/or others). A failure to confront these behaviors could even be viewed by the patient as tacit acceptance or approval of the behavior (Langs, 1973, 1974). This would not be a good thing. Interpretations are usually required to reach a fuller understanding of these issues, but confrontations can cast them into sharper relief and encourage the patient to reflect.

For example, a male patient with borderline personality organization came to session and reported that he recently committed a minor (but risky) "white collar" crime in his personal business. After he spent some time minimizing the importance of this event, he abruptly changed the subject. I confronted this by saying, "I remember you telling me recently how much you valued your personal ethics. I also recall how troubled you said you would be if your professional reputation was sullied. Can you see how I might be having some trouble making sense of what you just disclosed?" I did not attempt to explain his self-destructive behavior with an interpretation (as I only had a vague sense of his true motivations) but instead pointed out the discrepancy between his past words and his recent deed. This confrontation also refocused attention back to the disclosure he seemed all too willing to avoid.

Box 12.2.

Reasons to Confront a Patient

- The patient denies an unavoidable reality.
- The patient avoids an important clinical matter.
- The patient manifests resistance toward the treatment process.
- The patient overlooks or forgets something important for the treatment.
- The patient underestimates or overestimates their true capacities (i.e., seeing themselves as either less or more capable than they are).
- The patient violates the terms of the treatment contract.
- The patient thinks, feels, or behaves inconsistently (e.g., differences between verbal and non-verbal behaviors).
- The patient "acts out," "acts in," or otherwise behaves in inappropriate or dangerous ways.
- The patient is unwilling to look at an important (and usually unflattering) aspect of themselves (e.g., their jealous behavior).
- The patient is not taking a topic as seriously as the therapist would like.
- The patient lies or otherwise corrupts the process of therapy.
- The patient is unable or unwilling to see an important connection (e.g., between the past and present or between ostensibly different situations).
- The patient makes statements that seem overemphasized.
- The patient preemptively denies a particular wish, thought, or emotion without being asked.
- The patient makes a potentially meaningful parapraxis.

Confrontations are also indicated when patients make statements that seem a bit too emphatic. In the poetic words of William Shakespeare (1988), "the lady doth protest too much, methinks" (p. 77). Therapists are wise to be suspicious of overly emphatic statements, as they often indicate intentions that are the exact opposite of the stated words. They also point to patient conflict. Fink (2007) helpfully termed these statements "overemphasized assertions" and "unprovoked denials" (pp. 41–42). As an example of the former, a male patient might say, "There is no doubt about it, I absolutely and with 100% certainty always love my kids. How could anyone think otherwise?" In this case, the gentleman doth protest too much.

As for unprovoked denials, a patient once said, "I'm not trying to personally attack you," and then proceeded to do just that. Perhaps not surprisingly, this made me a tad suspicious of her prefatory remark and also quite curious. It was almost as if she wanted to defensively negate the conclusion that she fantasized I was going to reach. Interestingly, she did this before I had even reached it. Therefore, I thought it wise to redirect her attention by asking, "What do you make of the fact that you began by saying that you weren't intending to attack me and then proceeded to give me a fairly personal criticism?"

Finally, it may be important to mention confrontations of patients' personal capacities (see Chapter 14). Specifically, it can be helpful for some patients to recognize their actual strengths and limitations. A primary goal of psychodynamic therapy is to accept unchangeable realities, and this is the case whether the realities are pleasant or not. Sadly, people are oftentimes poor judges of their true abilities, and other people they are close to (e.g., friends, parents) may have any number of motivations to *not* provide honest feedback. If not dealt with, these situations can have a dramatic impact on clinical work and the patient's broader life.

For instance, imagine a patient who is crippled by insecurity. He selectively attends to (perceived) instances of his incompetence in employment situations all the while ignoring evidence to the contrary. Some cognitive biases are rigid and probably none more so than confirmatory biases (Oswald & Grosjean, 2004). A well-timed confrontation may help to "shock" such a patient out of their usual ways of thinking. In this case, the therapist might say, "You seem quite certain that you would never 'measure up' and be successful if you were to take the promotion. However, you've given me a number of examples—several over the past month—of you taking over your boss's responsibilities and receiving good feedback. I wonder what makes it difficult for you to acknowledge your successes?" Here, the therapist is far from being an overly optimistic "cheerleader" but is merely reminding the patient of prior achievements that are being ignored (i.e., they are preconscious). In situations such as these, it is helpful for therapists to have a good memory of prior communications.

Other patients may need to be confronted with the opposite message (i.e., that they may be unrealistically *optimistic* about their abilities). Given that these sorts of confrontations can trigger feelings of pain, loss, or sadness—or even be narcissistically wounding—a great deal of empathy and finesse are required. These messages are often easier for the patient to face if they come from a combination of the patient's own words and those of trusted others. Any "bleed-through" of the therapist's personal judgments will likely elicit defensiveness. Fortunately, with all patients that I have encountered, the larger world has given them some amount of helpful (if disappointing) feedback, but for whatever reason this has been hard for them to recognize, "take in," and explore. Therapist reminders can facilitate this process.

DIFFERENT TYPES OF CONFRONTATIONS

It would be impossible to catalogue all the many possible confrontations. Instead, I have listed three broad subtypes in Box 12.3 for didactic purposes. They each perform slightly different functions and also differ in their overall level of "forcefulness." Some specific confrontations made in session may fall under multiple subtypes (e.g., a confrontation that is both connective and prohibitive), and this is obviously fine. The boundaries between each of the categories are not assumed to be firm.

Box 12.3.

THREE DIFFERENT TYPES OF THERAPIST CONFRONTATIONS

- *Spotlight confrontations* direct a patient's attention to a specific matter of clinical importance (e.g., pointing out a particular statement or behavior; reminding the patient of a previous statements)
- *Connective confrontations* link two or more pieces of clinical material (e.g., bringing together an inconsistency; indicating a similarity)
- *Prohibitive confrontations* call attention to the unacceptability of a patient's behavior and direct patient attention to consequences of subsequent repetitions of this behavior (e.g., termination of the treatment)

Spotlight Confrontations

Spotlight confrontations are intended to draw the patient's attention to an area of clinical importance. Like an actual spotlight, they focus the patient on a specific piece of clinical material (e.g., words or actions). These confrontations interrupt the patient's chain of free association and let them know that the therapist believes another matter (conscious or preconscious) should take clinical priority. As such, they are not terribly forceful but certainly fall under the rubric of a confrontation. So, if a normally obsessive patient nervously started fidgeting while recounting a story, but appeared to be unaware of this nonverbal shift, the therapist might say "I notice that your leg is shaking as you are telling me this." This confrontation shifts the patient's center of attention from their words to the nonverbal behavior. Note that no explanation for the fidgeting was provided—in fact, the therapist may not even have one formulated yet—and it is left up to the patient to decide what to do with the new focus.

Similarly, therapists can use this technique when patients make parapraxes (i.e., slips of the tongue). For example, imagine that a middle-aged patient reflecting on his life and career said, "I came to the sudden realization that I didn't have as much sex as I'd like," when the context indicated that he likely meant to say "success." Now imagine that the patient did not register or follow up on this slip. The therapist could gently confront him by saying, "as much *sex* as you'd like." The outward form of this confrontation may appear outwardly similar to a clarification (especially the repeating back of words with a shift in emphasis). However, the intention is not to have the patient clarify their meaning, but to instead recognize their statement.

Spotlight confrontations are also useful with tangential, circumstantial, or avoidant patients. Clearly, these three behaviors are slightly different and imply different clinical meanings, but they can all lead to difficulties with session focus. They may also limit opportunities to work on a particular session "theme." Therapists can use spotlight confrontations to help these patients stay on task and avoid glossing over crucial details. This can be done in a supportive way. For instance, if a patient disclosed something that the therapist felt was clinically relevant and then quickly changed topics, the therapist could say (with a bit of genuine enthusiasm), "What you just told me sounds really important. I wonder if it might be worthwhile for us to take a closer look at that." As is hopefully apparent, this confrontation is far from being "confrontational" in the traditional sense of the word.

It might also be useful to consider spotlight confrontations as a means of asking patients to go back a bit and *rewind*.[4] Therapists may need to occasionally say, "Why don't we go back to what you discussed at the beginning of session?" As this is somewhat directive and refocuses the patient, it is technically a confrontation, though obviously it is a fairly gentle one.

Relatedly, *therapist reminders* could be considered to be spotlight confrontations. Similar to the previous example, it is often useful to draw a patient's attention back to something said in a prior session that the therapist believes may possess a current, yet unrecognized relevance. This is particularly helpful with avoidant patients who may give what has been called a "doorknob gift" or "exit line."[5] When this occurs, so long as it is not a legitimate crisis, it is a good idea to at least note the importance of the exit line and suggest that it be discussed at the subsequent session. If, after a reasonable amount of time has passed during the next hour, the therapist could remind the patient of their suggestion.

As spotlight confrontations are relatively gentle, they can be a good first step in the process of confrontation prior to utilizing more "forceful" ones (see the following sections). Shifting a patient's focus to something else is usually experienced as less stressful than indicating potential inconsistencies/incongruities/troubling similarities. These are hallmarks of the next subtype.

Connective Confrontations

One definition of confrontation is to "set together for comparison" (Arvidson, 1973, p. 165). Consistent with this, *connective confrontations* (Box 12.3) join two or more pieces of clinical information.[6] In most cases, the patient is not attending to at least one of them (i.e., it is preconscious) and is seemingly unaware of a potential connection or contradiction. Like all confrontations, though, the therapist does not provide "an answer" or resolve the inconsistency *for* the patient, but merely draws attention to a matter through the confrontative juxtaposition.

Any number of connective confrontations could be made (e.g., between the patient's past and present, between different relationships, important inconsistencies, important similarities). However, they are probably most easily formulated by paying close attention to the different channels of communication (Yeomans et al., 2015; also see Chapter 8). For instance, patients' nonverbal communications (Channel 3) often betray their true reactions far better than their more easily filtered speech (Channel 1). It is not uncommon for patients to deny with words (e.g., "I'm not sad") what they assert in action (e.g., a solitary tear on their cheek). Therapists can easily reveal discrepancies by bringing the mismatch to light (e.g., "I'm struck by the fact that you say you're not sad but appear to be crying"). Similarly, therapists can even incorporate their subjective countertransference reactions into a connective confrontation if they are made known to a patient first (e.g., "It feels like something changed in here after I made my last statement"). The therapist could then link other observations (e.g., signs of an alliance rupture).

As noted by Boris (1973), confrontations often induce conflict. This is particularly the case with this subtype. Connective confrontations of patient inconsistencies can be particularly challenging because (a) patients may become defensive or feel "attacked" as a result of the intervention and (b) therapists run the risk of eliciting negative patient reactions due to confusing or inelegant phrasing. Despite these risks, connective confrontations can be very helpful in dealing with patient denial and acting out.

For instance, patients with substance abuse problems are well known to minimize or deny the ramifications of their behaviors (Milhorn, 2018). They often keep these unpleasant realities outside of conscious awareness by suppressing them into their preconscious. To deal with this defense, a therapist might say, "I hear you saying that your drinking is not affecting your life. I must say that I'm a bit confused by that, as you told me last week that your boss gave you a warning at work and your wife gave you an ultimatum. How do you understand that discrepancy?" Clearly, this is a bit more forceful than the previous examples but is neither hostile nor judgmental. When looked at objectively, it is merely a restatement of the patient's own words.

In a similar way, I had to repeatedly confront a patient with bipolar I disorder who incorporated his diagnostic label very strongly into his identity. He was very motivated to do so because mania served as a convenient excuse for some of his more destructive and ego-dystonic behaviors. For instance, whenever he was in a manic episode, he would cheat on his partner. Regardless of whether he was actually "caught" by her or only disclosed his indiscretions to me in session, he would inevitably blame his "brain chemicals" to absolve himself of responsibility.[7] This was a reliable pattern and appeared to have dynamic meaning. However, he found it inordinately difficult to explore despite a number of gentler questions and confrontations. After another iteration of his behavior, I said,

I'm really interested in this pattern. What we know about manic episodes is that they do indeed make people more impulsive. However, I'm struck by the fact that you always do the same thing during your manic episodes. Your brain chemicals don't make you go gambling in Atlantic City or buy $5,000 worth of Zagnut bars. You always cheat on your girlfriend. It seems that, for whatever reason, it's really hard for you to entertain the possibility that this behavior might have causes other than your biology.

In this instance, you can see a bit of frustration, or "countertransferential snarkiness" (especially the "Zagnut bar" comment) leaking into that intervention which I wish I had omitted. However, the point was made despite my unpolished phrasing, and, after some defensiveness, this confrontation led to some useful introspection on his part and an eventual shift in his destructive pattern.

Prohibitive Confrontations

The last type of confrontation (see Box 12.3) is the most directive and, as such, is very likely to elicit negative patient reactions (e.g., defensiveness, alliance ruptures). Regardless of the risk, prohibitive confrontations have their place in psychodynamic treatment, especially during intense moments and when working with lower-functioning patients. The hallmark of a *prohibitive confrontation* is the therapist directing the patient's attention to an aspect of their behavior that the therapist deems to be unacceptable. During these confrontations, the therapist imposes a *limit* or reminds the patient of a component of the treatment contract that, if crossed, will lead to negative consequences (i.e., up to and including ter- mination of the treatment).[8]

An example may help. I once worked with an extremely low-functioning pa- tient at a community mental health center. He had a lengthy history of inpatient hospitalizations and serious suicide attempts. Though usually functioning at a lower-level borderline personality organization, he would occasionally "dip" into transient psychosis. After five months of therapy, he experienced a sudden and significant decline in his overall level of functioning and began to engage in dan- gerous, risky acts (e.g., discontinuing his medications; having unprotected sex with strangers whom he knew to be intravenous drug users with violent criminal histories). He also lost some contact with consensual reality (i.e., he was not fully "psychotic," but on the border).

Along with manifesting a callous disregard for his own safety, he stopped participating in therapy in any appreciable sense of the term. He neither worked in session nor was willing to explore his dangerous behaviors. He also arrived late and no-showed twice in a row. Subsequent communication with his case manager revealed that he left his temporary housing shelter without disclosing his new lo- cation to either of us.

When he arrived at our next regularly scheduled session, I was relieved that he was alive but extremely troubled by his current condition. He disclosed even more dangerous situations, including one where he was almost shot. His nonchalance during these descriptions was quite unsettling and disturbing, and I found myself in the strange position of feeling far more concerned for his well-being than he appeared to be. I also felt frustrated and powerless to help.

After considering my own countertransference reactions and attempting to understand his subjective state of mind, I began to intervene. I first used some spotlight and connective confrontations to focus him on both his denial and his recklessness, but he was unwilling to engage in this process. I also suggested that, in my professional opinion, his current condition indicated a need—at least short-term—for a higher level of clinical care (e.g., ranging from more frequent therapy sessions up to and including hospitalization; see Chapter 15). He remained adamant that he was "all right" and that I was "being too sensitive." Thus, we found ourselves at an impasse; I was very concerned about his current situation, and he was unwilling to consider these concerns.

As my attempts to focus him on his pathology and engage his observing ego failed, few therapeutic options remained. Interpretations would be of little use (and possibly harmful) given his impaired reality testing. Psychoeducation already failed, and he refused to engage with standard confrontations. Further, the option of just "waiting it out" until he returned to baseline would be clinically irresponsible.

Therefore, given that treatment had stalled and the alliance had ruptured, I made a prohibitive confrontation. I said,

> It seems to me that we're stuck. I'm very concerned about your health and your safety, as you've told me some scary things. However, you dismiss my concerns as overly sensitive, seem unwilling to look at your dangerous behaviors, and refuse to meet regularly as we agreed. Though I am more than willing to keep seeing you, I am not willing to continue therapy as it is. Not only would it be unhelpful, but it would be dishonest, as we would both be acting as if we were involved in a real treatment when we were not. If you are interested in continuing, we need to seriously talk about these things and find a solution. If not, I can provide you with a referral.

This was not a standard therapy situation and, in most clinical practices, might be a relatively infrequent occurrence. It is also not a very pleasant process for either the patient or the therapist. Many beginning psychodynamic therapists would be quite uncomfortable intervening like this, as it feels too forceful, "paternalistic," or perhaps, *confrontational*. However, it is important to remember that it is the therapist's job to maintain the integrity of the treatment and model responsible behavior. At times, and regardless of best intentions, this integrity can be compromised. In these situations, it does not make sense to continue with the status quo. Instead, a prohibitive confrontation is intended to (a) "shock" a patient out of significant denial/complacency, (b) confront them with the realistic limits of the therapy and the therapist, (c) focus them on their realistic choices in treatment and the fact that they are indeed making a choice regardless of their ultimate decision, and (d) hopefully move toward a solution.

If no forward solution is possible, it is appropriate to terminate or refer the patient to a new provider. In general, all therapists need to be prepared to let their patients go[9] if fundamental aspects of the therapy are absent or no longer working. The alternative of conducing what could be called a "sham" therapy would be both unproductive and unethical. Fortunately, prohibitive confrontations may help return a disturbed treatment to baseline.

HOW TO PRESENT CONFRONTATIONS TO THE PATIENT

As will be shown with interpretations, confrontations could also be thought of as *high risk, high gain* interventions (Gabbard et al., 1994). As such, they should rarely be used impulsively or without considering their potential clinical ramifications. Lothane (1986) even recommended asking a series of questions prior to confronting (e.g., "For the sake of whom? To what end? . . . Is it done out of concern for the patient or for the benefit of the therapist?"; p. 210). Even if one does not go through a meticulous series of steps, it is nonetheless important to be thoughtful and deliberate. This helps model appropriate reflectiveness for the patient.

Tone is particularly important. In most situations I recommend confronting with a tone of confused, yet earnest curiosity. This can be intermingled with surprise and even humor at times (e.g., see Buie & Adler, 1973), but the patient should know that the confrontations are coming from a place of therapist benevolence. Though they may be presented forcefully, patients should never have any objective grounds to doubt the confrontation's well-meaning origins. Thus, condemnation is never appropriate, not even when making a prohibitive confrontation. The therapist should respect the patient's right to autonomy even if it results in termination. As noted by Welpton (1973), a therapist who pressures their patient through confrontations is inadvertently aligning with the patient's superego. This is rarely advisable.

The context of the confrontation (i.e., in terms of timing and patient readiness) is also critically important. Langs (1973, 1974) and Levin (1973) both noted the importance of good timing and as well as making sure that the "dose" of confrontation was appropriate. Confrontations are worthless if the patient is unable to hear them or feels too overwhelmed to explore them. In such cases, it is better to keep the confrontation in mind for a later session. As Sifneos (1973) wisely advised, "confrontation creates pain. The therapist who plans to use it must be fairly certain that it will help set in motion a process of self-understanding that eventually will be beneficial to the patient" (p. 373).

It is also a good idea to make direct reference to the *adaptive cost* of symptoms or behaviors that are being confronted (Langs, 1973, 1974). Adaptive costs are the negative consequences of patient behaviors in terms of relationships, personal judgments (e.g., guilt), limits on freedom (i.e., choosing not to be free in some way), or limits on functioning (e.g., symptoms keeping a patient from fully living their life). At the risk of repetition, these negative consequences should come from the *patient's* words, not the therapist's. The former are not only more relevant and powerful, but are also far safer. Injecting the therapist's personal opinions into session will likely only lead the patient to feel "judged." Instead, use your patients' own words against them, but for their own benefit.

For example, during a different session with the bipolar I patient previously mentioned, I confronted his tendencies to be controlling and critical of others, most notably his girlfriend. I noted this by saying,

So it sounds like you're really uncomfortable letting your girlfriend be in charge of household chores and don't really trust that she will do them correctly. I also recall that you feel very resentful that so much of your own time is spent cleaning. This certainly seems like a dilemma that has some important impacts on your relationship.

When confronting like this, it is important to convey to the patient (either implicitly or explicitly) that *they* are contributing in some way to their own pain. This is far from a criticism but is more accurately a description of a situation that they do indeed have some control over. Harnessing your knowledge of the patient's values and intrinsic motivations may help them to resolve such inconsistencies.

A SPECIFIC EXAMPLE OF THE PROCESS OF CONFRONTATION

Although a number of examples have been presented, a longer vignette might better illustrate the process of confrontation. Specifically, I hope to demonstrate how connective confrontations can be used to defuse requests for gratification and move past a clinical impasse.

I was once working with a 26-year old man who made an appointment with me to treat his panic attacks. Upon completion of a diagnostic interview, he met criteria for panic disorder without agoraphobia and a mild depressive episode. He was neurotically organized per the *Structural Interview* (Kernberg, 1984; Yeomans et al., 2015). After completing these tasks, the patient felt comfortable enough to discuss the *real* reason he presented for treatment: He was a fundamentalist Christian who was also gay. He reported being attracted to men for as long as he could remember. Given that he believed in the literal truth of the Bible (i.e., that it was indeed the word of God), this resulted in an intense intrapsychic conflict. He felt that acting on his sexual urges would be a sin but that not acting on his urges would be inconsistent with what he believed to be his authentic self. Interestingly, and due to no direct intervention on my part, his panic attacks went into remission after he articulated this weighty conflict to me. The profound anxiety and dread that surrounded his issue, however, did not remit.

We spent several sessions exploring his conflict further, primarily through the use of questions and clarifications. He then directly asked me what *I* thought he should do. I initially answered his question with a counterquestion and asked what *he* thought he should do. Though answering a question with a question is almost a psychodynamic cliché, it is appropriate at times (Chapter 10). I also encouraged him to articulate his fantasies of what he thought I might say in response to his query. This was all to no avail, and he continued to press me for answers.

When presenting this case to students, I usually stop at this point and ask them what they would do. The responses usually run the gamut, but many discussed potential "compromises" that were inevitably in line with their own values. The majority of these compromises clearly came out in favor of him choosing to be more accepting of his homosexuality and, therefore, modifying his religious belief system (e.g., finding a church that was more accepting of homosexuality or finding "softer" translations of the Bible). Regardless of the answer, though, the students' responses usually reflected whether they valued social liberalism or religion more fully. To be honest, as a secular person, I was inclined to feel similarly. However, if I were to act on these beliefs, I would be foisting my own values onto him and, in this case, doing so *knowingly*. This would not be consistent with how I conceptualize psychodynamic therapy (e.g., see Chapter 04).

Instead, I utilized serial questions (summarized in a condensed form in the following discussion) to set the stage for a connective confrontation. I said to him,

> I understand that you would like an answer, and it's not an unreasonable request. But let's focus on the implications of your question.[10] How would you feel if I told you, You know, I think your relationship with God is the most important thing in your life and you need to suppress these urges to maintain your relationship with him?

He replied that he would feel that I was respecting his religious beliefs but discounting his sexual orientation. I then said,

> Ok, what if I told you that, Life is short, and God would want you to be happy and find love with a partner you're attracted to. After all, you feel that God made you this way, so why shouldn't you go out there and find someone to be with?

Not surprisingly, he said that, in this case, I would be accepting of his sexual orientation but dismissive of his faith. I then made a connective confrontation and said,

> So, it seems to me that, regardless of which way I answer you, it would be upsetting and make you feel bad about therapy. It might even make you feel bad about me and leave you wondering if I really accept all of you. You may begin to wonder if you can actually be yourself in here. Even more fundamentally, though, it is really not my place to weigh in on such an important decision. I'm sure you have lots of people in your life with strong opinions on this matter, but this is your life to lead. I want to help you find your own way.[11]

He agreed with this intervention, even if it was unsatisfying in the sense that he was still left to struggle with his unanswered question. Throughout the remainder of my work with him, I had to remain continually vigilant that my own values and beliefs did not subtly creep into session.

As I write this, I surmise that some readers might disagree with the "neutral" approach that was taken in this vignette. From my perspective, situations such as these cast the ineluctably value-laden nature of psychotherapy into sharp relief. They also warn us how easy it is to potentially move beyond our usual therapeutic role and influence our patients with our own values (sometimes without even realizing it). This is one of the dangers of the power differential between patient and therapist and the fact that there are any number of people that we meet who do not see the world as we do. The use of standard dynamic techniques (i.e., questions, clarifications, and confrontations) in conjunction with the psychodynamic stance help us to not only make these values more apparent, but also guard against patient manipulation

POTENTIAL DANGERS IN THE PROCESS OF CONFRONTATION

There are some other dangers in the process of confrontation. Along with the previously mentioned warnings about good timing and being mindful of alliance ruptures, there is also the issue of frequency/appropriateness. Confrontations are potentially disruptive interventions; they can generate insight and anxiety, sometimes simultaneously. In other words, it is very easy to use either too many or too few and, as with most clinical techniques, there is likely a "sweet spot" that varies according to patient and circumstance. Further, as will be detailed further, the way that we apply confrontations might tell us a bit about ourselves.

Overuse of Confrontations

Some therapists overuse confrontations.[12] This may occur in supportive therapies or when working with patients who could tolerate more interpretive work. When this pattern is evident, therapist introspection is in order—possibly with the help of a supervisor or their own therapist—as overuse of confrontations usually indicates one of at least three potential problems.

First, overuse of confrontations may indicate a lack of therapist knowledge. Novice therapists may simply not understand case formulation or basic psychodynamic processes at an adequate level. As a result, they might shy away from their patient's unconscious communications because they are not sure what they are looking for and what may be important. They instead stay closer to the surface by using confrontations, clarifications, and questions. Beginning therapists often suffer from self-doubts (e.g., "Am I seeing this the right way?" "What if I'm wrong with my interpretation?") and may decide to focus on more easily observable material as a way to avoid mistakes. However, despite their hesitancy, they still want to help their patients and, as a result, use a preponderance of confrontations in session to help generate limited insight. Additional experience and familiarity with the psychodynamic literature usually leads to more interpretive work and a more appropriate technical balance.

Some therapists have an adequate (or even exquisite) knowledge of psychodynamic theory but suffer from a more general discomfort with "deep" material. They have difficulties understanding theories on an *experiential* level and applying them directly to their patients and themselves. Unconscious communications—especially more primitive ones—may make them feel uncomfortable. Thus, just like the novice therapists mentioned previously, they prioritize confrontations and avoid interpretations, but for very different reasons. This clinical obstacle may be overcome if the therapist decides to begin their own expressive work.

A third reason that confrontations may be overused is countertransference problems (Langs, 1973, 1974). I am referring to countertransference in the *classic* sense of the term here (i.e., as an unresolved issue in the therapist that negatively impacts a patient's treatment; see Chapter 8). Some therapists may unhealthily use confrontations as a means of preserving relational dominance. They may experience discomfort when the patient directs sessions or when they are not the center of the patient's attention. Other therapists may use confrontations, especially the more "confrontational" ones, to gratify their own aggressive impulses. In other words, they unconsciously (or consciously) want the patient to feel ill at ease, on guard, defensive, or inferior in order to make themselves feel steadier. This aggressiveness may come out in confrontations that are distracting, insensitive, or even demeaning. Similar to the second type, problems such as these may indicate a need for supervision and personal therapy.

Underuse of Confrontations

Underuse of confrontations can be just as problematic. Confrontations are powerful and even necessary interventions with a high potential for patient growth. As such, a conspicuous absence of confrontations in any psychodynamic therapy is noteworthy. Some therapists may avoid them due to discomfort in their role as an authority figure or "expert." For although patients should—all things being equal—primarily drive the action of sessions, therapists need to frequently adopt an active role. Some find this activity level anxiety-provoking. They may fear challenging the patient (or even potentially hurting them) through confrontations and opt instead for questions and clarifications.

Unresolved personal issues might also drive an underuse of confrontations. Langs (1973, 1974) hypothesized that therapist with their own ego deficits may have problems confronting patients, especially about acting out behaviors. Some therapists may experience any number of countertransference problems that lead them to avoid confrontations. As previously noted, though, a failure to confront unacceptable and/or dangerous behaviors could be construed as an implicit sanction of these behaviors.

NOTES

1. Karpf (1986) makes the case that Bibring's (1954) definitions of manipulation and clarification largely encompass our more contemporary ideas of confrontation.
2. In doing so, I will be incorporating material from the relevant works of Langs (1973, 1974), Mann (1973), and Yeomans, Clarkin, and Kernberg (2015).
3. As noted in Chapter 13, though, this is not always the patient's response to a good interpretation.

4. Mentalization-based therapy has a specific procedure called "the process of re-wind" (Bateman & Fonagy, 2016, pp. 203–205) that partakes of elements of both confrontation and clarification as discussed in this book.

5. In other words, the patient withholds an important piece of information until the end of session. This ensures, whether consciously planned or not, that no significant clinical attention can be devoted to the topic (Gabbard, 2010).

6. Three examples of connective confrontations were previously provided (i.e., the man who committed a crime, the "I'm not attacking you" patient, and the employee who was worried about "measuring up").

7. In other words, he essentially gave himself what Rockland (1989), among others, termed a "benign introjection" (pp. 96–97). These interventions locate responsibility for a symptom or behavior outside of the psychic self (i.e., in this case, in his "brain chemicals"). These are described further in Chapter 15.

8. Corwin's (1973) concept of "heroic confrontation" has a good bit of overlap with this construct, but I find the current phrasing to be a bit more intuitive. See also Welpton (1973) for additional discussions of using confrontations in a prohibitive manner.

9. This can be very difficult, especially if you see a great deal of potential in a patient. However, it does no good for a therapist to be held hostage in what could be called a therapy in name only.

10. This is a spotlight confrontation.

11. I have called this technique, which shows the untenable consequences of such a therapeutic dilemma, "reduction to destruction" (i.e., showing how this leads to the destruction of the therapy) or, as things usually sound more impressive in Latin, *reductio ad exitium.*

12. Langs (1973, 1974, p. 443) called these therapists "confrontationists."

13

The Process of Interpretation

INTRODUCTION TO INTERPRETATION

Interpretations are probably the most misunderstood (and fetishized) techniques in the history of psychodynamic therapy. Though they certainly play a key role in expressive work, they are not supernatural in their power or in their origins. Sadly, a naïve reader of certain older case studies could come away with a mistaken impression that interpretations only emerge—already fully formed[1]—from the brilliant minds of master therapists. Although it is true that some interpretations come about from a sudden and "eureka-like" moment of clinical inspiration, far more are carefully deduced from a combination of good case formulation and meticulous clinical observation. My hope in this chapter is to make the case that interpretations, though complex, are actually fairly intuitive interventions. Even novice therapists can use them to good effect so long as they are thoughtful and deliberate. It may also be important to note that interpretation is a skill that only develops gradually, but which can become an almost preconscious activity with sufficient practice (Dewald, 1971; Levy, 1990).

After briefly discussing interpretations in the context of psychodynamic therapy, a six-step procedure for making interpretations will be described. This will be followed by a detailed clinical vignette to illustrate the process.

INTERPRETATIONS IN PSYCHODYNAMIC THERAPY

The proper use of interpretations presupposes the knowledge of other psychodynamic techniques. Therefore, it might be useful to briefly review and compare "the big four" listed in Table 13.1. Interpretations distinguish themselves from the others through direct use of *unconscious* patient material. Like some forms of confrontation, they also make links. Unlike confrontations, however, interpretative links are based upon premises that the patient is unaware of, but that appear necessary to explain the patient's pattern of thoughts, feelings, or behaviors. These unconscious premises could be thought of as the missing pieces of a jigsaw puzzle which make the picture emerge. In other words, they help confusing clinical behavior become clearer.

This linkage of the apparent (i.e., conscious or preconscious) to the concealed (i.e., something unconscious to the patient but surmised by the therapist) constitutes a very different sort of intervention than the other three. Instead of merely asking for information, trying to "get on the same page," or pointing out

Table 13.1. DEFINITIONS OF CLASSIC PSYCHODYNAMIC TECHNIQUES

Technique	Definition/Purpose
Questions	Efforts to generate patient information that is unknown to the therapist but potentially needed for the treatment (i.e., CS or PCS). Questions may be used to facilitate free association or to gain more specific information about the patient, their problems, and the unique ways that they think, feel, behave, and respond to the therapeutic process.
Clarifications	Efforts to expand upon and/or clarify readily available patient/therapist information (i.e., CS or PCS). The process of clarification may involve the patient or therapist describing, elaborating upon, reordering, or restating material to the other party. This is done to facilitate mutual understanding.
Confrontations	Efforts to direct attention (at varying levels of forcefulness) to important but overlooked/denied/incongruous patient communications. Confrontations may be used to (a) encourage the patient to resolve inconsistencies between different channels of communication and/or CS and PCS materials, (b) note denial or acting out behaviors, (c) help the patient face an uncomfortable reality, or (d) indicate that clinical material has psychodynamic importance.
Interpretations	Efforts to connect manifest (i.e., CS or PCS) feelings, thoughts, and behaviors (e.g., symptoms) to the UCS materials that gave rise to them. Interpretations may consist of therapist observations and/or the presentation of a hypothesis which goes beyond what the patient already knows (i.e., it contains UCS material presumed by the therapist to be accurate and important). The process of interpretation requires content generated from at least one of the other techniques.

Notes: CS = conscious. PCS = preconscious. UCS = unconscious.

an inconsistency, the interpreting therapist offers the patient a hypothetical *res-olution* to a clinical mystery. Further, this is a resolution that the patient did not arrive at on their own, but is given by the therapist. These unique aspects of interpretation are partially responsible for the complexity of psychodynamic therapy. A brief digression may help to explain.

Interpretations raise an interesting question about psychodynamic process. Namely, how can the therapist recognize material that is unconscious to the *patient*? It may seem counterintuitive that a relative stranger would be more likely to recognize hidden patterns and wishes than the person who is most directly involved. However, as noted in Chapter 4, people are not always transparent to themselves. The therapist, being at least partially outside the patient's psychical system, may be able to observe the patient in ways that they themselves may not (e.g., by using the four channels of communication and psychodynamic theory). Thus, therapists often arrive at very different conclusions than their patients (Lemma, Roth, & Pilling, 2008). A patient's patterns would not just be "how things are" to a dynamic therapist, but would instead be potentially meaningful objects of the therapist's suspicious curiosity.

Now, to be clear, it is necessary to be humble when making interpretations. If you do not at least entertain the possibility that your seemingly well-thought-out interpretation could be wrong—or even complete nonsense—you may find your clinical effectiveness limited.

The Empirical Basis of Interpretation

Interestingly, there is a growing empirical literature on psychodynamic interpretations.[2] Although the findings are fairly complex and, at least in some ways, counterintuitive, they nonetheless provide some practical guidance for therapy. For instance, although the exploration of interpersonal themes (Klein, Milrod, Busch, Levy, & Shapiro, 2003; Slavin-Mulford, Hilsenroth, Weinberger, & Gold, 2011) and affect (Diener, Hilsenroth, & Weinberger, 2007; Lilliengren, Johansson, Town, Kisely, & Abbas, 2017) both appear to be positively associated with outcome, interpretations are not so clear cut. Any simplistic notion that "more [interpretation] is better" is not supported by the literature (Barber et al., 2013, p. 478). Other factors, such as the strength of the alliance, level of object relations, and type of interpretation—transference or otherwise—may affect the relationship between outcome and interpretations (Hoglend et al., 2011; Ogrodniczuk & Piper, 1999; Piper, Azim, Joyce, & McCallum, 1991). In general, though, therapists who use interpretations in a cautious and deliberate manner are on safe ground, at least empirically.

The relation between *accuracy* of interpretations (i.e., how well they correspond to the case formulation) and outcome is a bit more straightforward. Numerous studies have identified a positive relationship between the two (e.g., Andrusyna, Luborsky, Pham, & Tang, 2006; Crits-Christoph, Cooper, & Luborsky, 1988). Accurate interpretations are also positively associated with the alliance (Stigler, de Roten, Drapeau, & Despland, 2007). As such, it makes both clinical and empirical sense to devote considerable attention to formulations and logically derive interpretations from them.[3]

On the Different Classes of Interpretation

Entire books have been written on interpretations (Levy, 1990) with individual chapters devoted to different subtypes (e.g., transference, resistance). This section will not be able to reach that level of detail. However, it may be useful to briefly discuss several different classes or subtypes of interpretations.

General interpretations (also known as superficial interpretations) are the vaguest class (Langs, 1973, 1974). As the name implies, they are potentially applicable to any number of people, as they lack patient-specific unconscious detail (e.g., "It seems like you might be reacting to your boss as if she were your mother"). They are also relatively self-evident and nearer to the surface than *specific* interpretations. However, like any interpretation, they have the possibility to generate insight, but it is usually of limited depth. They help the patient look inward but not too far. Perhaps not surprisingly, most psychodynamic therapists do not solely rely on general interpretations, but instead use them in a preparatory manner for more specific interpretations or as a way to assess the patient's general capacity for expressive work (Etchegoyen, 2012).

Specific interpretations, on the other hand, are far more detailed. They focus on a particular patient's unconscious materials and are formulated in a more individualized fashion. As such, they are presumed to be far more mutative and powerful than general interpretations. Unless there are compelling reasons to the contrary, general interpretations should not be used when specific interpretations are possible.

One subtype of specific interpretation, the *genetic interpretation* (Dewald, 1971), deserves special mention, if only for the purpose of terminological clarity. The "genetic" part of genetic interpretation refers not to DNA or biological genetics but to the psychological *origin* of a clinical problem. This is usually one or more experiences from the patient's remote past. In a "classic" genetic interpretation, unconscious material is not only explained but also directly linked to these early formative events. Cabaniss, Cherry, Douglas, and Schwartz (2011) recommended using genetic interpretations sparingly and only when the patient was in touch with the affect associated with these earlier events (p. 182). Regardless of class or subtype, though, the similarities between interpretations far outweigh their differences.

THE PROCESS OF INTERPRETATION

As was the case with other interventions, it is helpful to think of interpretation as a *process*. Good interpretations are not just isolated pieces of wisdom that are handed

Box 13.1.

STEPS IN THE PROCESS OF INTERPRETATION

1. The patient generates clinical material (i.e., conscious, preconscious, and unconscious).
2. The therapist organizes the material into one or more clinical problems.
3. The therapist synthesizes the material into a series of possible interpretations.
4. The therapist presents an initial interpretation to the patient.
5. The therapist listens for evidence of support or disconfirmation.
6. The therapist either begins the process anew or makes subsequent, augmentative interpretations to help the patient "work through" the insights and experiences.

to the patient like an unexpected gift. They are better thought of as variations of an important message that the patient needs to hear or as chapters of a book that the patient needs to read. Competent interpretation requires the therapist to not only plan a few steps ahead but to also understand their patients at a sophisticated level.

In order to get a better sense of how to formulate an interpretation, I have broken the procedure down into six consecutive steps (see Box 13.1). With practice, the process will become less effortful than during initial attempts. When starting out, it is useful to go through these steps in a deliberate fashion and to physically write out the first four. More generally, drafting lengthy *therapist notes*[4] after each session also helps to ensure that the subtle derivatives of unconscious processes are not missed or forgotten.

Step 1: Material Is Generated from the Patient

Before you can make an interpretation, you obviously need something to interpret. This is where careful psychodynamic listening (with a liberal dose of suspicion) and the proper application of other techniques comes into play. The combination of all these components makes interpretations possible. The alliance also needs to be strong.

To get the best information, sessions should feel like a collaboration in which both parties work hard to understand the patient. The therapist's role is both to participate and observe and also make the patient feel comfortable enough to introspect and self-disclose. As noted by Gabbard (2014), "surgeons need anesthesia before they can operate. The psychotherapist needs to create a holding environment through empathic validation of the patient's experience before offering an interpretation of unconscious dynamics" (p. 452). Genuine curiosity and respect go a long way in helping a patient peer into the darker, lesser-known regions of their psyche.

Listening for Themes and Patterns

The process of listening shifts over time (Langs, 1973, 1974). In the beginning, it is "looser" due to the simple fact that the therapist has few hypotheses available with which to focus their listening. As such, questions and clarifications are frequently used during this time. The derivatives of the patient's unconscious come out in many ways, so there is usually a great deal to think about. It is therefore important for the therapist to be open to many possibilities. Freud's (1964) suggestions for listening are worth quoting here:

> We gather the material for our work from a variety of sources—from what is conveyed to us by the information given us by the patient and by his free associations, from what he shows us in his transferences, from what we arrive at by interpreting his dreams and from what he betrays by his slips and parapraxes. All of this material helps us to make constructions about what happened to him and has been forgotten as well as about what is happening in him now without his understanding it. (p. 177).

These and other sources of information are summarized in Table 13.2. In general, the full range of session content is important to consider, and this includes the therapist's empathic and sympathetic introspection.

As listening proceeds, it shifts from being looser to more focused. For example, the therapist notices that what formerly seemed like an isolated incident in the

Table 13.2. Sources of Material for Interpretation

Events in session	Events in the recent past
Events in the distant past	Resistances to the psychotherapy process
Symptoms	Defense mechanisms
The patient's transference reactions	The therapist's countertransference reactions
Knowledge of the patient's wishes	Knowledge of the patient's fundamental fears
Repetitive patterns	Things that the patient avoids
Content from fantasies and dreams	Psychological testing data
Historical information from the patient's medical records	The patient's contributions to their own suffering
Parapraxes	Meaningful omissions or patient dissimulation
The patient's acting out behaviors	

patient's life is nothing of the sort. It may instead be nonrandom and pregnant with meaning. Thus, one or more clinical *themes* or *patterns* emerges that selectively attract the therapist's attention (e.g., self-sabotaging behavior; pushing loved ones away when they are needed most). These themes/patterns will be helpful in formulating the problem generated in Step 2.

This is an exciting and interesting part of the psychodynamic process. Therapists feel that they are "on to something" and beginning to understand their patients at a deeper level. However, this can also be a risky time. All people—therapists included—have a natural tendency to find patterns where there are none.[5] This is especially the case if one *really wants* to find a pattern.[6] Thus, mistakes are always a possibility.

Therapist *confrontations* tend to be more frequently used as these themes and patterns emerge. Confrontations help set a patient to work, as they direct attention to important topics and indicate potential similarities (or inconsistencies) in patient narratives. They usually make patients curious and more inclined to recognize aspects of themselves that they do not understand (e.g., "Why do I always get depressed during holidays?"). As noted in Chapter 12, it is not uncommon for patients to gain insight from confrontations alone. This leads to the generation of "deeper" material needed for interpretive hypotheses.

Confrontations also help therapists determine whether they are "on the right track." Before material can be usefully organized into a problem or an interpretation, it should first be vetted for accuracy. For instance, a therapist might confront a patient by suggesting similarities between two instances of personal rejection and then determine whether they constitute an actual trend/pattern (unconscious or not). Additional clarifications and questions may be needed as well. Regardless of which techniques are used, though, therapists should continually assess for potential links to unconscious material that can be catalogued and understood further.

WHAT IF NO THEMES OR PATTERNS EMERGE?

If no themes emerge and deeper content remains elusive, the psychodynamic literature provides us with some guidance. First, material that is charged with affect is thought to be particularly important (Strachey, 1934). There is some empirical evidence that exploring affect is a good clinical strategy in general (Diener et al., 2007). Second, therapists can return to the patient's presenting symptoms and reasons for treatment (i.e., their current adaptive context; Langs, 1973, 1974). In shorter-term therapies, this narrower focus is critical (Busch, Milrod, Singer, & Aronson, 2012). Third, any communications that strike the therapist as puzzling, incongruous, contradictory, or obtuse should be explored (Lemma et al., 2008). More generally, whenever a patient discusses a matter that deviates significantly from the "normal" or "expectable" range of human experience, it may point to important issues and conflicts. Clarifications and confrontation are useful with this seemingly anomalous content. Finally, the regular avoidance of particular topics may serve as another guidepost.

Step 2: The Therapist Organizes the Material into One or More Clinical Problems

After information is collected in Step 1, the therapist next identifies one or more clinical *problems* that could be helped by interpretation. In general, a combination of the patterns/themes previously described and the therapist's case formulation guides the selection of the problem. It could be a conflict, a symptom, or a puzzling behavior. Regardless, to be a good candidate for interpretation, it should satisfy several criteria. First, it should be responsible for patient suffering. Like any "disorder" (*Diagnostic and Statistical Manual of Mental Disorders [American Psychiatric Association*, 2013] or otherwise), the problem should cause clinically significant distress and/or clinically significant interference. If it does not, there will be little patient motivation for deep introspection and change. Second, the problem should be relatively chronic or pervasive (i.e., occurring frequently or across multiple settings and time periods). For example, if it is an interpersonal problem, it would be reasonable to expect it to occur in session with the therapist, across recent relationships, and in the patient's past relationships.

The problem should also be confusing to the patient. If they already possessed a full psychodynamic understanding of it, further interpretation would be superfluous. Therefore, it is important to select problems that betray some degree of unconscious involvement. Any number of behaviors could indicate this. Some patients say they want something, yet never seek it out. They may even summarily reject it when it is within their grasp or directly offered to them. Other patients are emphatic that they *do not* want something yet appear to seek it out with a dogged, almost single-minded purpose. Still others seem compelled to relive a pattern over and over again to their obvious detriment. Situations like these (and many more) indicate a disconnect between the patients' conscious and unconscious awareness. As such, they could readily be formulated into clinical problems.[7]

Step 3: The Therapist Synthesizes Patient Material into a Series of Possible Interpretations

Once one or more suitable clinical problems has been identified, the therapist next begins to formulate interpretive hypotheses. This should not be rushed, and it may be reassuring to know that few find it to be a quick or easy process. Ferenczi (1955) noted:

> One gradually becomes aware how immensely complicated the mental work demanded from the analyst is. He has to let the patient's free associations play upon him; simultaneously he lets his own fantasy get to work with the association material; from time to time he compares the new connexions that arise with earlier results of the analysis; and not for one moment must he relax the vigilance and criticism made necessary by his own subjective trends. One

might say that his mind swings continuously b/w empathy, self-observation, and making judgments. The latter emerge spontaneously from time to time as mental signals, which at first, of course, have to be assessed only as such; only after the accumulation of further evidences is one entitled to make an interpretation. (pp. 95–96)

From my perspective, if Sandor Ferenczi finds the interpretive process to be challenging, we should all try to be patient with ourselves.

So how do we start "connecting the dots" and making interpretations? Our patients provide us with so much material, even over the course of a single session, that they sometimes lose the forest for the trees (Menninger, 1958). Part of our job as therapists is to maintain a broader, panoramic perspective. More accurately, we need to facilely attend to the seemingly inconsequential trivialities of the patient's life, the larger themes/patterns/problems, and everything in between. It is easy to get lost, as everything seems potentially meaningful.

Therefore, it is useful for therapists to ask themselves a series of basic questions. Some of these are listed in Box 13.2. The last three are particularly decisive, as interpretations should convey a broad, experience-near, and clinically useful message. They should also be logically connected to one's case formulation. If the identified problem does not meet these three criteria, it may be time to either reconsider the problem or modify the case formulation.

In a nutshell, the goal of Step 3 is to marshal evidence for (a) the importance of the problem, (b) the pervasiveness and rigidity of the problem, (c) the consequences of the problem (i.e., both good and bad; both conscious and

---

Box 13.2.

Useful Questions for Formulating Interpretations

- To what extent is the patient aware of the problem?
- What is the patient trying to accomplish or avoid through this problem?
- What are the missing unconscious components that help to make sense of the problem?
- Does this problem manifest during sessions with the therapist?
- What are the recent manifestations of this problem in the patient's life?
- When did the problem first manifest in the patient's life?
- What does the patient get from their current "solution" to the problem?
- What patient behaviors or interpersonal reactions from others maintain the problem?
- How is the problem related to the patient's case formulation?
- How is the problem related to the current patient themes/patterns noticed in Step 1?
- Would work on this problem be useful for the patient?

---

unconscious) and, most importantly, (d) the potential *solution* for the problem (i.e., a dynamic understanding of the problem that will help the patient feel better and increase their personal freedom). This evidence could come from any and all of the sources detailed previously in Table 13.2.

It is important to alternate between sticking fairly close to the clinical data and making conjectures that go a bit beyond. After all, unconscious links are, by definition, hidden, and require some degree of speculation to be identified. The patient has presumably been unable to do this for themselves, so the unconscious links to manifest behaviors are likely to be subtle.

For example, imagine a patient who unequivocally states that she wants to fall in love with a "good man." However, her dating history reveals repeated disappointments, as she regularly chooses men who are unavailable to her in some fundamental way (e.g., they have another partner they are unwilling to leave) or emotionally abusive. Assuming the patient is being truthful to the best of her ability, this is a puzzling pattern, as the outcomes run contrary to her stated wishes. Looked at from an objective, logical perspective, it just does not make sense. Why would a person who wants one thing always choose its opposite?

A dynamic therapist would not see her problem as random, illogical, or the result of "bad luck." They would instead view it as a potentially meaningful repetition with an internal logic of its own. However, the logic has not yet been revealed. Something is missing from her tale that would cause the pattern to make sense. But what is the missing unconscious premise? This question should occupy the therapist's curiosity as they ponder the case and review material. After putting several pieces of evidence together (e.g., the patient's numerous downward social comparisons during session, a history of critical comments from caregivers), the therapist would be better situated to generate a tentative interpretive hypothesis. For instance, the therapist might hypothesize that the patient unconsciously chooses the men *she feels she deserves*, not the men she consciously wants. That is to say, her choices are in keeping with her critical self-evaluations, not her stated wishes. This initial interpretive foray could then serve as a basis for other interpretations. Some may be more specific than this (e.g., a very precise interpretation of what happened during a recent date), and some may be more general (an interpretation connecting her current sense of self to internalized criticisms from her parents).

As will be discussed in subsequent sections, interpretations are rarely helpful if they are isolated clinical events. Their power is augmented when they are repeated and organized around a central interpretive *message* (see Step 6). It is therefore important to prepare a *series* of rough interpretations. This process benefits from a therapist's creativity, empathy, access to their own unconscious patterns, experience with other patients, and use of supervision. However, knowledge of the psychodynamic literature and the use of good clinical texts can also stimulate interpretive hypotheses.

Though interpreting patient material is an individualized process, some general guidance may be helpful. It is a good idea to really let your "sympathetic imagination" come out to play at this stage (Boris, 1986). Allow yourself to enter your patient's subjective world and try to understand and resonate with their unconscious patterns. Your own capacities to mentalize are helpful here. Further, try to avoid judging yourself too harshly on interpretive accuracy until you are in a better position to do so. Excessive criticality will only inhibit brainstorming, and improbable interpretations can always be filtered out later.

As a rule, you should generate several interpretations that cover a full range of the patient's problem. More specifically and, of course, depending on the problem, it is ideal to have at least one interpretation for each of the following: (a) the current therapeutic situation (e.g., related to transference), (b) a current life event (e.g., related to a current friend), (c) a recent life event (e.g., a past partner), and (d) events in the patient's remote past (e.g., early parental relationships). Psychodynamic goals are often quite broad (see Chapter 3), so operating with a longer-term time horizon is critical. Further, as it is impossible to anticipate when a specific interpretation will be needed, having several prepared in advance will help the therapist to be maximally responsive.

After generating a series of interpretation, you will be in a better position to determine which ones are most likely to be accurate, clinically useful, and "heard" by the patient.[8] This is another time when it helps to revisit the case formulation. If interpretations are consistent with your formulation and logically deducible from it, you will be better able to justify and explain these interpretations to your patient. If they are incompatible with one another, one (or both) may need to be modified. Formulations are useful but imperfect and incomplete human constructions. They must be periodically evaluated and modified regardless.

Step 4: The Therapist Presents an Initial Interpretation to the Patient

Step 4 is the moment of application (i.e., when the therapist presents an interpretation to the patient). This step requires some additional planning.

PREPARATION

Therapists must first decide on the most appropriate interpretation to present. In other words, which part of the overall interpretive message does the patient need to hear? By this time the therapist hopefully has a good sense of what the patient knows, what they do not know, and how they typically protect themselves (i.e., characteristic defense mechanisms). This being the case, which interpretation would be (a) most helpful and (b) most capable of being understood?

Two of the most repeated "rules of thumb" for dynamic interpretations note that they should proceed from present to past (i.e., reverse chronological order) and from surface to depth (e.g., Langs, 1973, 1974; Levy, 1990).[9] All things being equal, then, recent and shallower material should be interpreted before older and deeper material. These rules were not empirically derived, but they make good clinical sense. Interpretations always transcend the patient's level of self-understanding. If they are too obvious, the patient will not gain any insight. If they are too deep, the message will be lost as the interpretation either bounces anemically off the patient's defenses or is dismissed as nonsensical. Therefore, high-impact interpretations aim to be only a step or two ahead of the patient's understanding (i.e., just out of the patient's immediate reach but potentially graspable) with no large gaps between conscious awareness and unconscious inference (Freud, 1958d).

Next, it is a good idea to practice *justifying* the interpretation. Demonstrate—using clear and jargon-free language—how you arrived at your conclusion. I have found it helpful to error on the side of too much preparation here rather than too little. After all, it is very possible that you may have misjudged your patient's level of psychological mindedness, resulting in a "Huh?," but the interpretation might still be salvaged if you can connect the dots and make your case.[10]

The phrasing of an interpretation is similarly critical. Though interpretations are not qualitatively different from other psychodynamic interventions (e.g., see suggestions in Chapter 6), they tend to require a bit more stylistic nuance due to their inclusion of unconscious content. As a result, the usual rules (e.g., concision, avoiding jargon) are doubly important.

HOW TO PRESENT AN INTERPRETATION

Interpretations are best presented as relatively simple, declarative sentences. In most cases, they should be worded in a tentative and "one-down" manner (e.g., "Could it be the case that . . . ?" "I wonder if . . .")[11]. This is another situation in which a variation of the "slow, not too bright therapist" approach described by Levy (1990) can be disarmingly effective (p. 24; see also Chapter 10). In general, a tentative phrasing indicates that the therapist could be wrong and implicitly invites the patient to correct the therapist as needed.[12]

It is also wise to anticipate patient reactions as you formulate. For interpretations that might be particularly wounding, you might begin and end with supportive/empathic statements (e.g., "I understand that it might be difficult to consider X, but I also know that you have been able to face difficult things in the past").

Relatedly, it is often helpful to reference the adaptive cost of the problem (i.e., how it interferes with the patient's life and/or the therapy). This helps ensure that the message is not merely an abstract one but also holds a personal relevance. Try to make the case that the patient's problem is far worse than the difficult therapeutic work needed to remedy it.

Finally, if the interpretation is complex (i.e., more than a few sentences), break it down into smaller "chunks" or check in with the patient to ensure that they received the entire message. In the latter case, you could end the interpretation with, "I understand that what I just said was pretty complicated. Could you tell me in your own words what you heard me say?"

Since wording is so important, it is often helpful to practice interpretations several times. Some therapists rehearse them silently to themselves (Gabbard, 2014), and others write them down verbatim into their therapist notes. Regardless of method, it is usually reassuring for new therapists to know that they have essentially committed the interpretation and its many nuances to memory. At that point, they just have to wait for an opportunity to use it and adjust the specific content as necessary.

Although preparation is critical, it is just as important to ensure that you are not "mechanical" when interpreting. Interpretations must strike the patient at emotional and cognitive levels simultaneously if they are to be maximally effective. This requires both nuance and sensitivity, as the material is very real and potentially troubling to the patient. It is also likely intertwined with any number of profound emotional experiences. Thus, it would be a little strange to give the patient a coldly rational interpretation (Strachey, 1934). As noted by Boris (1973), "interpretations do not need to smell of antiseptic" (p. 300).

WHEN TO PRESENT AN INTERPRETATION

Of course, the best time to present an interpretation is at the exact right time, but I have a feeling that this tautological (yet accurate) answer will ultimately be unsatisfying. The classic advice from Freud (1958b) would be to wait until patients are just one short step away from making the interpretation themselves (p. 140). This lends the interpretation far more power than if it was obvious or several steps removed from their experience. Although few could deny that this is sage advice, other criteria may be helpful.

Patient context is critically important. Namely, is the patient in a good position to receive the interpretation and make use of it? There are two overlapping considerations here, one personal and one situational. The personal piece is not just related to patient capacity for insight—which is obviously important—but also to the patient's openness and amount of ego strength. Can they "hear" the interpretation or will it be taken as an unanticipated personal attack or psychological intrusion? Making the matter more complex, this readiness can vary from session to session. For example, a patient may be able to take in a very "unappealing" interpretation of his unconscious romantic patterns during a "normal" session but would have far greater difficulty accepting it on the day that his wife served him with divorce papers. Considering therapist competence more generally, knowing when *not* to intervene is important (Sharpless & Barber, 2009).

One of the most important patient contextual factors relates to affect (Strachey, 1934). Some patients can tolerate (and benefit) from interpretations when they are in a heightened emotional state, but others cannot. Fred Pine's catchy way of capturing this technical dilemma is knowing whether to strike "when the iron is hot" or "when the iron is cold" (Pine, 1985, p. 175). This metallurgical metaphor is apt, as hot metal is far more malleable (i.e., potentially altered) than cold metal. Personality structure is important to consider here as well. In the vast majority of cases, you should not attempt to "strike" psychotically organized patients at all. Interpretations are inappropriate techniques for them that will likely only foster further regression and serve to diffuse already weak ego boundaries. Neurotics, on the other hand, are excellent candidates for the "hot" option. They can tolerate the provocative mix of insight and affective immediacy that characterizes a mutative interpretation. There is less consensus with how best to interpret with borderline organized patients. Some advocate striking when the iron is cold due to the emotional lability of this population. I tend to strike when hot with higher-level borderlines and when cold with lower-level borderlines.

In terms of *situational* context, it's always a good idea to check the session clock. Interpretative work benefits from having sufficient time to process the many implications. It is rarely prudent to make an interpretation near a session's end. After all, you do not want to give your patient the therapist equivalent of a "doorknob gift." Patients may even experience this as a "parting shot" from the therapist (Levy, 1990, p. 200), which only serves to increase their anxiety. With particularly important interpretations, it is preferable to present them early in session (Dewald, 1971). If there is no way to smoothly transition to the general topic of the interpretation, therapist patience may be required. [13] If the matter is truly important, it should theoretically repeat again and again in the patient's free associations.

Step 5: The Therapist Listens for Evidence of Corroboration or Disconfirmation

As noted in Chapter 07, the best thing to do after making any intervention is to stop talking and pay attention. It can also be useful to anticipate your patient's reaction before you interpret (Dewald, 1971, p. 190). If their response is wildly different than expected, something may have been missed or not formulated well.[14]

The reader may have noted that this section heading does not include the word "confirmation." This is for good reason. Given the inevitable vagaries of clinical work and the fact that it is an active process of attempted understanding from beginning until end (i.e., not just a passively neutral "collecting of facts"; Spence, 1982), I am uncomfortable with interpretations being labeled as "true" or "confirmed." Instead, I take a page from Popper's (2002) philosophy of science and prefer to view them as *tentatively supported* or *corroborated* (p. 280). In other words, corroborated interpretations (a) make sense to the patient, (b) are clinically useful, and (c) provide a "good enough" understanding of an aspect of the patient's existence for the time being with no expectation of being the final word.[15] However, I am far more inclined to view an interpretation as "disconfirmed" if it does not prove its clinical mettle.[16] A nondefensive listening to patient responses facilitates these judgments (Lemma et al., 2008).

INDICATORS OF SUPPORT

Any number of patient reactions may indicate a good interpretation. Clearly, if a patient expresses direct agreement or has a "eureka" moment (or even unexpected, non-mocking laughter in certain cases) these are usually good signs. However, care must be taken if the patient in question displays unassertive tendencies or characterological dependence. Such patients might be uncomfortable letting the therapist know that an interpretation fell short. In these cases, it may be helpful to pay even more attention to nonverbal information and countertransference reactions (i.e., Channels 3 and 4) and present interpretations in an *extremely* tentative manner (e.g., "I'm not sure, but do you think it's possible that . . .").

Patients might also generate new material (e.g., novel connections) as they work to test out and integrate the new insight (Stocking, 1973). If the material becomes broader or deeper, this is another good sign. Relatedly, an increase in patient emotionality (e.g., real anxiety or sadness at the recognition of an uncomfortable unconscious motivation) or significant decrease (e.g., in response to a reassuring insight) may be similarly informative. However, the former reaction could also arise if the patient felt that the therapist failed to understand them.

Although these responses represent some of the short-term indicators of corroboration (see Chapter 7), good interpretations should also have long-term support. After all, some interpretations require repetition or a bit of an "incubation period" to take hold. Insight from interpretations should lead to shifts in patient perspective that impact upon the patient's internal representations of self and other. In general, good dynamic therapy, with or without interpretations, should also result in narrative change (see Summers & Barber, 2010).

INDICATORS OF DISCONFIRMATION

Direct patient disconfirmation of an interpretation (e.g., "No, that's just not right") should be taken with deadly seriousness. Unless there is an extremely compelling reason to the contrary, the therapist is wise to defer to the patient's assessment. Even if the patient does not disconfirm in such a straightforward manner, there are other indications. For instance, they may just look blank or appear to be confused (for other indicators, see Chapter 7). Displaced references to the therapist's inaccuracy are similarly informative (e.g., the patient describes a friend who either does not understand them or is too "pushy" with their judgments).

Step 6: Working Through or Starting Anew

The final step of the interpretive process is predicated upon the results of Step 5. If the interpretation is disconfirmed, the therapist should return to Step 3 and revisit their case formulation. Some tweaking is clearly needed. If it is tentatively corroborated, though, the therapist next begins "working through" the interpretation.

As with other key dynamic constructs, the definition of "working through" varies somewhat according to author (for a review, see Solomon, 1992). I typically describe it as an ongoing process in which patient and therapist work together to (a) expand upon the results of interventions and (b) better incorporate them into the patient's day-to-day experiences.[17] By way of analogy, the process of working through could be thought of as weaving the strands of individual interpretations into the tapestry of an overall interpretive message (e.g., a new perspective on self and/or others). Rarely is it the case that one specific interpretation is sufficient to produce sustained patient change.[18] It is far more common for patients to require reiterations and novel variations of the overall message (Fenichel & Brunswick, 1941).

Morton Shane proposed a developmental process of working through (Shane, 1979, p. 376). It may be useful to consider this process to be *iterative* as well.[19] The four levels are:

1. Receiving and understanding the new insight
2. Applying the new insight and testing out new perspectives and behaviors
3. Viewing oneself differently as a result of the application of the insight
4. Mourning and overcoming the loss of old self and/or attachments to old objects (adapted from Shaw, 1979)

As is hopefully apparent, working through an interpretation is not a purely cognitive activity. In fact, the psychotherapy research literature indicates that interpretations are more associated with symptom improvement when followed with emotional processing (McCullough et al., 1991; Milbrath et al., 1999), and this is consistent with Shane's four levels. In general, the process of working through helps insights trickle down into intrapsychic, interpersonal, emotional, cognitive, and behavioral changes. After all, abstract understanding is fairly useless in the absence of real-world change.

ADDITIONAL TIPS FOR WORKING THROUGH

Working through occupies a good bit of time in expressive therapy. It is an individualized process with a pace and intensity determined by the patient's psychological mindedness, level of mentalization, defenses, and resistance to change. The "sweet spot" is somewhere near the edge of the patient's comfort level without overwhelming them. Pace/intensity is also determined by the therapist's skill in recognizing unconscious material.

Therapists can also facilitate working through by being systematic in their approach. The interpretive "rules of thumb" discussed in Step 4 (interpreting from present to past, etc.) are useful to follow here. All things being equal, good interpretive work starts out as narrow and superficial and then moves increasingly toward breadth and depth.

Finally, and as discussed in prior chapters, resistance to change (including the process of interpretation) is not only normal but expected. Dynamic therapists see resistance not as an impediment to treatment, but as a part of the treatment, and especially the process of working through. Resistance provides many opportunities to learn more about the patient and the ways that they organize experience and manage distress (Lemma et al., 2008). As such, it is very common for therapists to develop more precise interpretations as a result of patient resistance.

A CLINICAL EXAMPLE OF THE PROCESS
OF INTERPRETATION

Now that the process of interpretation has been discussed in some detail, it may be useful to explicate the six steps using a case vignette. This will not include a full psychodynamic case formulation (for examples of these, see Summers & Barber, 2010, 2015) but will only focus on aspects of the case that are relevant to the process of interpretation that took place during the first few months of a longer-term treatment.

Step 1

The patient, "Mark," is an African American doctoral student (biology) in his early thirties who presented for treatment at a training clinic housed in a community mental health center. He described difficulties with his productivity and "interpersonal problems." These included numerous altercations (some physical in nature) with people who "annoyed him." He also felt that other students in his program were "out to get" him due to "petty jealousy." In terms of his romantic life, he reported irritation that he was still "fixated" on a breakup that happened during his undergraduate years. Mark's current romantic life consisted of brief sexual encounters (i.e., "hook-ups"), and he noted that these were quite easy for him to arrange given his self-described "charm and good looks." He had several male friends in his life, only one of which he spoke to about "personal" matters. The others were primarily "drinking and activity buddies."

He was administered the *Anxiety and Related Disorders Interview Schedule* (Brown & Barlow, 2014) and the *International Personality Disorders Examination* (Loranger, 1999) by a clinical psychology graduate student at the clinic. Mark met full diagnostic criteria for narcissistic personality disorder (i.e., the primary diagnosis) and posttraumatic stress disorder. When he began seeing me, I administered Kernberg's (1984) *Structural Interview* over our first two sessions and situated his personality structure at the high borderline level.[20]

I found Mark to be extremely bright, moderately insightful, and motivated for change. Though it was hard for him to directly admit it, he had the vague sense that something was "very wrong" with him which he feared might ultimately limit his chances for "happiness."

To give the reader a better sense of the clinical data-gathering process with Mark, I placed snippets of content from the first few sessions into Box 13.3. This material (in no particular order), came from Mark's free associations as well as my use of questions, clarifications, and confrontations. The reader is encouraged to take a moment and read through these clinical "snapshots" and identify patterns and themes.

Though any number of themes and patterns could be potentially extracted, I found myself most struck by Mark's:

Box 13.3.

Some of "Mark's" Step 1 Clinical Data

- Mark reported several fist fights resulting from interpersonal slights and feeling "disrespected" by other men.
- His father was physically abusive and neglectful, only showing affection when Mark was similarly "tough" on his classmates.
- Mark noted repeatedly that he has no problem "getting" women but does not want a "real relationship" at this time. When these women express a desire for more commitment and/or more time with him, he abruptly stops seeing them.
- Mark reported always feeling like "the poor kid" when he left home for his undergraduate program. He described trying to dress like others and mimic their behaviors to fit in better.
- Mark identified a pattern of drinking to the point of "black out" when he felt sad. He was not sure why he did this.
- He described an incident in which he publicly "humiliated" a fellow student in front of their peers and the student's girlfriend. Additional questioning revealed that this man criticized him earlier that day in class, but Mark did not initially make that connection.
- Mark noted that he wears so many "masks" in front of other people that he's not sure what might actually be behind the masks.
- During a rare moment in which he seemed to be in touch with feelings of sadness, Mark said that he worried he might be "too damaged" from his upbringing to be a good husband or father.
- When working with Mark, I occasionally felt "pulled" into power struggles for session dominance. I also felt pulled into defensive reactions when he would make mildly derisive comments toward me. These are not common reactions for me to have during therapy sessions.
- When arriving late to one session (a rare event), Mark expected me to criticize him. He disclosed that he strongly considered walking right past the clinic due to this fear.
- Mark's stories (indirectly) indicated that he was very devoted and caring toward his pet. However, he either avoided these feelings or experienced a great difficulty articulating these feelings to me.
- He reported a recurrent dream in which he is harassed and followed by a woman he hurt in the past. Though the specific woman varies, the other aspects remain constant.
- After I made an empathic statement in reference to his abuse history, Mark laughed dismissively, said it was "no big deal" and moved on to detail a recent academic success.
- Mark reported hosting a party at his home where underage drinking occurred. When I asked for his thoughts about the potential academic and legal consequences of this party (i.e., through a connective confrontation),

he eventually explored these issues, but only after first making a dismissive comment about psychology being a "soft science" and questioning the rigor of psychological research methods.

- Though blustery, aggressive, and off-putting at times, I genuinely liked Mark and found him to be interesting and likable in a number of ways. I also felt a strong desire to help him find ways to be happier and treat others better. These were his self-identified goals.

---

1. Impression management (i.e., bragging, dismissal of problems)
2. Tendency to keep people at an emotional distance
3. Liberal use of aggression when feeling "hurt" by others
4. Difficulty soothing himself when upset
5. Strong feelings of shame and/or inadequacy that he actively tries to avoid.

Step 2

After thinking carefully through the clinical material and the themes identified in Step 1, a *sensitivity to criticism* appeared to be Mark's primary problem. It seemed to be a common thread linking his other patterns. This problem not only impacted several different areas of his life but also led to personal suffering and the potential for real harm (i.e., both physical and academic). Further, Mark appeared to have limited awareness of the pervasiveness of the problem and seemingly little personal control when criticized. The latter often manifested in session when he felt that I criticized him. Thus, it appeared to be a problem that could be helped through psychodynamic interpretation.

Step 3

With a problem identified, I next had to make logical sense of his ostensibly puzzling behaviors. Specifically, why would a bright person put his physical safety and academic future at risk because of "drunk assholes" who criticized him? Why would someone who states that he wants closer connections with others negatively react to empathic statements and push people away who wanted to get close to him? Again, looked at from purely "surface-level" perspectives, none of these patterns made sense. However, attempting to answer some of the questions in Box 13.2 led me to identify unconscious premises that made these behaviors not only understandable and meaningful, but even reliably *predictable*.

Consistent with the psychodynamic literature on narcissism (Kernberg, 1975; Meissner, 1979), I hypothesized that his sensitivity to criticism resulted from a fundamentally weak and depleted sense of self (i.e., a low self-esteem). The combination of his swagger and overconfidence was, in actuality, a brittle patina covering up the belief that he was fundamentally inadequate. Though he wore a mask of calm self-assurance, he was exceedingly vulnerable to the whims, perceptions, and judgments of others. If people criticized him or did not display the proper amount of deferential respect, his self-esteem was wounded. When wounded, he defensively compensated by either (a) wounding the other in return (i.e., dragging them down to his "lower" level) or (b) aggrandizing himself through prominent displays of strength or achievement.[21] These two "solutions" (often unconscious or only recognized in retrospect) were not terribly effective and enacted a high toll on his day-to-day functioning.

In order to formulate a series of interpretations that were consistent with the broader interpretive message (i.e., he reliably and repetitively deals with blows to his fragile self-esteem by engaging in partially unconscious and maladaptive compensatory behaviors), I had to deal with an interesting technical dilemma. Specifically, how do you tell someone who is exquisitely sensitive to criticism and feeling "less than" that you can help explain a repetitive pattern that he does not understand and, further, that you know that he is far more fragile than he would like to be? The activation of Mark's narcissistic compensatory strategies seemed inevitable. To some extent, this was indeed the case (see Step 6), but careful wording and appropriate timing makes any interpretation easier to accept. A sample of interpretations for Mark's primary clinical problem can be found in Table 13.3.

Step 4

As noted throughout this book, unconscious patterns tend to repeat, so it did not take long until I had an opportunity to make an initial interpretation. Toward the end of one session, Mark disclosed a painful event from his childhood. It was a horribly sad story, and he began to cry. I found myself tearing up as well. When he regained his composure, I could tell that he felt uncomfortable crying, especially in front of another man. I noted that sharing this with me must have been difficult. I also gave him the message that a combination of exploring difficult subjects and taking chances like that would ultimately make therapy more helpful for him. He appeared to begrudgingly accept this and thanked me at the end of session.

I found myself wondering about Mark over the intervening days and worried that he might no-show the following week. I wished I had "inoculated" him against some of the emotional reactions that I surmised might follow in the wake of his disclosure. However, he showed up on time the next week.

He began session by informing me that he slept with three different women over the course of the last weekend. The reader is again encouraged to stop for a moment and speculate on the psychodynamic *function* of this disclosure within the context of recent therapy events. Since my proposed interpretation (noted in the following discussion) involved the immediate therapy context, was not too "deep," and was consistent with the overall interpretive message formulated in Step 3, it appeared to be a promising option.

Table 13.3. SOME POSSIBLE INTERPRETATIONS FOR "MARK"

Interpretive Context	Interpretation
In-session event	"After I said, 'That must have been painful for you,' you quickly criticized me. I wonder if my comment might have made you feel a bit vulnerable in here or somehow 'less than.'"
Current life event	"Do you think that telling your friend that he was 'stuck selling cars' while you were 'presenting research at international conferences' might have been a means of making things right in some way after he made fun of your apartment being small?"
Recent life event	"When you found out that your girlfriend in college cheated on you, you hid that knowledge from even your closest friends. I'm struggling to understand that, as it must have left you feeling very alone with all that pain. Is it possible that you kept it from them so they wouldn't see you as you may have seen yourself during that time: as 'not good enough'?"
Remote past	"I wonder if your current difficulty 'letting people in' may be part of a very old pattern. From what you've told me, your father only gave you love and praise when you were 'tough like him.' The rest of the time you felt weak, worthless, and inadequate. Is it possible that those old feelings are still with you? Maybe it feels safer to be 'tough' than to let them know how you really feel. A part of you may worry that they'll hurt you in some way or use your vulnerability against you just like he did. Does any of that sound accurate?"

As it is always more powerful to discover things for oneself, I resisted the urge to immediately interpret and instead asked him, "What do you think made you start session with that?" He said, "I don't know . . . because it happened." I replied, "Sure, but the timing is interesting. This is the very first topic that you chose to discuss since we last met. Do you think that might be meaningful in some way?" He answered confusedly with a terse, "Not following you."

Since I judged that he was only a step or two away from making the insight and likely to "get it," I made the following interpretation:

OK. I'll try to explain what I mean. From what I recall, you worked really hard in here last week and told me a painful story about your father. This affected you, and you felt a lot of sadness. From my perspective, I thought it took courage to do that. However, I wonder if part of you thought it wasn't such a good thing. Maybe you worried on some level that I would see you as "weak" or lose respect for you as a man. So, when you came to see me today you wanted me to know that you were still manly by telling me you had sex with three women in as many days.

Step 5

After presenting the interpretation to him, I studied his reactions. His eyes drifted away from my face as he thought his way through my statement. After a moment or two, he laughed, said "Huh" in a curious (not questioning) manner, and looked at me as if to say "You got me." It was almost as if I had just bested him in a game of chess.[22] In general, he reacted less defensively than I predicted. He then proceeded to provide me with two more examples that instantiated this same pattern. These all seemed like good indications that the initial interpretation was corroborated. Toward the end of this session, I encouraged him to continue to look closely at himself. He noted that it was a "good session" and left.

Step 6

The limited insight that Mark gained into his compensatory behaviors set the stage for a lengthy process of working through this central interpretive message. It included variations of all the interpretations listed in Table 13.3. This work also strengthened our alliance, and he came to increasingly rely upon both me and the therapy as a means of support for personal exploration.

To be clear, this was not always a smooth, easy process. Some interpretations (e.g., the "recent life event" interpretation in Table 13.3) were more difficult for him to take in than others (i.e., they were wounding). As such, they elicited typical defensive reactions. In general, when working with patients who suffer with narcissistic disorders, such wounding is inevitable. Talking about the wounding in a supportive way and having them articulate their feelings of shame, anger, or envy is a critical component of treatment.[23]

The overall clinical results from this process of working through provided additional corroboration for the interpretive message. He not only began to more easily notice his narcissistic reactions after the fact but began to preemptively avoid them. For instance, when at a dinner party with some new people, one of the guests "flirted" with Mark's new girlfriend right there in front of him. Whereas this would have resulted in a fist fight several months previously, he was able to control his feelings of rage and jealousy and only reacted with mildly aggressive undercutting remarks. Though this was certainly not sublimation, it was progress nonetheless.

POTENTIAL DANGERS IN THE PROCESS OF INTERPRETATION

As previously noted, interpretations are high-risk, high-gain interventions with the potential to not only generate insight if done well, but to also create alliance ruptures and unnecessary patient distress if done poorly. Along with the "technical" issues scattered throughout this chapter, there are fundamental dangers with the overuse and underuse of interpretations.

Overuse of Interpretations

Overuse of interpretation constitutes a serious threat to patient outcome and retention. It sometimes results from an error in assessment such that patients are believed to be able to tolerate more interpretative work than they really are. This may especially be the case when working with "healthier," neurotically organized patients or those who are reticent to discuss their discomfort in session. In such cases, a simple technical recalibration may be in order (e.g., increase the use of clarifications and confrontations and limit interpretations).

If this overuse constitutes a reliable pattern, therapist personality characteristics or regular countertransference problems may be to blame. For instance, some therapists may be somewhat insensitive to patient anxiety (Etchegoyen, 2012). They may have mentalization deficits themselves or not properly realize the intrapsychic perturbations that result from intense expressive work. Others may gravitate toward interpretations because they find themselves titillated by the "primitive fantasies" hiding beneath their patient's surface behaviors. As a result, they neglect important, but less "sexy," aspects of psychodynamic work (i.e., clarification; confrontation). In these cases, introspection and/or additional supervision may be helpful.

Other therapists overinterpret due to unresolved narcissistic issues that become enacted during session. In this case, it is important to recognize that all forms of therapy include unavoidable power differentials. David Heller adumbrated many of the powers that dynamic therapists hold such as "the power to decide what constitutes transference and resistances. . . . The power to choose what should be interpreted" (Heller, 1985, p. 87). If you think about it, the process of displaying that which was formerly concealed also has the power to "wow" a patient with the keen intelligence and perspicacity of the therapist (Langs, 1973, 1974). All of these can be seductive and unwittingly become vehicles for *therapist* gratification instead of patient growth. In these cases, close supervision or personal psychotherapy may be indicated.

Underuse of Interpretations

Interestingly, the reasons for *underusing interpretations* are the very same reasons for *overusing confrontations* (i.e., a lack of knowledge of psychodynamics, discomfort with unconscious processes, and countertransference problems; see Langs, 1973, 1974). More generally, some beginning therapists associate interpretations with great *personal* anxiety, as they fear they might "mess up" their patients with a mistake. This is understandable to some degree, especially given the admittedly speculative nature of the unconscious premises contained within an interpretation. It may be important to remember that patients generally let therapists know when they are wrong, at least in some fashion. In fact, it can be quite therapeutic for certain patients to learn that even their therapists make mistakes, and nothing truly bad happens. More fundamentally, though, if interpretations are not used with the patients who could benefit the most from their insights, the treatment process will become unnecessarily prolonged.

NOTES

1. Almost like Athena being birthed from Zeus's head as a fully grown woman in a suit of armor.
2. For a more thorough review of this literature, see Barber, Muran, McCarthy, and Keefe, 2013.
3. Along with more global formulations, the use of a *core conflictual relationship theme* is a straightforward and clinically useful means of focusing interpretations (Book, 1998; Luborsky, 1984)
4. In the United States, a therapist can maintain private "therapist notes," which are incapable of being subpoenaed so long as they are kept physically separate from the patient's medical record (i.e., the "progress notes"). Therapist notes are a good place to document and organize patient material that is useful for interpretations. Since they are private, therapists can be far more speculative when generating treatment hypotheses than would be appropriate for the "official" medical record.
5. This is termed "apophenia" in the cognitive psychology literature.
6. Confirmatory biases are particularly troublesome at this stage of the interpretive process.
7. If it is difficult to identify a problem to work on, the reader might find it helpful to review the six core psychodynamic problems listed in Summers and Barber (2010) and/or the many different personality styles described by McWilliams (2011).
8. If you are feeling "stuck" at this step, it can be helpful to take a break from the process and do something nonclinical (e.g., play music for a while). If worse comes to worse, let your own unconscious get to work on the material when you go to sleep later that night.
9. Other "rules of thumb" encourage us to interpret patterns before specifics, anxieties before defenses, defenses before wishes, derivatives before deeper material, there before here, and now before then (Boris, 1986).
10. Preparation also facilitates therapist flexibility, as it is unlikely that the interpretation can be given exactly as planned. Adjustments are usually needed.
11. There is some disagreement in the field on this point. Levy (1990) and Yeomans, Clarkin, and Kernberg (2015) often recommended presenting interpretations less tentatively. Of course, patient characteristics should ultimately drive the form of presentation.
12. All interpretations presented to the patient should be, at least in principle, falsifiable.
13. Strupp and Binder (1984) noted that a lack of patience is one of the biggest difficulties that young therapists face (p. 190).

14. Although these types of predictions are far more common in cognitive behavioral approaches, they can also be used to assess the assumptions of psychodynamic therapists.

15. The matter of "proof" or "truth" in clinical psychology is a thorny one, and one that cannot be adequately addressed here. The interested reader might explore Spence (1982), Messer, Sass, and Woolfolk (1988), and Miller (1992).

16. This is again a pragmatic decision, as interpretations can no more be proven absolutely false than they can be proven absolutely true. Further, Fink (2007), among others, has noted that, due to the polysemic nature of speech, we cannot always assume that our patients are responding to interpretations as they were intended and may instead substitute any number of idiosyncratic meanings.

17. Cognitive-behavioral therapists (Barlow, 2014) are correct that real change requires the generalization of new skills. Working though is the psychodynamic equivalent of generalization.

18. In fact, this has only happened once since I began to do clinical work, and I am not terribly optimistic that it will happen again.

19. It is also a process in which the patient's understanding of themselves as a *psychical whole* is established by reference to the individual interpretations, and the patient's understanding of individual interpretations is established by reference to their psychical whole. Thus, I would argue that this process constitutes a *hermeneutic circle* (Bernstein, 1983; Gadamer, 1975).

20. For a number of reasons, my formulation of Mark was more in keeping with Kernberg (1975) than Kohut (2001). I saw him as alternating between a grandiose, surface-level self and a more hidden, *depleted* self.

21. When trying to understand narcissism, it is helpful to consider such things as power, intelligence, prestige, and influence as "zero-sum games." For instance, if the narcissistic patient believes that you have more of one of these qualities, they have less. They will therefore feel unconsciously compelled to correct this perceived imbalance.

22. This reaction was very consistent with his narcissistic dynamics and agonistic worldview, but I chose not to interpret it at the time. I thought it more important to see whether he generated new clinical material.

23. For a good introduction to narcissistic pathology and treatment, see McWilliams (2011).

The Expanded Range of Psychodynamic Therapy Techniques

Supportive Therapy
Techniques Part I

Chapter 5 discussed the supportive–expressive continuum and noted key differences between these two overlapping approaches. Section II then focused on expressive techniques as epitomized in the process of psychodynamic interpretation. This and the following chapter will elaborate on what therapists can do when working on the other side of the continuum.

WHY DO WE NEED SUPPORTIVE THERAPY TECHNIQUES?

Supportive psychodynamic therapy has a long history. Early psychoanalysts such as Sandor Ferenczi and Otto Rank quickly found themselves dissatisfied with a one-size-fits-all approach to treatment (i.e., traditional psychoanalysis) and proposed substantial modifications to theory and technique (Ferenczi & Rank, 1986). Some of these innovations are still with us (e.g., no longer requiring use of the analytic chaise), but others are not (e.g., manipulative variations of Franz Alexander's corrective emotional experience; see Chapter 7). This willingness to expand the range of psychodynamic therapy continues to the present.

A number of patients seen by psychodynamic therapists today are simply not appropriate for an insight-oriented approach (e.g., a psychotically organized patient). Some may not event want it. I once worked with a physical scientist with schizoid traits who could have greatly benefited from interpretive work. However, he made it clear to me that he had no interest, could not be convinced otherwise, and wanted to focus on a circumscribed symptom (i.e., insomnia). In cases such as his, the only realistic options would be to (a) continue as planned and risk termination, (b) provide a referral, or (c) apply a supportive approach and scale back the focus on unconscious exploration.

Fortunately, patient insight is not necessarily even required for clinical change. Though much remains to be learned about the therapeutic actions/mechanisms of change for *all* forms of psychotherapy (Lambert, 2013), it would be difficult to argue against that statement. For instance, behavior therapy can result in lasting benefits without any direct exploration of the patients' unconscious whatsoever (e.g., Perlis, Jungquist, Smith, & Posner, 2005). This is in no way a criticism or argument against the importance of expressive work, but merely instantiates the point that there are any number of pathways to change. Many patients require the therapist to *deviate* from using interpretation. Kurt Eissler famously termed these deviations technical "parameters" (Eissler, 1953, p. 110). He believed that they were indeed necessary for some patients, but should be used sparingly (i.e., as little as is necessary) and dispensed with as soon as possible.[1] For some patients, though, a prolonged supportive approach is indicated.

Supportive therapy should not be viewed as a "second-class" treatment approach or one that is professionally unsatisfying. It is not a simple therapy that consists of just being nice or merely listening to patients and giving advice like a bartender might. It requires thoughtfulness and skill (Rockland, 1989). Good supportive therapy requires a theoretical sophistication such that the therapist understands the myriad ways supportive therapy differs from expressive work. Table 14.1 summarizes many of these differences. It may be important to note again that all psychodynamic therapies possess some admixture of supportive and expressive elements and that finding the most appropriate balance of techniques for each patient is key.

SPECIFIC SUPPORTIVE THERAPY TECHNIQUES

There are hundreds of techniques that could be used in supportive therapy. So long as they are thoughtfully implemented, consistent with case formulations, and not disruptive to psychodynamic processes or values, they are likely appropriate with certain patients. In the following pages I will describe a sample of techniques representing six different, yet overlapping, therapy intentions: (a) supporting self-esteem, (b) supporting the development of skills and knowledge, (c) reducing anxiety, (d) supporting self-awareness, (e) supporting patient growth through remedial parenting, and (f) supporting the therapeutic alliance.[2] Some techniques serve multiple functions (e.g., using praise to support self-esteem and also build the alliance).

Table 14.1. DIFFERENCES IN PSYCHODYNAMIC THERAPIES ACCORDING TO THE
SUPPORTIVE OR EXPRESSIVE EMPHASIS

A More Supportive Therapy	A More Expressive Therapy
CASE FORMULATION	
Solid psychodynamic formulation required	Solid psychodynamic formulation required
SESSION FREQUENCY	
Generally lower	Higher (at least once per week)
SESSION DURATION	
Shorter sessions as appropriate	Full 45-50-minute sessions
SESSION STRUCTURE	
More structured and more therapist-driven	Less structured and more patient-driven
FOCUS ON PATIENT DEFICITS	
Stronger focus on patient deficits	More limited focus on patient deficits
TEMPORAL FOCUS	
Primary focus on present and future; less attention to past events	Focus on past, present, and future as appropriate; more attention to the past as sessions unfold
USE OF TRANSFERENCE	
Therapist attempts to have patients maintain a healthy, positive transference; avoids strong transferences; interpretations are rarely the session focus	Therapist fosters patient transferences through anonymity and abstinence; actively works with transferences in session
WORK WITH DEFENSES	
Less focus on removal of defenses (unless they are particularly maladaptive); therapist encourages the use of relatively adaptive defenses and eschews nonadaptive defenses	Defenses are actively worked with and challenged; therapist focuses on removing unhealthy defenses and increasing the flexible use of healthier defenses
THERAPIST SILENCE	
Limited use	Extensive use
USE OF FREE ASSOCIATION	
Limited use (i.e., modified free association)	Extensive use
AMBIGUITY	
Limited, appropriate therapist disclosures	Therapist is ambiguous; self-disclosures are rare

(continued)

Table 14.1. CONTINUED

A More Supportive Therapy	A More Expressive Therapy
ABSTINENCE	
Appropriate therapeutic gratifications	Limited gratifications
TECHNICAL NEUTRALITY	
Occasional deviations from neutrality but remains aligned with the patient's observing ego; nonjudgmental stance	Therapist remains between conflicts and is aligned with the patient's observing ego; nonjudgmental stance
CONTRACTING	
More extensive and detailed; least restrictive contract necessary for treatment	Limited unless issues arise; least restrictive contract necessary for treatment
IMPORTANCE OF THE THERAPEUTIC ALLIANCE	
Extremely important	Extremely important
USE OF QUESTIONS	
Appropriate	Appropriate
USE OF CLARIFICATIONS	
Appropriate	Appropriate
USE OF CONFRONTATIONS	
Appropriate (though usually less "confrontational")	Appropriate
USE OF INTERPRETATIONS	
Inappropriate in most cases	Appropriate in moderation

Techniques to Build and Support the Patient's Self-Esteem

A sense of realistic self-esteem is lacking in many patients. This problem appears to be a common endpoint for any number of patient disturbances ranging from inadequate parenting (Miller, 1981) to a disparity between the patient's *ego ideal* and how they actually are (Bibring, 1953). Perhaps not surprisingly, self-esteem is often compromised in sicker patients. They not only view themselves in inaccurate ways but also feel subjectively bad at a visceral level or feel altogether "empty." As a result, they often withdraw from life and the many opportunities/challenges that it presents, preferring the safety of routine and personal isolation instead. They may also utilize compensatory behaviors to manage their low self-esteem (e.g., Kohut, 2001; Summers & Barber, 2010). Three flexible techniques for buttressing a patient's low self-esteem are listed in Box 14.1.

Box 14.1.

TECHNIQUES TO SUPPORT SELF-ESTEEM

- Praise
- Encouragement
- Allowing a limited idealization of the therapist

PRAISE

Praise can exert a powerful influence on self-esteem. It is sad to consider, but praise may be a rare gift for some of our patients to receive. In general, the sicker the patient and the lower their self-regard, the more reasonable it is to utilize praise (Winston et al., 2012). It acts as a powerful reinforcer for the appropriate use of adaptive skills (see the following discussion) or for "taking chances" in life. Of course, the praise's impact depends upon the patient's view of the therapist. If the latter is held in high regard, praise can be very meaningful.

When using praise, psychodynamic principles should nevertheless be followed. Thus, the praise should be about the patient and minimize therapist involvement to the greatest extent possible. For instance, saying "Wow! You're really good at that," "That was really brave of you," or "I'm happy that you were able to go there" may be appropriate for lower-functioning patients. In contrast, statements such as "You're getting a lot of good feedback from people," "Even though it was scary, you still tried it," or "It sounds like it was important for you to go there, and I hope that feels good" would be more appropriate for healthier patients. This is because the latter statements involve the therapist's opinion to a lesser degree. Both approaches praise the patient, but the first statements convey a message of "That was good, and I am proud of you" whereas the second imply, "That was good, and you should be proud of yourself."

ENCOURAGEMENT

Encouragement can also be used to bolster self-esteem and, indirectly, self-sufficiency. The main message of encouragement is "I believe that you can do it, and it is important for you to try." As with praise, it may be difficult for therapists to dial in the appropriate level of encouragement. This is because therapists should only encourage behaviors that are within the patient's capacity but remain challenging enough to still require a "nudge" or a "push" (Misch, 2000). The border between challenging and overwhelming may be very narrow indeed. Good case formulations are needed here.

So what behaviors should be encouraged? Our more impaired patients may need the therapist to prompt them to get up in the morning, be more active during the day,[3] or even maintain good personal hygiene. Relatively healthier patient may need encouragement to discuss tough subjects, engage in secondary process thinking, or apply for a job. Even in the most expressive psychodynamic therapies, though, patients are at least *tacitly* encouraged to experiment with new ways of being, thinking, feeling, and behaving.

In the case of behaviors that make the patient nervous, encouragement could include reminders of the patient's true capacities or the progress they have already made in treatment. In other words, encouragement can be combined with a gentle confrontation. For instance, when a patient expressed reluctance to ask a woman out on a date, I encouraged him by saying, "Of course nobody likes to be rejected, but you've had success asking women out in the past. From what you've told me, she has been giving you some signs that she enjoys spending time with you. I know that you've felt lonely for some time, so I wonder if your fear or excitement will win out here." Implicit in all encouragement is a sense of hope that the patient's life can significantly improve. When done correctly, it can both inspire and motivate.

ALLOWING A LIMITED IDEALIZATION OF THE THERAPIST

This is not a technique per se but an important technical consideration in supportive psychotherapy. Patients at a lower developmental level or who suffer from certain forms of psychopathology may idealize others as a way of feeling better about themselves. In other words, they try to bolster their weak self-esteem though their connections with people they have "put on a pedestal" (Busch, Rudden, & Shapiro, 2016). This *idealizing transference* can occur in any form of therapy, but is handled differently in supportive approaches and in the early phases of self psychology as well (Kohut, 2001). Instead of analyzing and interpreting this transference, a supportive therapist might instead allow it to continue so long as it did not disrupt other therapy processes. With time and patient progress (i.e., the functions performed by others are now performed by the self), more expressive work could then take place.

Techniques That Build Knowledge and Skills

Some patients lack knowledge or skills. These deficits negatively impact their ability to navigate the complexities of interpersonal relationships and life more generally. In such cases, it is perfectly acceptable for patients to use therapy as a safe place for remediation. Any number of techniques could be applied, and not only from psychodynamic sources (e.g., some cognitive and behavioral techniques may be appropriately integrated into treatment; see Barlow, 2014; Beck, Rector, Stolar, & Grant, 2009; McMullin, 2000). Several techniques commonly discussed in the psychodynamic literature can be found in Box 14.2. It may also be helpful to note that many of the topics fall under what has been termed *ego-lending*, or the way in which therapists may temporarily loan their ego capacities (e.g., reality testing, impulse control) to patients whose own egos are compromised.

Box 14.2.

TECHNIQUES THAT BUILD KNOWLEDGE AND SKILLS

- Psychoeducation
- Providing information
- Naming emotions and helping the patient put feelings into words
- Problem-solving
- Rehearsal/anticipatory guidance
- Reality testing

PSYCHOEDUCATION

Regardless of their location on the supportive–expressive continuum, all patients require some amount of *psychoeducation*. This term is specifically reserved for information relevant to mental health issues and treatment (e.g., psychopathology, prognosis, etiology, psychotherapy approaches, psychopharmacology). In most cases,[4] it is very reasonable for patients to want to know what they are suffering from, how it may have developed, what the field knows, and if the therapist's approach is likely to work. This information might be useful for their day-to-day lives and even improve their capacity to perceive themselves objectively. Patients may also require psychoeducation if they suffer from specific errors in psychological knowledge (e.g., believing that chronic depression is "untreatable"). If left uncorrected, some beliefs may perpetuate or intensity a patient's illness (see Etchegoyen, 2012, p. 318). Therefore, it is important to understand both your patient and the current professional literatures. Even with best efforts, though, no therapist could realistically know everything. If you are asked a question you cannot answer, you should feel comfortable acknowledging this fact and let the patient know that you will find out prior to the next session.[5]

Clarity is important in psychoeducation. When working with supervisees, I have noticed that their level of understanding appears to be strongly correlated with how easily they can translate esoteric clinical concepts into language that is understandable to their nonexpert patients. This takes time and practice. It is often helpful to rehearse this process of "translation" with friends and family first and to also anticipate the patient's response.

For instance, if you want to provide treatment recommendations to a patient suffering from a *personality disorder*, it may help to first step back and consider patient reactions. How might the patient feel upon learning that their personality is "messed up" in some way or "defective" (at least according to their lay understanding of "disorder")? When patients possess a limited understanding of diagnostics, this bit of psychoeducation may only result in hostile or dismissive reactions. An alternative to jargon would be to ask the patient to describe how *they* see their problem, correcting them as appropriate. You could also provide an experience-near description of your understanding of their problem and continually check in on their own. In the specific case of borderline personality disorder, you might say, "From what you've told me, you have a lot of ups and downs in relationship that often leave you feeling unsatisfied and hurt. You've also told me how the drastic changes in your moods often confuse you and some-times lead you to do things that you wouldn't do if you were feeling better. Finally, you noted that you don't really know who you are as a person. Did I capture that accurately?" If the patient agrees, the therapist would then discuss treatment options, etiology, and prognosis (Bateman & Fonagy, 2016; Clarkin, Yeomans, & Kernberg, 1999; Yeomans, Clarkin, & Kernberg, 2015). Ultimately, clinical judg-ment determines whether diagnostic labels are used for anything other than of-ficial medical records and reimbursement purposes, but patients have a right to know what they suffer from. If they ask, it may be reassuring to know the reality of the situation: that diagnostic labels are required but are of limited clinical value and that good psychotherapy presupposes that the therapist always views the pa-tient as a unique individual.

PROVIDING INFORMATION

Nonprofessional information may also be needed. If the therapist is familiar with the standards and practices of the patient's culture and relatively less impaired than the patient, they can correct confusion and provide the patient with tools needed to better understand their world. To be clear, the tools that are given should ide-ally be principles and facts (e.g., there are legal consequences for not paying taxes; thoughts *and* emotions are useful when making big life decisions), and only rarely mere therapist opinion. Therapists, being rational and informed people who are hopefully "familiar with the unwritten rulebook of life" (Winston et al., 2012, p. 63), can genuinely help their lower-functioning patients by imparting such knowledge. This teaching, however, should always be *needed* by the patient and focused on improving their function. Further, when information is given, it is often a good idea for the therapist to help generalize it (i.e., work it through). An example may help.

When I was in training I shared a bus route with an intellectually disabled male patient with poor interpersonal boundaries. As I boarded the bus one morning and stood toward the front, I heard his booming voice coming from the rear. "Hey Brian! I got a lot to tell you tomorrow," he shouted, and then proceeded to describe a recent sex act he performed with his girlfriend. He then got up from his seat, stood beside me, and continued reporting the details of his intimate en-counter at only a slightly reduced volume. I told him—as discreetly as I could, given the circumstances—that it might be better for us to save this topic for a dif-ferent time. This appeared to satisfy him, and he only made "small talk" with me for the rest of the ride. When he came in the next morning—on a different bus than me—I thought it prudent to bring our previous encounter up. I first asked him what it was like to see me outside of the therapy office. After this, I encouraged him—using developmentally appropriate language—to reflect upon the potential consequences of his public disclosures and what he thought about them. As he had some trouble with this, I felt more confident that his actions might be due to a lack of information and poor judgment rather than other motivations (e.g., a desire to make me or others uncomfortable). As we chatted, I gave him three pieces of information. First, I informed him that no one would know that he was a patient of mine unless he told them (i.e., I reiterated confidentiality and his role in maintaining it). Relatedly, I also told him that, should we meet outside the office again, I would only chat with him if he spoke first (i.e., I would "follow his lead"). Finally, I informed him that intimate sex acts are not usually discussed in front of strangers, and that this could result in any number of listener reactions that he would be unable to control (e.g., embarrassment, titillation, disgust, curiosity).[6] Note that I did not tell him *what he should do* with any of these matters but only provided him with information he could use to make his own choice (see the discussion of advice in Chapter 15). More important for therapy, though, the discussion of this specific incident led to a broader consideration of his interpersonal boundaries and their impact on others.

Naming Emotions and Helping the Patient Put Feelings into Words

Emotions are also important sources of information (Bateman & Fonagy, 2016). More specifically, the ability to recognize and describe interior emotional states not only facilitates interpersonal relationships but also fosters patient *self-understanding*. When therapists are engaged in empathic observation using the four channels of communication (see Chapter 8), they are usually able to detect patient emotions rather easily. Of course, the patient's own abilities may be more tenuous and require deliberate and repetitive work.

These efforts are often rewarded, as the simple act of naming an emotion performs at least three functions relevant to supportive therapy. First, putting a label to the indescribable (or the ineffable) may lead to a reduction in unnecessary patient anxiety. Misch (2000) noted that this process was analogous to a patient in pain learning that they have a specific medical illness rather than an unknown problem. Second, emotional recognition is likely an important step toward emotional self-control (i.e., the ability to maintain an appropriate baseline). With both a label and an understanding of themselves, patients may be better armed against the emotional repercussions of life events (e.g., an unexpected pregnancy) or better able to predict how they might feel in advance. Third, and possibly most important, psychodynamic therapy presupposes an ability for patients to observe the many connections between feelings, behaviors, motivations, and actions.[7] This process is hampered if patients are unable to recognize and describe their emotions.

Problem-Solving

Many patients in supportive therapy have difficulties solving "real-world" problems. They may become overwhelmed during the process or mistakenly believe that worrying about a problem is the same as trying to solve it.[8] Regardless, bolstering a patient's capacity for problem-solving is not something that supportive therapists should shy away from (Misch, 2000; Rockland, 1989). If you think about it, this skill is critical for independence.

The classical sequence of problem-solving involves a series of sequential, interacting steps: (a) define the problem, (b) generate solutions, (c) evaluate the likely consequences of each solution, (d) implement the best solution, and (e) evaluate the consequences. Should this not result in an acceptable outcome, the problem is redefined and the process is repeated until sufficiently "fixed" (e.g., see Sears, Rudisill, & Mason-Sears, 2006, p. 21).

As is apparent, it is a relatively simple and straightforward procedure to learn. However, as the old saying goes, *the devil is in the details*, especially when conducted in the context of psychodynamic therapy. Appropriate problems must first be mutually agreed upon (i.e., Steps 1 and 6). Further, the problem should be at least partially under the control of the patient. If not, it may be better to help the patient accept it or otherwise ignore it.[9] Patients often get stuck when asked to generate potential solutions (Step 2). If this happens, therapists should facilitate (but not control) the process and support patient self-esteem, as patient confidence is critical (Woody & Ollendick, 2006). Therapists could also ask: (a) how they solved similar problems in the past or (b) what they might advise a friend to do in the same situation (Beck, 2011). This latter suggestion encourages both emotional distancing and mentalization. In general, a nonjudgmental stance and the occasional use of humor (e.g., coming up with ridiculous scenarios) may increase patient comfort and lead to more solutions (Borkovec & Sharpless, 2004). During Steps 3 and 5, when evaluation and judgment are required, patients may benefit from therapists "lending" their objective ego capacities. Therapists can also help the patient anticipate unexpected consequences or the likely responses of others who are involved in the problem (if relevant). However, the lending of therapist capacities should only take place when the patient's own abilities have reached their limit. Finally, patients at the implementation stage may benefit from encouragement prior to action and praise afterwards. As increasing the patient's overall skill at problem-solving is likely more important than any individual outcome, they should be praised for taking action regardless. Even if they choose poorly, they will likely learn something new that they would not have otherwise (e.g., see Kierkegaard, 1980).

To be clear, supporting the development of patient problem-solving is not equivalent to therapist problem-*fixing*. It does not require a deviation from the therapeutic stance (Chapter 4). Autonomy is encouraged except in the most egregious of circumstances (e.g., dangerous patient behaviors). Further, problem-solving should also be conversational (instead of "didactic"), appropriately exploratory, and focused on the patient's forward development. Finally, as with any patient communication, therapists should be on the lookout for new patient patterns and connections with other relevant dynamic issues (e.g., unnecessary dependence).

REHEARSAL/ANTICIPATORY GUIDANCE

Rehearsal (also known as anticipatory guidance) is a supportive technique intended to better prepare patients for stressful life events (Winston, 2014). It may be a particularly useful strategy for patients with pronounced ego deficits in judgment, forward planning, or flexibility. Similar to problem-solving, the first step is to identify the stressful situation as well as the desired outcome (e.g., a patient with schizoaffective disorder who wants to regain control of her finances from her nonimpaired sister). The therapist then helps the patient to vividly anticipate, from beginning to end, the many intervening steps and necessary interactions along the way.[10] If the patient paints an unrealistic or overly simplified picture (e.g., "I think she'll say 'yes' without discussion"), the therapist should inject realism and propose alternate possibilities (e.g., "It sounds like you would be very happy if she agreed, but what would you do if she didn't?"). Further, the therapist should ensure that they are not just sticking to "facts" alone, but also anticipating emotional and physical reactions (e.g., "How is your body reacting as you're arguing with your sister?"). The purpose of the rehearsal is not to successfully predict the actual outcome—this is likely a futile task—but to help prepare the patient for a wide range of possibilities. Coping is generally easier when the patient is not blindsided by the unexpected. Good preparation may help maximize chances for success and increase confidence.

Rehearsal can also illuminate patient dynamics. This is because the therapist gains a fairly immediate access to patient fantasies (e.g., what they fear) and can more easily see their characteristic resistances, defenses, and conflicts. All of this knowledge is informative and may point to more pervasive patient patterns. Even if expressive work is not clinically indicated, these insights are useful for case formulation and treatment planning.

REALITY TESTING

From a psychodynamic perspective, reality testing is often defined as the ability to discriminate between internal and external stimuli (Bellak, Chassan, Gediman, & Hurvich, 1973). This occurs along a continuum: patients with extreme deficits suffer from vivid hallucinations (i.e., they mistakenly perceive an internal sensory experience as emanating from the external world) and frightening delusions (i.e., rigid beliefs that do not change with contrary evidence) whereas those with milder deficits may subtly distort their experiences or hold strong—yet nonbizarre—interpretive biases. What links all these phenomena is an inability to distance oneself from beliefs and/or entertain the possibility that one could be wrong.

Solomon (1992) noted the personal nature of assessing a patient's degree of contact with consensual reality. Therapists must use their own senses and judgment here.[11] Accuracy presupposes some familiarity with patient cultural norms as well. If these are not attended to, an overestimation or underestimation of psychopathology may result (see Gray-Little, 2009).[12] When in doubt, open-ended questions and clarifications may provide a useful window into a patient's compromised thought patterns (see Chapters 10 and 11).

Once deficits are identified, therapists can begin to intervene. With less impaired individuals, any number of cognitive therapy (CT) techniques could be used. Reality testing is strengthened through entertaining multiple perspectives on events and evaluating evidence for and against personal beliefs. These CT techniques are generally consistent with many supportive psychodynamic approaches (Abend, 1982), but may differ in execution if not in intention (i.e., CT and psychodynamic therapy operate according to different therapeutic stances). Robert Leahy (2017) proposed that CT is actually a form of reality testing or "reality therapy" (p. 79), and I very much agree with his assessment.

With more impaired patients, though, it is unwise to directly challenge the veracity of hallucinations or delusions. Making a "full-scale frontal assault" would likely only result in further regression, an alliance rupture, and possibly even the incorporation of the therapist into the delusional system (e.g., "You're against me just like everyone else!"). When working with psychotically organized individuals, therapists need to essentially balance themselves on a razor blade. They neither totally dispute the hallucinations/delusions nor agree that they are true.

The reader may wonder what options are left. There are indeed some. It is important to remember that, no matter how "crazy" the psychotic experience is, the corresponding emotions feel absolutely real to the patient. Thus, reality testing is best combined with empathic statements and a respectful, supportive atmosphere. I used this approach extensively with a treatment-refractory patient suffering from paranoid schizophrenia. One day he described a particularly scary hallucination to me that dovetailed into his extensive delusion system which involved alternate dimensions, UFOs, and Nazis. He then suddenly slumped down into his chair and said, "You don't believe me either." After pausing a moment to consider his communication, I replied, "Well, I don't have the same experience of the world that you do, but I can clearly see that you're scared, and I hope we can figure out a way for you to feel safer than you do right now." The first clause was a gentle reminder that reality was not exhausted by his own, rigid perspective, especially if he accepted the fact that I was being truthful with him. It also conveyed the subtler message that there were firmer boundaries between people than he realized (i.e., people cannot read each other's minds). The second part of my statement indicated that I was there for him and took his feelings seriously.

When not decompensated, I could more systematically augment and support his own reality testing. My primary goal was to introduce—ever so gently—some flexibility into his delusional system. So, when he reported that a man in a passing car shouted "Demon!" at him, I did not tell him that was unlikely. I instead asked him if it was possible that another word might have been uttered. This was intended to prompt his own ego capacities. With a great deal of repetition and "working through" this and similar situations, his delusional thinking softened a bit, but obviously did not go away. The combination of supportive therapy and clozapine significantly reduced his hospital stays, but it would be unrealistic to expect a complete remission of his severe psychotic symptoms.

In ending this section and chapter, it may be useful to briefly note several other common problem areas that may be helped via skill-building in supportive psychodynamic therapy:

- assertiveness
- social skills
- self-care
- logical reasoning

- attention/focus
- learning difficulties
- memory difficulties

Psychoeducation, information, rehearsal, problem-solving, and skill-building techniques could all be used to remediate these deficits. Further, and as previously noted, an integration of nondynamic techniques is not only possible in supportive therapy but encouraged. So long as the integration makes clinical/theoretical sense and does not push therapists beyond the boundaries of their professional competence, therapists should feel free to enlarge their technical repertoires.

NOTES

1. For a lengthier discussion of parameters, see Etchegoyen (2012).
2. Five of these categories overlap with those formulated by Winston, Rosenthal, and Pinsker (2012, pp. 53–70).
3. This is what behaviorists often term *behavioral activation*.
4. I use "most" here because some patients may ask a number of ostensibly "reasonable" questions as a way of avoiding important aspects of the therapy process (see Chapter 10).
5. Fortunately, it is easier than ever to access professional literature without going to a library (e.g., Google Scholar, researchgate.net, and other free resources).
6. Though not relevant here, I also tried to foster mentalization by asking him to speculate on how his girlfriend would react to learning of his public disclosure.
7. Cognitive-behavioral therapists also believe in the therapeutic importance of understanding these connections, but differ from psychodynamic therapists in their stronger emphasis on conscious and preconscious material.
8. This is particularly common in patients diagnosed with generalized anxiety disorder or who otherwise suffer from chronic worry (Woody & Ollendick, 2006).
9. Stoic philosophers have long made this point. For a contemporary perspective, see Irvine (2009).
10. For patients who experience difficulties visualizing the scenario, the "slow, not so bright therapist" approach described in Chapter 11 may be helpful here.
11. As every therapist has "blind spots," idiosyncratic appraisals, and interpretive biases, a personal course of psychotherapy may facilitate accuracy.
12. For an example of this, please see the case of *Ode Ori* described in Sharpless and Doghramji (2015, pp. 12–13).

15

Supportive Therapy
Techniques Part II

SPECIFIC SUPPORTIVE THERAPY
TECHNIQUES CONTINUED

Chapter 14 described how therapists can support patient self-esteem and foster the development of important adaptive skills. This chapter details the use of four more groups of clinical interventions and ends with a discussion of the process of "working through" in supportive dynamic therapies.

Techniques to Reduce and Prevent Unhelpful Anxiety and Other Emotions

Whereas the proper use of expressive techniques may require a temporary *increase* in patient anxiety (see Chapter 13), this is not a primarily intention of supportive therapy. Patients appropriate for supportive approaches may instead need help *mitigating* or *containing* in-session anxiety. There are any number of ways to do this. Although therapists should obviously be creative and flexible here, a sample of some of the more common psychodynamic anxiety reduction techniques can be found in Box 15.1.

Box 15.1.

TECHNIQUES TO REDUCE AND PREVENT UNHELPFUL ANXIETY AND OTHER EMOTIONS

- Supportive bypassing
- Supportive redirection
- Activating and encouraging defenses
- Normalizing
- Reassurance
- Reframing
- Benign introjections
- Benign projections
- Upward explanations

SUPPORTIVE BYPASSING AND SUPPORTIVE REDIRECTION

When you know a patient well, you may be able to predict their reactions to certain "tender" subjects in advance. You may also know which conversational paths inevitably lead to doors that are better left unopened. If so, steering away from these topics may help the patient avoid unnecessary emotional tumult. Supportive bypassing and supportive redirection are a means to do this when the patient either cannot or will not do it for themselves (Cabaniss, Cherry, Douglas, & Schwartz, 2011).

Supportive bypassing is relatively simple to do but may feel somewhat antithetical to "standard" psychodynamic procedure. For instance, when a patient in expressive therapy makes a provocative or emotionally charged comment, the therapist usually "homes in" on that comment like a laser and encourages further associations. If, on the other hand, a supportive therapist decides that further discussion would be detrimental to the patient, the therapist silently registers the comment to themselves but ignores it in session (i.e., they *bypass* it).

In the closely related supportive *redirection*, the therapist again recognizes that a chain of associations could lead to negative consequences (e.g., uncontrollable negative affect; decompensation). However, instead of ignoring the communication, the therapist shifts the focus to a "safer" topic or a more solvable part of the problem. This helps the patient better maintain homeostasis and not become overwhelmed. For example, as I neared the end of an early session with a lower-functioning female patient suffering from severe trichotillomania, she made an important disclosure. She reported that her mother (now deceased) was the first person to pluck her hair and that, despite the pain, these were some of the only memories she had of receiving noncritical attention from her. Given the sudden shift in the patient's mood and the clinical reality that 10 minutes would be grossly inadequate for helping her deal with the emotional complexity of this issue, I said, "That sounds like a really important piece of the puzzle, and I'm glad you felt comfortable enough to share that with me, but in the time we have left I wonder if it might be best to figure out what we should do about your hair-pulling before we next meet?" We returned to the topic of her mother when she was feeling more emotionally centered.

Though both of these techniques have a role in supportive therapy, they can easily be overused. Patients—regardless of their level of functioning—need opportunities to "vent" and express their feelings. Thus, therapists should only interrupt these processes when clinically warranted and return to the topic at a more appropriate time.

ACTIVATING DEFENSES

Defense mechanisms are not necessarily "bad" (Freud, 1966; Reich, 1990). Everyone has at least some in their psychological repertoire and, if used well (i.e., flexibly and appropriately), they perform important homeostatic functions. There are times when therapists want to encourage or even *activate* patient defenses to better allow them to cope with distressing material. The more "mature" defenses should be prioritized here (e.g., sublimation; also see Gabbard, 2014, p. 39), but therapists need to be mindful of their patients' realistic capabilities. Suppression (e.g., "When you take the exam, it might be helpful to ignore those voices in your head") can be particularly useful as an immediate "stopgap" measure. I have also found humor to be effective for dealing with tough circumstances, especially if this is first modeled by the therapist (Misch, 2000).

NORMALIZING

The intention of normalizing is to essentially make the patient feel more human. When you normalize, you let them know that their reactions are not unreasonable or out of bounds, but are roughly equivalent to what others would experience in the same situation. Certain patients, especially those who are psychotically organized, may have scant opportunity to receive normalizations from the outside world. Their odd behaviors or idiosyncratic communications create distance between themselves and others, and a lack of normalization only widens the gulf of understanding. It can also foster terrible anxiety. To help remedy these feelings of difference, simple therapist statements such as "I think most people would feel sad if that happened" or "Anyone would be affected by that" help to make patients feel more "normal."

Further, some psychodynamic therapists (McWilliams, 2011, p. 76) have noted that therapist self-disclosures of emotional matters—including those intended to normalize—are appropriate for sicker patients. I concur and, when circumstances demanded it, have even used them with certain higher-functioning patients. For example, it might be very helpful for a psychotic patient to hear their therapist say "You know, I would feel the same way" or "I found myself tearing up as you told that sad story." In general, though, I am less inclined to disclose historical facts about myself than the specific emotional reactions that I have had (or am currently having). But, again, there is intertherapist variability on this matter (see Chapter 4).

REASSURANCE

Reassurance aims to alleviate a person's fears or misgivings.[1] Patients in supportive therapy often have deficits in ego functions (e.g., judgment, reality testing) that may cripple them with *unrealistic* anxieties. In such cases, is it appropriate for therapists to reassure them? If so, how? There has been some disagreement over the answers to these questions (Dewald, 1971; Glover, 1955). Further, one could surmise that many patients received reassurance from others in their life, but to no avail. If so, why would a therapist's efforts be more successful?

I essentially agree with Rockland (1989), among others, who stated that reassurance can be used to good effect in supportive therapy,[2] but that certain precautions were necessary. First, the reassurance should never be unrealistic. As noted in Chapter 4, psychodynamic therapists aim to set themselves apart from other people in the patient's life by providing honest and *non-self-interested* feedback. Second, therapists should only reassure a patient after they have determined the true nature of the patient's fears (Dewald, 1971, p. 104). Otherwise, the reassurance may miss the mark or be experienced as "fake" because it is presumptuous. Finally, care must be taken to not create unnecessary dependence (Etchegoyen, 2012). When therapists reassure, they tell the patient some variation of statements such as "Knowing what I know, I believe that you will be OK, and therefore you should believe that you will be OK, too," "We'll get through this together," or "You did the best that you could given the circumstances." Though palliative interventions like this may be needed at times to maintain patient equilibrium, they should not be used too frequently due to the attendant risks for dependence.

REFRAMING

Reframing is a broad term encompassing many different strategies to shift patient perspectives. Though probably most associated with cognitive therapy (Fruzzetti & Fruzzetti, 2008), it is certainly not alien to psychodynamic work (Misch, 2000; Wachtel, 2011). Given that a discussion of reframing could easily expand well beyond its role as a specific supportive therapy technique (e.g., the role of reframing in shifting global patient narratives), it may be helpful to use a more specific definition. For the purposes of this chapter, then, the meaning of reframing will be restricted to therapist attempts to change a *conscious*, distressing, and unrealistic patient perspective to one that is less troubling and more adaptive.[3]

Therapists can reframe in many ways. Probably the simplest way is to add a "but" to the patient's specific viewpoint or, better yet, have the patient add it (Beck, 2011, p. 243). For example, if a patient said, "I suck at painting, just like everything else," the therapist might help them realize, "*but* the last time I picked up a paint brush was 30 years ago and the whole point of painting is to relax, not to be the next Caravaggio." Further, symptoms that are viewed by patients as moral failings or personal weaknesses could be reframed as well-intentioned (but failed) attempts at adaptation. So, if a patient with tendencies to withdraw from others became self-critical, you might say, "I wonder if this pattern of 'pulling back' might have actually been a way for you to keep yourself emotionally safe when you were younger. Unfortunately, this way of coping seems to have outlived its usefulness, as it's causing you some problems in your current life." This will hopefully lead to less self-debasement and shift the patient's attention to working on their *current* problem. More generally, therapists can help patients find the "silver lining" in bad situations that elicit anxiety (Misch, 2000, p. 181). As one more example, if a patient suddenly lost her job and was in the depths of a formidable depression, the therapist could remind her of the ambivalence she felt about the job. Perhaps she was bored with work, felt "deadened" by it, and could better manifest her talents elsewhere. The new-found freedom may present opportunities never previously considered.

Several other technical considerations are relevant. First, the goal of reframing is not to give a patient *the* viewpoint (i.e., the only right, accurate, and "true"), but to provide a useful alternative to their current one. Most events can be viewed from multiple perspectives, and patients may suffer from limited vision. Second, it is important for therapists not to be "Pollyannaish" or overly optimistic. If the patient is lucky enough to have reassuring friends or family, they likely receive enough unbridled optimism. The therapist's role is to suggest a better, yet still plausible perspective. Finally, patients should be given the opportunity to reframe before the therapist. For instance, after the patient articulates a negativistic perspective, the therapist could simply ask, "I understand that's how you view it right now, but can you see it any other way?"

BENIGN INTROJECTIONS

Whereas reframing shifts patient perspectives, benign introjections shift the focus of *responsibility*. More specifically, they shift the "blame" for a symptom or behavior away from the *psychological* patient (i.e., the self-reflectively aware and agentic self) and toward the *biological* patient (i.e., genetics and physiology, of which the individual has little to no control). This technique is intended to help absolve them of unnecessary guilt and, if the symptom is chronic, move them closer to acceptance.

Though this technique may seem strange, it can be used to good effect in certain situations. For example, if you are working with a patient who is riddled with guilt for having a symptom, you might let them know that this symptom is associated with deficits in specific neurotransmitters.[4] This may not only lead to a reduction in patient responsibility (i.e., "It's not just because I am 'weak'"), but could also prompt interest in getting a medication referral.[5] As another example, Rockland (1989) described using benign introjections to help a psychotically organized patient by saying, "Your illness is due to difficulties with your stimulus barrier. These problems make it difficult for you to separate your own thoughts and feelings from stimuli coming from outside, predisposing you, for example, to hear voices or to misinterpret what others are saying you" (p. 97).

BENIGN PROJECTIONS

Benign projections are very similar to benign introjections. However, they shift the responsibility for symptoms outside of the patient's self and onto other people (especially those found in the patient's past) or external circumstances (e.g., time spent in a foster home or in a gang). Personally, I find these a bit more dangerous to use than benign introjections, as they entail the risk of inadvertently demonizing an important person in the patient's life. Therapists rarely gain first-hand knowledge of these people, and instead see them only as they are filtered through their patient's eyes (i.e., therapist judgments may be wildly inaccurate). Further, blaming (m)others for patient's miseries may feed into some common and inaccurate psychodynamic stereotypes (see Chapter 4). If it is clinically helpful to assign blame, it is far safer to blame circumstance.

Note that in all the examples of both benign projections and benign introjections, the traditional psychodynamic explanations for symptoms were omitted entirely in favor of other, less anxiety-provoking causes. They were not left out because they were irrelevant—psychodynamic processes are operative even in the lowest-functioning patients—but because the therapist made a judgment that the current context was more suitable to a different kind of explanation. When working supportively, and especially when insight is not a primary goal, traditional psychodynamic interpretations may be useless or harmful.

It may also be important to note that neither of these techniques should include falsehoods. Therapists instead present the patient with a helpful approximation of the "fuller" understanding of their difficulties. Just like the process of interpretation, therapists must decide what the patient is ready to hear. As patients progress—and hopefully they do—they may be able to tolerate "deeper" and increasingly detailed explanations for their problems.

UPWARD EXPLANATIONS (UPWARD INTERPRETATIONS)

Another supportive intervention has been called the "upward interpretation" (Werman, 1984, p. 38). The purpose of this technique is to limit patient anxiety when associations drift into uncomfortable areas which may be difficult to face. Thus, whereas a "normal" interpretation encourages the patient to look downward (i.e., toward "deeper" unconscious material and past events; see Chapter 13), upward interpretations focus on recent events and material that is either conscious or preconscious. This "shallower" approach can help organize the patient, make them feel less vulnerable, and possibly even lead to increased self-awareness.

To be clear, though, "upward interpretation" is a bit of a misnomer. Werman (1984) noted that this technique does not directly link unconscious material and might be more accurately described as an *explanation* (pp. 83–84). Therefore, to avoid conceptual confusion I will refer to them as *upward explanations*. Regardless of terminology, they are useful interventions. For instance, a female graduate student that I supervised was assigned a low-level borderline-organized male patient. He reported intense and troubling violent fantasies, and the objects of his fantasies were usually female supervisors at work.[6] The therapist's formulation included a hypothesis that these women served as relatively safer displacements for the person he was *really* angry with (i.e., an older sister who sexually abused him as a child and was currently his roommate). When he next disclosed these fantasies, he was in a highly agitated state. The therapist very appropriately judged that it was not the right time to interpret, and instead provided an upward explanation. She said, "I know these violent images are very troubling to you, and I wonder if they might represent the intense reactions you have to feeling criticized by your bosses." This was not inaccurate, but only represented an approximation of the therapist's full formulation. It was also limited to what the patient already knew (i.e., he has these fantasies, and he becomes intensely angry when his bosses challenge him) and focused on his present life, not the past.

Another example may help. If a lower-functioning patient developed an erotic (or eroticized) transference, psychodynamic interpretations may be too troubling. Therapists could instead provide an upward explanation that noted how these "romantic" feelings are not uncommon in therapy (i.e., a normalization) and that they might represent the patient's feelings of closeness to the therapist as well as their trust in the therapeutic process.[7]

Patients in general, and lower-functioning patients in particular, often feel terrified and overwhelmed when they face some of their more "primitive" (i.e., id) urges and conflicts. Langs (1973, 1974, p. 589) noted that sexual urges may be even more difficult to accept than violent ones. In these cases where interpretations are not indicated, upward explanations help shift the patient from upsetting and "unacceptable" feelings to the more acceptable *derivatives* of these urges (e.g., troubling sexual desires are explained a desire for interpersonal connectedness). Thus, they may help reduce anxiety and buoy a weakened ego.

Techniques to Support Self-Awareness

As noted in Chapter 5, limited insight and increased self-awareness are appropriate goals for supportive therapy. Even if the primary treatment objective is to keep the patient out of the hospital, there will be many in-session opportunities for the patient to better understand themselves. After all, the primary difference between expressive and supportive work is the *active* use of unconscious patient material (e.g., transference interpretations). Thus, each of these techniques has already been discussed (see Box 15.2).

All things being equal, I would argue that the connective subtype of confrontations (see Chapter 12) are likely be the most awareness-building of the three techniques. This is because they encourage the patient to recognize

---

Box 15.2.

TECHNIQUES TO SUPPORT SELF-AWARENESS

- Clarifications
- Confrontations
- Upward explanations

---

and *resolve* inconsistencies. Unlike interpretations, therapist confrontations do not provide a "solution" but rather encourage the patient to look closely at the "problem." Any resulting insight into conscious or unconscious processes is due to the patient's effort and ingenuity.

Supportive "Parenting" Techniques

Several theorists described the parallels between supportive therapy and good parenting (Rockland, 1989; Werman, 1984). Misch (2000) noted that it may be the most helpful strategy for guiding the supportive therapy process (p. 175). This analogy is not meant to infantilize or demean the patient, though. It instead recognizes the fact that many lower-functioning patients possess deficits that may be helped through, for lack of a better term, "parenting" strategies.[8] Consider all the things that "good enough" parents do that many of our patients have never received. They not only keep the child safe but also provide structure, limits, advice, and many of the other things listed in Box 15.3. Ultimately, good parents want their children to become fully realized and independent persons, not just extensions of themselves. Good supportive therapists hold similar attitudes. Therefore, they are careful when using interventions that limit patient autonomy. However, they also understand that supportive work occasionally entails the therapist serving as an "auxiliary ego" for patients whose own capacities are lacking (Mitchell & Black, 1995).

Containing Affect

Good parents help their children cope with emotions. Children easily become overwhelmed and feel out of control, and the presence of a stronger other may help make emotions more bearable. This applies to patients in supportive psychotherapy as well. When patients are in emotional tumult, interpretations are rarely helpful (Yeomans, Clarkin, & Kernberg, 2015, p. 286). At times, *any* technical activity (e.g., questions, clarifications) may only further upset the patient or feed into negative transferences.

Another option is not to intervene on the feelings but to *sit with them* in a particular way. Specifically, the therapist connects to the patient's emotions but

---

Box 15.3

Supportive "Parenting" Techniques

- Containing affect
- Advice
- Environmental manipulation
- Setting limits

---

tolerates them better than the patient and does not become overwhelmed.[9] If so, the therapist helps to *contain* the affect. With repetition, this technique is believed to help the patient better regulate their own emotions. Summers and Barber (2010) noted that therapists who use this technique essentially convey the message that "I am OK because my analyst has been able to tolerate and contain me, and I am now able to tolerate and contain myself" (p. 220). When patients return to a more even keel, other strategies can help them better clarify what happened and "work through" the experience.

An empathic connection is the key to effective containment. If therapists are not actually "in touch" with the feelings, but distract themselves or resort to other defenses, the patient will likely sense this disconnect and experience it as a painful emotional withdrawal (and they would be correct in their assessment). Sharing a patient's pain is not easy, especially for therapists who operate at the emotional extremes (i.e., those who have difficulty experiencing strong emotions or those who feel them too strongly). Honest discussions with clinical supervisors may help to calibrate a useful emotional balance and minimize countertransference interference.

Advice

Advice is free, and few of us are at a loss for finding people to tell us what we ought to do. Parents, teachers, friends, and many others—book authors included—all have viewpoints that they may be inclined to share. Therefore, when acting in a therapeutic capacity, we should all be cautious about providing those same services at much higher prices.

Just like parents and other authority figures, therapists are inevitably in a power-privileged position (Heller, 1985). This not only makes their advice carry more weight, but also implies some degree of responsibility. As psychodynamic therapists want patients to better make their own decisions, advice should be a rare event in expressive therapy (McWilliams, 2011, p. 78) and used sparingly in supportive therapy.

In fact, there are at least four very good reasons *not* to give advice. First, advice can deprive patients of the opportunity to solve their own problems (Langs, 1973, 1974). People in supportive therapy often require more independence and autonomy, not less, and further deference to the wishes of others may be counterproductive. Second, therapists may inadvertently funnel their own needs into the advice that they give. As noted by Silver (1986) and Rockland (1989), unhelpful countertransference reactions (e.g., frustration with the progress of therapy; desires to control the patient; desires to have the patient act as the therapist does) could be the motivating force behind advice instead of the patient's needs. Therefore, it is usually a good idea for therapists to explore the reasons for their advice and search for any elements of self-interest. Relatedly, some patients may unconsciously "pull" for the therapist to behave in a dominant (or even infantilizing) manner. If these enactments are not recognized, they will perpetuate old patient patterns and may eventually corrupt the therapy. Third, therapists may be very wrong in the advice that they give. In almost every instance, therapists base their advice upon partial information, and usually far less than the patient possesses (Langs, 1973, 1974). This dangerous reality should give us all pause before we recommend a course of action. Bad advice could not only lead to negative patient consequences but may also damage the alliance. Finally, and perhaps most important, therapists do not have special knowledge on how to live. We struggle to conduct our own lives as best as we can, and it would be quite presumptuous to assume that we can help other people better than we can help ourselves. Though we may have training in assessment, therapy, and psychopathology, we do not have a secret decoder for life's mysteries.[10] Therefore, given all this discussion, psychodynamic therapists should be very cautious about the advice that they give and the manner in which they give it.

However, despite all these caveats, advice is not necessarily incompatible with psychodynamic therapy. So long as it is based upon a solid understanding of the patient's motivations, capacities, character style, and needs, and is also applied conservatively, advice can be used to good effect. In general, it should only be used when the patient has failed to find their own solutions (e.g., through therapist clarifications and joint problem-solving). For instance, after a lower-functioning patient began missing sessions due to a train station closure, we began problem-solving (e.g., asking a friend for a ride, taking the bus). When these options were exhausted, I suggested that she contact the county mental health office to see if she could schedule their medical appointment van for our meetings.

As another example, a patient with histrionic personality disorder (who was also a recovering heroin addict) wanted to start taking classes at a local college. She reported feeling much better than when treatment began and was understandably very excited to get her life "back together." I was excited for her as well. However, as she discussed the details of her upcoming semester, I learned that she signed up for 15 credits of coursework and was also planning to maintain part-time employment. Given what I knew of her ability to tolerate stress, I feared a relapse if she were to become overwhelmed. I initially encouraged her to reflect upon her competing time demands. After some discussion of the upsides and downsides of her plan, she remained resolute in taking a full course load, and I decided to intervene. I said,

> I'm glad you are so excited about classes, and it sounds like this really fits in with your long-term goals. However, I am concerned about your schedule. As you told me a few minutes ago, you haven't taken a class in over 10 years, and I am worried that it might take some time for you to readjust to school, especially at a college level. Since you've been doing so well, it would be a shame if you became so overwhelmed that you didn't do as well as you'd like during your first semester. I wonder if nine credits might be a safer way to start.

We then discussed the pros and cons of that approach, and she eventually chose to follow my advice.

I would like to raise another consideration before ending this section. Since therapist advice is a low-frequency event, even in the most supportive of psychotherapies, patients will often register it as a "shift." They may also have fantasies about what the shift represents. Does it mean that the therapist cares about them and, like a good parent, wants to help them succeed? Perhaps it means that the therapist fundamentally distrusts their judgment and wants to control them so they do not "screw up" again. These fantasies are likely consistent with whatever transference is dominant at the time. Regardless, as advice-giving is provocative in its ambiguity, it is wise to provide patient-appropriate explanations whenever possible. It is also prudent to pay close attention to any reactions to the advice both before and after it is given.[11]

ENVIRONMENTAL MANIPULATIONS

Supportive psychotherapy cannot always be conducted in isolation. Patients' lives continue past the 50-minute hour, and they spend far more time *outside* of session than with us. Their environments and the personal decisions that they make might not be conducive to psychological health and personal safety. In these cases, therapists need to act like good parents and, in effect, make decisions *for* the patient by altering their environment. This should never be undertaken lightly or without considering the broader clinical implications (e.g., loss of patient autonomy, risk of alliance rupture). In most cases, these are interventions of last resort, to be used only when the need is a great and the patient cannot or will not alter their environment for themselves. Two examples will be provided including (a) altering the patient's level of professional care and (b) enlisting the aid of others to make environmental changes.

Changing the Level of Care

All therapists hope to keep their patients safe—and not just emotionally. Unfortunately, some patients receive a level of professional care that is inappropriate for the seriousness of their condition. It is obviously preferable for the *patient* to reach out for additional help and support, but if this does not occur the therapist or a third party will need to intervene.

There are a wide range of possible options depending upon how much care is needed. The simplest approach is to offer a temporarily increase in session frequency. More contact provides additional opportunities for the therapist to "check in," help maintain homeostasis, and monitor for any further declines in functioning. Medication referrals can be provided, and sicker patients may also benefit from a partial hospitalization program. If patients balk at these recommendations, though, the therapist is faced with a dilemma. Do they capitulate and allow the patient to continue with what they perceive to be a subpar level of care or, alternately, do they take a "hard line" approach and insist on additional services as a prerequisite for continuing treatment? Unless the patient can provide very compelling reasons to the contrary (and even if it runs the risk of premature termination), the therapist should stick with the most ethically defensible decision.[12]

The most dramatic need for additional care arises from acute suicidal (or homicidal) risk. These situations obviously trump therapeutic neutrality and any other session priorities (Yeomans et al., 2015, p. 225).[13] If a patient's judgment is so compromised that *nonbeing* seems enticing, therapists are required (and mandated) to take immediate action and, in effect, loan their healthier egos to the patient. These threats may require changes to the patient's environment and personal routine up to and including involuntary hospitalization. As with the other modifications previously described, it would be best for the patient to initiate a voluntary hospitalization, but if they do not, the therapist is required to take action (e.g., contact the police or nearest emergency department; Winston, Rosenthal, & Pinsker, 2012, pp. 135–137).

These dramatic actions are not without consequences. Involuntary hospitalizations may lead to alliance ruptures, premature termination of therapy, and so on, but these are obviously preferable alternatives to the patient's demise. Fortunately, if the patient is willing to return to treatment, even for one session (and, in my experience, most are willing to do so), the therapist can explain their decision. This process of *therapist clarification* may allow therapy to resume.

Enlisting the Aid of Other People to Make Environmental Changes

Aside from the previous examples, therapists are fairly limited in their ability to effect changes to a patient's environment. Advice may be given but could be ineffective for any number of reasons (e.g., it may be ignored or incapable or being followed). Therapists may therefore need to enlist the aid of other people in the patient's life to make changes (e.g., friends, relatives, case managers). This may be one of the most conspicuous differences between the more purely supportive and expressive psychotherapies. Though not without challenges, these environmental changes could be very meaningful.

For example, one patient I worked with displayed such severe hoarding tendencies that he was in danger of being evicted from his Section 8 housing unit. During this session, my patient gave the distinct impression that his landlord was going to insist on a swifter solution than psychotherapy usually allows (i.e., he had an apartment inspection scheduled in three weeks). After discussing the matter further and expressing my concerns for his possible eviction and homelessness, we enlisted the aid of his case manager. After a joint session, the two of them formulated a plan to reduce the clutter and provided me with regular updates.

Whenever other people become directly involved in psychotherapy, relatives or otherwise, there are a number of issues to consider. For instance, the patient and therapist must be clear on their respective expectations for confidentiality. External parties should only receive "need to know" information that is (a) *directly* relevant to their involvement with the task and (b) agreed upon in advance by the patient. A broad summary of the patient's psychotherapy is inappropriate. Further, therapists need to be mindful of the all-too-human reality that opinions will differ and that the person enlisted to aid the patient may have different motivations and/or expectations. They could even be operating at cross-purposes to the treatment (e.g., they have a vested interest in keeping the patient dependent on them). If so, this places the patient in a difficult position, as they may be forced to—at least from their perspective—"choose" between their therapist and this other person. Clearly, situations are rarely so black and white, but therapists need to be mindful of the many attendant risks when involving others in treatment.

SETTING LIMITS

Just as therapists sometimes need to alter the environment for the good of the patient, they may also need to *impose limits* for the good of the therapy. With sicker patients, these limits are usually negotiated during the contracting phase (see Chapter 9) and continue throughout the remainder of the treatment. However, if other maladaptive behaviors emerge (e.g., poor attendance, acting out), or if the contract is broken, the therapist may have to add additional prohibitions (Yeomans et al., 2015).

Limit-setting is usually preceded by therapist confrontations (i.e., spotlight or connective). After all, it is far better for the therapeutic alliance if a patient recognizes and modifies their own behaviors as opposed to a therapist imposing a firm limit. If this approach fails, prohibitive confrontations may be necessary (see Chapter 12).

To be clear, limit-setting can be done in a less than heavy-handed way. Limits arise from authentic concern for both the patient's welfare and the integrity of the treatment. However, patients may view limits quite differently. They may experience them as overly paternal and rigid punishments (Langs, 1973, 1974). Any number of reactions are possible, and these are partially dependent on which transferences are activated by the limit. The experience can be softened somewhat if the reasons behind it are clearly articulated (e.g., "If you don't come to treatment regularly, it is unlikely that you will feel better"). Regardless of patient reaction, though, if the limit is deemed critical for therapy and the patient refuses to comply, termination and referral to another provider may be indicated.

Techniques the Build and Sustain the Therapeutic Alliance

Last, but certainly not least, there are a number of techniques that therapists can use to support and sustain the therapeutic alliance. The alliance and each of its three components (i.e., agreement on goals, agreement on tasks, and a patient–therapist bond; Bordin, 1979) are broadly viewed as predictive of psychotherapy success (Muran & Barber, 2010). Therefore, all of the techniques listed in Box 15.4 are not only relevant to supportive therapy but also to expressive therapy. It may also be worth noting that many of the techniques described in the previous chapter can also help foster a good alliance (especially praise, encouragement, reassurance, and normalizing).[14]

TECHNIQUES FOR SUPPORTING THE PATIENT–THERAPIST BOND

Therapies are hard to sustain if patients and therapists do not feel connected (Safran, Muran, & Eubanks-Carter, 2011). Given the nature of psychodynamic therapy, though, some of the paths that normally lead to feelings of closeness are

Box 15.4.

TECHNIQUES THAT BUILD AND SUSTAIN THE THERAPEUTIC ALLIANCE

- Displaying interest
- Displaying understanding
- Displaying empathy
- Displaying trust
- Using the language of explicit joining
- Sharing agendas
- Contracting
- Discussing and jointly determining goals

---

inappropriate (e.g., reciprocal self-disclosures). Fortunately, there are a number of ways to feel close to patients without deviating from one's stance, and none of them are complex. In fact, it may even be a conceptual stretch to call them "techniques," as this description almost removes some of their intuitive "warmth."

An old supervisor used to say, "When in doubt, be human." I have found this simple maxim to be helpful not only in strange clinical situations where a clear path was missing, but in almost every initial session. When meeting a new patient, therapists often have little sense of what they will say or how they might respond to the therapy process. Therefore, to make them feel comfortable, and prior to getting the chance to know them, therapists are open and "human." They display authentic *interest*. They do not multitask or stare at the clock but sit in rapt silence and pay exquisite attention to all the information flowing through the four channels of communication. Earnest expectancy is the atmosphere that is created as therapists wait for more information. Good questions are used to foster more dialogue. When appropriate, therapists nod or otherwise let patients know that they *understand* them and what they are trying to say. If something important is missed or does not logically follow from the patient's associations, therapists politely interrupt them and clarify until understanding returns.

Empathy and trust also facilitate the bond. Interspersing empathic comments such as "That must have been hard" or "The look on your face right now makes me think you felt good about that" can go a long way toward increasing feelings of closeness. Such comments also lead the patient to trust that you will "get" them even if they struggle with words or do not know how to articulate their feelings. Trust is bidirectional, though. To have a strong bond with patients, the therapist needs to trust *them* as well. If therapists are not confident that the patient is telling the truth, the bond will be limited. It hopefully goes without saying that anything which inhibits the bond should be noted and discussed with the patient.

GAINING AGREEMENT ON TASKS AND GOALS

Regardless of the strength of the bond, therapy will not feel very steadying for the patient if they have no idea where they are going or how they should get there.

Therefore, even in the most open-ended of expressive therapies, goals and tasks merit discussion (Safran & Muran, 2000). Patients in supportive therapies may require a great amount of detail conveyed in a developmentally appropriate manner. Most important, though, the goals and tasks must be *jointly* created by the therapist *and* the patient. If not, treatment adherence will likely be poor, and the patient will feel left out of the process.

Sharing the agenda is critical. "Translation" of the patient's goals into the language and scope of psychodynamic therapy is key to a good alliance, but this can be challenging. Patients may need to be educated about what constitutes a realistic therapy goal (e.g., something within the patient as opposed to something wrong with another person or "society"). Tasks may also need to be "translated" and explained or else confusion may occur (e.g., "So why do I need to start sessions for this to work? You're the therapist, so why don't you tell me what you need to know?"). Techniques such as clarification and psychoeducation may augment these discussions. Therapy contracts are also relevant (see Chapter 9).

THE PROCESS OF WORKING THROUGH IN SUPPORTIVE THERAPY

Prior to ending this chapter, mention should be made of "working through" the results of supportive therapy techniques. In essence, this process is identical regardless of the patient's location on the supportive–expressive continuum. Therapists ultimately intend to help their patients increase their personal freedom, build upon their successes, learn from their mistakes and failures, and become more fully transparent to themselves. This takes repetition, patience, and the hard work of all relevant parties.

NOTES

1. This helps to differentiate reassurance from encouragement (see Chapter 14). The latter is intended to prompt patients toward confident action as opposed to making them feel better.
2. Some theories argued for the role of reassurance in expressive therapies as well. For instance, Winnicott (1955) wrote, "It is foolish to deny that reassurance is present in the classical analytic situation. The whole set-up of psycho-analysis is one big reassurance, especially the reliable objectivity and behaviour of the analyst, and the transference interpretations constructively using instead of wastefully exploiting the moment's passion" (p. 25).
3. For a fuller discussion of the differences between reframing and traditional psychodynamic interpretation, see Wachtel (2011).
4. At first glance this might appear identical to psychoeducation (see Chapter 14), but the intention is not just to educate the patient, but to reduce their excessive feelings of responsibility for the problem.

5. For an interesting discussion of pharmacotherapy in the context of psychodynamic work see (Gabbard, 2014, Chapter 5).

6. The therapist conducted a threat assessment and the patient denied any intent, plan, or history of violent behavior.

7. For a lengthier description of psychodynamic work with a lower-functioning patient who also manifested an erotic transference, see Sharpless (2014).

8. Elements of Kohut's (2001) self psychology are consistent with this.

9. One of my supervisors described this as "being the anchor in a storm."

10. Even worse, we often do not know what we do not know.

11. In certain cases, when therapist advice is not accepted, it may be appropriate to reinforce the patient's independence and confidence in their choices. This is, of course, based on the assumption that the choice they wish to make is not a damaging one.

12. If the patient refuses services, it is appropriate for the therapist to provide referrals and let them know that therapy could resume in the future if they altered their level of care.

13. For a discussion of psychodynamic approaches to suicide, see Busch, Rudden, and Shapiro (2016, Chapter 14). Another good clinical resource which details an interpersonal theory of suicide is Joiner (2009).

14. For a summary of some of the therapist and patient factors that may predict the alliance, see Sharpless, Muran, and Barber (2010).

16

Repairing Ruptures in the Therapeutic Alliance

INTRODUCTION

As noted throughout this book, the therapeutic alliance is a key ingredient of any successful therapy. It emerges[1] (along with the transference, real relationship, etc.) out of a therapeutic encounter between two or more people (Barber, Khalsa, & Sharpless, 2010). However, once formed, it cannot be taken for granted. Like most aspects of a human relationship, an alliance takes work, and it is important to look after it throughout the entire course of treatment. Indeed, numerous studies indicate that the alliance is not static, but varies both within and across sessions (e.g., Gelso & Carter, 1994; Stiles & Goldsmith, 2010). One of the more dramatic variations is an alliance *rupture* or deterioration/strain in the alliance.

Ruptures occur along any or all of the three components of the alliance. For instance, they can manifest if there is patient–therapist disagreement on either the *goals* or *tasks* of therapy or if a solid emotional *bond* is lacking between the parties (Bordin, 1979). Ruptures range from relatively minor events (e.g., what might be described as a minor empathic failure; Kohut, 1984, pp. 66–67) to massive, potentially treatment-ending conflicts.

The challenging nature of psychodynamic therapy—or any form of therapy, for that matter—makes the occurrence of ruptures essentially inevitable. When using confrontations, interpretations, or other powerful techniques that could be jarring for the patient, the possibility of a rupture increases. However, as I hope will become apparent in the following discussion, ruptures are not simply "bad things" that can be avoided, but are better viewed as opportunities to model good relationship skills. They may even help move the therapy forward (Muran & Safran, 2017) or lead to corrective emotional experiences (Sharpless & Barber, 2012; also see Chapter 7). This is not say that they should be *encouraged* to occur, but ruptures can be used to good effect if they are handled in a thoughtful and respectful manner.

The primary focus of this chapter will be on the specific techniques involved in resolving alliance ruptures. As rupture resolution strategies are essentially transtheoretical (Muran & Barber, 2010), they can be seamlessly integrated into psychodynamic work (i.e., both short- and long-term approaches).[2] The *process* of rupture resolution, which emphasizes exploration, honesty, empathy, and understanding, also fits very well with the psychodynamic tradition. To be clear, this brief summary will not be a substitute for more advanced training, but may help start the process of better identifying and managing ruptures that take place over the course of therapy.

EMPIRICAL RESEARCH ON ALLIANCE RUPTURES

Ruptures are frequent clinical events.[3] For example, outside observers identified ruptures in 41% to 100% of therapy sessions (Safran, Muran, & Eubanks-Carter, 2011). This was a higher overall frequency than therapist (43%–56%) or patient (19%–42%) ratings, but ruptures appeared to be ubiquitous regardless of the type of rater that was used. Existing research also indicates that it is unwise to ignore ruptures (i.e., leave them unresolved). If therapists do so, a premature and unilateral termination may result (Muran et al., 2009; Safran et al., 2011).

The research on *therapist* alliance skills is particularly interesting, and two important findings will be noted here. First, it will probably come as no surprise that therapists differ in their ability to form and maintain good therapeutic alliances (Del Re et al., 2012). Not all therapists are equal (Castonguay & Hill, 2017). Indeed, Del Re et al.'s (2012) meta-analysis found that therapist variability in the alliance, not patient variability, was a significant predictor of subsequent patient outcome. So, clearly, the therapist is an important factor, but is alliance work a trainable skill or more of an innate characteristic?

Existing evidence indicates that therapists can be taught to form stronger alliances and resolve ruptures more effectively (Crits-Christoph, Crits-Christoph, & Connolly Gibbons, 2010). One model, *alliance-focused training*, works to develop three interrelated core therapist skills: self-awareness, affect regulation, and interpersonal sensitivity (Eubanks-Carter, Muran, & Safran, 2015, p. 169). In a nutshell, *alliance-focused training* helps therapists to (a) better understand themselves during ruptures, (b) better understand the needs of their patients during ruptures, (c) improve their overall tactfulness, and (d) improve their general skills at metacommunication. Rupture resolution training was found to yield small, but statistically significant clinical improvements compared to patients treated by therapists without this training (Safran et al., 2011). Thus, it provided the former with a slight clinical "edge" over the latter.[4]

THE PROCESS OF IDENTIFYING ALLIANCE RUPTURES

The ability to resolve ruptures[5] is predicated on an ability to *recognize* them. This is not always easy, as several of the *markers* of alliance rupture are subtle and require careful attention to the four channels of communication (Chapter 8). Safran et al. (2011) wisely noted that patients may be reticent to directly discuss their negative feelings in session. This may be due to a lack of assertiveness or a fear of therapist reprisal if they complain. As a result, it is incumbent upon therapists to covey a willingness to discuss *all* matters in psychodynamic treatment and not just the "pleasant" ones. This openness can be conveyed both verbally and nonverbally (for a review of other relevant therapist characteristics, see Sharpless, Muran, & Barber, 2010).

Alliance ruptures are typically classified into *withdrawal* and *confrontation* subtypes (Safran & Muran, 1996).[6] These categories have been widely used and possess a great deal of intuitive appeal. However, it is important to note that these distinctions should not be taken too literally or reified, as some ruptures may present as blends of the two (i.e., a mixed confrontation/withdrawal rupture).[7] Withdrawal ruptures will be discussed first.

Withdrawal Ruptures

During a withdrawal rupture, patients *move away* from either the therapist or the therapy (Safran & Muran, 2000). This withdrawal can manifest in many different ways. For instance, patients may become silent, disengage from their current emotional state by discussing trivial matters, or otherwise remove themselves from the treatment situation (Muran & Safran, 2017). In extreme cases, they may *physically* withdraw from therapy by abruptly leaving the office or ending session early. However, even if patients remain physically close to the therapist, they are distant in other important ways. During ruptures, they may suppress certain emotions or retreat into themselves. An unsuspecting observer might simply see the patient as anxious, bored, confused, or aloof. These superficial observations may very well be accurate, but do not convey the full picture. This is because a patient's true reactions during withdrawal ruptures are often well-hidden; they can be found bubbling under the surface of an otherwise calm or taciturn appearance. Therefore, therapists need to exercise a modicum of suspicion during session—especially during "intense moments"—and be willing to explore any unpleasant feelings that emerge.

Some common markers of withdrawal ruptures can be found in Box 16.1. These should be viewed as samples and not an exhaustive list. For just as each patient may have their own idiosyncratic way of responding to interventions (see

Box 16.1.

Markers of "Withdrawal" Ruptures

- The patient denies their true, apparent feelings (e.g., anger, upset) in order to avoid discussing them with the therapist.
- The patient denies or minimizes the importance of a relationship relevant to the therapy (e.g., with the therapist or others).
- The patient denies or minimizes the importance of an event relevant to the therapy.
- The patient goes silent or provides a minimal response to therapist questions/clarifications.
- The patient walks out of session or ends session early.
- The patient uses their cell phone or otherwise "multitasks" during session.
- The patient becomes overly intellectualized (e.g., moves away from affect).
- The patient becomes abstract, vague, or confusing.
- The patient tells irrelevant stories to avoid the therapy process.
- The patient shifts topics (often from serious matters to more trivial concerns or in rapid-fire succession) or filters their free associations.
- The patient becomes overly deferential to the therapist (i.e., to avoid conflict).
- The patient becomes overly appeasing of the therapist (i.e., to avoid conflict).
- The patient presents incongruous affect that does not correspond to the subject (i.e., a content/affect split).
- The patient becomes ruminative or reports hopelessness in a way that "shuts out" the therapist.
- The patient begrudgingly complies with the therapist's interventions.
- The patient engages in the therapy process, but expresses anxieties or doubts.

Sources: Derived and adapted from Muran & Safran, 2017; Eubanks-Carter, Muran, & Safran, 2015; and Safran & Muran, 2000.

Chapter 7), they may also have a particular way of indicating rupture. Some of these are not on this list (e.g., poor eye contact).

Interestingly, withdrawal ruptures may appear to be anything but that at times, as the patient "objectively" seems to move *closer* to the therapist (Safran & Muran, 2000). This is another instance where careful observation and a solid awareness of countertransference are needed. When patients "approach" the therapist in this manner, they are simultaneously moving away from their own subjective rupture experiences. As implied in Box 16.1, their conscious or unconscious intention may be to mollify the therapist through inauthentic compliance or deference (e.g.,

"Well, I trust that you know what's best"). Thus, the patient's approach behavior could be a means of maintaining their attachment with an important other (i.e., the therapist) regardless of the personal cost. It may also be a way to avoid abandonment.[8] Therefore, other aspects of the patient's interpersonal, intrapsychic, and transferential patterns are extremely relevant to their personal experience of rupture.

Confrontation Ruptures

Confrontation ruptures are a bit different from the withdrawal subtype. During confrontation ruptures, patients do not move away from therapists but instead move *against* them (Eubanks-Carter, Muran, & Safran, 2015). These events may involve outright hostility, but a more "polite," reserved, or inhibited patient may seem less antagonistic. For example, instead of yelling at the therapist or complaining, they may overjustify their behaviors or more subtly attempt to manipulate the therapist. The latter approach may manifest through inauthentic affiliation (e.g., flirting). Other markers can be found in Box 16.2.

Confrontation ruptures are quite heterogeneous. As is the case with the psychodynamic technique of confrontation (Chapter 12), a confrontation rupture does not need to be overtly *confrontational* to be meaningful. However, when the more aggressive confrontation ruptures occur they may be troubling for therapists and elicit reactions ranging from defensiveness and therapist counterattacks to subjective feelings of inadequacy. The last of these may be particularly common for beginning therapists. Any patient complaint or challenge to the therapist's authority or competence may quickly tap into natural (and somewhat reasonable) insecurities. For example, after having a confrontation rupture with one of my first patients (which was not well-resolved), I can vividly recall feeling thankful that the patient returned for our next session. This arose from a feeling that I had so little to offer him in the way of "skills." However, good rupture resolution techniques require the therapist to, in a sense, *bracket* any insecurities they may have and stay focused on the patient's complex communications, the present relational matrix, and the process of *metacommunication*.[9] As will be discussed, there is an appropriate time for therapists to take ownership of their actions and mistakes, but this need not reach unhealthy levels (i.e., self-castigation). If it did, it would essentially be a *therapist withdrawal* into rumination (see Box 16.2) that will only prolong or intensify the rupture.

The Importance of Context for Identifying Ruptures

The markers of alliance rupture are very context-dependent. For example, imagine that someone criticized your outfit. If this occurred during a therapy session with a well-known patient, the comment may very well indicate a rupture.

Box 16.2.

SOME MARKERS OF "CONFRONTATION" RUPTURES

- The patient complains about the therapist and/or expresses negative feelings (hostile, angry, etc.).
- The patient complains about the therapy and/or expresses negative feelings (hostile, angry, etc.).
- The patient dismisses/rejects the therapist's questions, observations, or clinical interventions.
- The patient expresses concern about the therapist's question, observation, or clinical intervention.
- The patient expresses concern about the existing therapy contract (e.g., session frequency).
- The patient expresses concern about their progress (or lack of) in therapy.
- The patient becomes defensive or overly justifies themselves in response to what they perceive to be therapist's judgment, attack, or criticism.
- The patient makes efforts to control the therapist or the therapy session.
- The patient tries to directly pressure the therapist into taking a particular course of action.
- The patient becomes overly friendly or seductive as a means of manipulating the therapist.

Sources: Derived and adapted from Muran & Safran, 2017; Eubanks-Carter, Muran, & Safran, 2015; and Safran & Muran, 2000.

If, on the other hand, a fashion reporter on a red carpet made the same comment prior to a movie premier, it may just indicate superficial cattiness. After all, you cannot really have an alliance rupture if an alliance never emerged in the first place. Similarly, prior to knowing the expectations of treatment (i.e., agreeing on tasks), many signs of a "rupture" (e.g., abstract communications, overly friendly or deferential behavior) may instead be rooted in patient uncertainty or misunderstanding. As noted several times throughout this book (see Chapters 4 and 9), psychodynamic therapy deviates from conventional social discourse in several important ways. Without sufficient explanation and patient socialization into treatment, rupture-like behaviors are a distinct possibility.

THE PROCESS OF RUPTURE RESOLUTION

A number of procedures have been formulated to repair ruptures (for a review, see (Safran et al., 2011, pp. 233–235). Many of these were based on task-analytic studies. The approach detailed below was primarily derived from the important work of Jeremy Safran, Chris Muran, and colleagues (e.g., Safran & Muran, 1996, 2000). They proposed a four-stage model of rupture resolution.

Stage 1: Noticing and Attending to the Rupture Marker

The first stage of rupture resolution is for the therapist to recognize that a rupture has occurred. Depending upon the subtlety of the marker, this may take some time. Therapists may first notice their own strong or uncharacteristic counter-transference reactions (e.g., boredom, annoyance at the patient) or certain inter-personal "pulls" to act in a non-therapeutic manner (e.g., a desire to be dominant or aggressive with the patient). Other ruptures (e.g., more aggressive confronta-tion rupture markers or a patient "shut down") might be far easier to detect.

Regardless, once the therapist notices a rupture, it is important to attend to it and not continue on with "therapy as usual" (Safran & Muran, 1996). If the al-liance is strained, additional work is unlikely to be successful, and ignoring the rupture could easily make matters worse. For instance, if a patient became upset after an interpretation, it would not be advisable to try to "work through" the in-terpretation or convince them that the therapist is in fact "right." It is far better to help the patient focus on the *here and now* of the therapeutic relationship and attend to the rupture. This can be accomplished through questions and/or gentle confrontation (e.g., "It feels a bit different in here. What do you think might be going on between us at this moment?" or "It seems like you and I might not be on the same page. Is that how it feels for you, too?").

Stage 2: Exploring the Experiences Involved in the Rupture

Once the rupture is recognized and situated as the main object of therapeutic in-quiry, the therapist next helps the patient to examine their subjective experiences. Do they feel hurt, neglected, angry, or disappointed? Do they want to leave session, terminate treatment, or retaliate in some way? The rupture will not be able to be resolved or put to good therapeutic use without adequate detail. Needless to say, explorations like these can only occur if the patient feels comfortable enough to speak, and the therapist's demeanor is critical. It is helpful to convey an authentic sense of openness, curiosity, nondefensiveness, and empathy during ruptures and in psychodynamic therapy more generally. The therapist must also be willing to tolerate the perceptions of the patient, even if they are critical, hurtful, and/or in-accurate. It is important to get the patient talking about their experiences during the rupture, not to preemptively "correct" their subjective appraisals.

Therapists can facilitate this process by actively (and non-defensively) en-couraging patients to share their perspective on how the *therapist* may have contributed to the rupture. If the patient is reluctant to do so, they can be asked directly. This can obviously be a delicate situation, as some patients are loath to "criticize" their therapist. Even if they do disclose their experience, they may quickly minimize or undo it (e.g., "Yeah, I was kind of hurt by what you said, but I probably just overreacted"). Safran and Muran (2000) termed this a "qualified assertion" (p. 145). When patients qualify, therapists are wise to encourage them to focus on the component that is most difficult to express (e.g., "Well, it might be helpful to say a bit more about how you felt hurt by me"). Therapists can also increase patient comfort by taking ownership of their own contributions to the rupture if they are truly authentic (e.g., "Yeah, I can see now how my use of that particular word could have made you feel bad").

Stage 3: Exploring Any Avoidance of the Rupture Experience

Consider the resolution process so far. First, the therapist noticed a strain in the alliance and shifted session focus to that tension. Next, the therapist invited the patient to explore their subjective experience of the rupture. As a result, the patient (hopefully) began to put their feelings into words and shared them. All the while the therapist listened to the patient with earnestness and displayed curiosity, openness, and authenticity.

For a number of our patients (especially those who are lower-functioning), this may be a novel experience. Stages 1 and 2 alone could very well defy their long-standing interpersonal expectations.[10] They may be more used to having their reactions met with dismissiveness (e.g., "Oh, you're always upset about something"), condescension ("Why are you being such a baby?"), or reciprocal hostility ("Oh yeah, well you do X too, and it really pisses me off!"). Even the sickest of patients may recognize the therapist's different way of responding to conflict, even if only tacitly.

Recognition of this difference, along with any number of other patient characteristics (e.g., dependency, level of insight), may lead to *blockages* in the patient's exploration of the rupture (Safran & Muran, 2000, Chapter 5). This is to be expected. When patients experience a withdrawal rupture, for instance, they are often reluctant to express their negative feelings. They may want to shut off their chain of associations as they approach the main reasons for the rupture (e.g., an interpersonal wish that was disappointed). Therapists can assist this process through noting any shifts away from the rupture and expressing their willingness to understand the patient (e.g., "It seemed like you were on the verge of an important insight there. What might have made it hard to continue?"). Just like all manifestations of patient resistance, though, they should be explored and understood, not ignored or attacked.

Blockages are expected to happen in confrontation ruptures as well. These often result from the patient avoiding or minimizing feelings of aggression and/or vulnerability after their initial disclosures. Regarding the avoidance of aggressive feelings, Safran and Muran (2000) noted, "Even those patients who are most overtly aggressive or hostile toward their therapists will experience moments of anxiety or guilt about the expression of such aggressive feelings and attempt to undo the harm they feel they have done." (pp. 161–162). Patients in this state might become stuck in a vacillation between anger, remorse, and minimization. With blockages caused by vulnerability, it may be far easier for patients to feel angry and aggressive than sad or disappointed. Thus, even if the patient is unwilling to engage with these more tender reactions, the therapist can note the shift and encourage exploration ("Right before you expressed your anger toward me, you looked like you were disappointed. Is that accurate? What might have caused that shift?").

Stage 4: Exploring the Wishes and Needs Associated with the Rupture

The last stage of rupture resolution involves the patient both accessing and *expressing* their underlying wishes and needs (Safran et al., 2011). Like other psychodynamic goals (see Chapter 2), this may take time. With certain patients, it may even take years or many inadvertent repetitions of the rupture (Safran & Muran, 2000, p. 162). Regardless, therapists can facilitate the process by continuing to be inquisitive, even-tempered, nondefensive, and open to the patient's expressions of discontent or annoyance.

After patient needs are sufficiently articulated, the therapist is faced with a dilemma: what should they do with this information to make the most positive clinical impact? For instance, should the therapist use the immediate rupture repair strategies described in the following sections, gratify the wish, or maintain therapeutic abstinence? There is no straightforward answer to this question, as it needs to be based upon multiple patient- and context-specific factors.

With regard to gratifications (see Chapter 14), these are more commonly used in supportive therapies. For example, the wish of a lower-functioning patient may be to be taken care of and guided by an important and powerful other. In this case, the therapist might make the decision to use advice, reassurance, or another supportive technique to gratify the patient at the minimally needed amount. The therapist would also ideally elicit the patient's reactions to the gratification as well. However, if this same rupture were to occur during a more expressive psychotherapy with a higher functioning patient, the therapist might instead validate and empathize with the wish instead of directly gratifying it. As always, gratifications should be used sparingly and thoughtfully so as not to decrease patient autonomy.

There are additional ways to use the rupture resolution process to maximize therapeutic gains. As one example, the rupture could be connected to more pervasive patterns in either the current therapeutic relationship (i.e., the transference) or the patient's broader interpersonal world (Eubanks, Burckell, & Goldfried, 2018). Not only would this increase patient insight, but might also help free them from maladaptive and repetitive patterns.[11] Another clinical option would be to link information gained from the rupture to other unresolved patient issues (e.g., interpreting the patient's disavowed wish for the therapist to take care of them to unmet needs with a parent).

Box 16.3.

SOME RUPTURE RESOLUTION TECHNIQUES

- The therapist clarifies a misunderstanding with the patient.
- The therapist changes or modifies one or more of the goals or tasks of therapy.
- The therapist repeats the rationale for a therapy goal or task.
- The therapist provides examples to better explain a therapy goal or task (i.e., the therapist makes a clarification).
- The therapist encourages the patient to discuss their reactions to the therapist.
- The therapist encourages the patient to discuss their reactions to the therapy.
- The therapist (appropriately) acknowledges their own contribution to the rupture.
- The therapist (appropriately) discloses their own personal experience of the rupture.
- The therapist empathizes with the patient's negative reactions.
- The therapist connects the rupture to a more pervasive interpersonal pattern in the therapeutic relationship (e.g., a connective confrontation).
- The therapist connects the rupture to a more pervasive pattern with other people in the patient's life (e.g., a connective confrontation).
- The therapist encourages the patient to further articulate their specific wishes or needs.
- The therapist validates the patient's resistance/defense (i.e., this may be similar to an upward explanation).
- The therapist redirects the patient to the task/topic at hand (e.g., a "flashlight" confrontation).
- The therapist provides a new relational experience to the patient (i.e., the patient has a corrective emotional experience).

Sources: This content was derived and adapted from Muran & Safran, 2017; Eubanks-Carter, Muran, & Safran, 2015; Eubanks, Burckell, & Goldfried, 2018; Safran & Muran, 2000; and Safran, Muran, & Eubanks-Carter, 2011.

Immediate Rupture Resolution Techniques

In addition to the four-part resolution process summarized previously, there are a number of specific techniques available to help resolve alliance ruptures. These can be found in Box 16.3. Some are specific to the component of the alliance that is strained (e.g., providing a rationale for a specific therapeutic task), and others are more general (e.g., empathizing with a patient's negative reaction).

ON THE INEVITABILITY AND UBIQUITY OF RUPTURES

In ending this chapter, it may be important to again underscore the point that all therapies of any significant duration will have ruptures. They are, in effect, inevitable. However, the alliance and its three components (agreement on goals and tasks and a workable bond) are necessary for many nonpsychotherapy relationships as well. For instance, a working alliance is necessary in clinical assessment, clinical supervision, research, and clinical consultation. The procedures outlined above can be readily adapted to these other situations.

NOTES

1. That is to say, it has a *supervenient* quality.
2. For an interesting discussion of the connections between rupture resolution and Luborsky's (1984) *core conflictual relationship theme,* see Safran and Muran (2000).
3. This is a very rich research area. Please see Muran and Barber (2010) for a summary.
4. For those readers who want to learn more, intensive training workshops are offered through the Center for Alliance-Focused Training in New York and a number of published resources are available (Safran & Muran, 2000). Operationalized ratings systems have been created for those who want to conduct research studies (Eubanks-Carter et al., 2015).
5. For a more in-depth discussion of alliance rupture markers and how they are operationalized, see Eubanks Carter et al. (2015).
6. They based this bifurcation upon Karen Horney's work with neurotics (Horney, 1950).
7. Jeremy Safran posted several video examples of ruptures, including a mixed confrontation/withdrawal rupture at https://www.youtube.com/channel/UCKdvsR6n658ZLR2XX5Jqr6w.
8. Though it may seem intuitive to view withdrawal ruptures as resulting from insecure patient attachment, these same ruptures can be found in secure patients as well (e.g., see Miller-Bottome, Talia, Safran, & Muran, 2018).
9. Safran and Muran (2000) defined this as "an attempt to step outside of the relational cycle that is currently being enacted by treating it as the focus of collaborative exploration" (p. 108).
10. In other words, they may set the stage for a corrective emotional experience (see Chapter 7).
11. This is also consistent with the process of "working through" (see Chapter 13).

My primary intentions for this book were to clarify and demystify psychodynamic interventions. I also tried to write it in such a way that it would have been helpful during my own doctoral training.[1] I suppose that the best that any author can hope for is to write something that they themselves would like to read with the implicit hope that others will feel similarly. And although I can clearly see weaknesses and omissions, I will allow the reader to assess the book's merit for themselves. Therefore, instead of a summary or an unavoidably biased evaluation, I prefer to conclude with some general remarks about what the field already knows about good psychotherapists.

Although this book focused almost exclusively on *technical skills*, there are obviously other pieces to the therapeutic puzzle that are worthy of examination.[2] We are still very much at an early stage of understanding (a) the specific role of techniques in therapeutic effectiveness (e.g., Anderson & Hill, 2017) and (b) which qualities make someone a good psychotherapist more generally (Castonguay & Hill, 2017).[3] However, some empirical findings recently summarized by Wampold, Baldwin, Holtforth, and Imel (2017) are intriguing and worthy of mention.

These authors identified four therapist characteristics that were associated with outcome, and three will be described here.[4] First, and perhaps not surprisingly, effective therapists demonstrate warmth, persuasiveness, verbal fluency, and other *facilitative interpersonal skills* (Anderson, Ogles, Patterson, Lambert, & Vermeersch, 2009). Given the complexity of therapy, it only makes sense that therapists with more relational acumen would be better able to enact positive clinical changes than those with less. Second, the amount of time spent in the *deliberate practice* of psychotherapy also seems to be important. Chow et al. (2015) defined this as a "solitary practice aimed at improving therapeutic engagement" (p. 338). In other words, deliberate practice is conducted alone and outside of session (e.g., by rehearsing the techniques described in Sections II and III or learning a new model of psychodynamic therapy; see the appendix). Again, it only makes sense that therapists who continually hone their craft are better than those who are indifferent or lackadaisical. Third, and perhaps not surprisingly, levels of *professional self-doubt* appear to interact with outcome such that therapists who are *less* confident in their abilities are more effective (e.g., Nissen-Lie, Monsen, Ulleberg, & Ronnestad, 2013). The reasons for this are not yet fully understood, but it seems reasonable to infer that a bit of self-consciousness or self-criticality prompts therapists to reflect upon themselves and their patients (Nissen-Lie et al., 2017). After all, it is well-known that anxiety, at least in smaller doses, can facilitate performance. Putting this all together, therapists who are interpersonally astute and practice their technical skills, yet who are not overconfident, seem to be better therapists. It is always nice when research findings converge with clinical intuition.

At an anecdotal level, but consistent with the previous discussion, the best therapists that I know—in other words, the ones that I would refer loved ones to without hesitation—can both think *and* feel their way through psychotherapy. They offer their patients intelligence, self-control, theoretical sophistication, and focused attention, but do not shy away from the strong emotions that people bring into the room. They instead want to understand these feelings at a visceral level and harness them for their patient's benefit. Good therapists can also *explain* what they are trying to do in session using clear, experience-near language.

Finally, and perhaps most importantly, the clinicians I respect the most are appropriately humble. They are willing to admit when they are wrong and can accept responsibility for their mistakes both inside and outside of session. These therapists are comfortable being what they truly are: fallible human beings no better or worse than the fallible human beings sitting across from them.

NOTES

1. A secondary intention was to differentiate these techniques in such a way that they might be useful for psychotherapy researchers.
2. Suggestions for other psychodynamic texts can be found throughout this work.
3. It may be worth noting that these two general statements are applicable to all forms of psychotherapy and not only psychodynamic approaches.
4. One of these characteristics, the ability to form an alliance across a range of patients, has already been extensively discussed in Chapters 2, 15, and 16.

APPENDIX

Psychodynamic Therapy Manuals and Models

PETER LILLIENGREN AND BRIAN A. SHARPLESS ■

	TRANSDIAGNOSTIC SHORT-TERM PSYCHODYNAMIC THERAPY MODELS			
	Supportive-Expressive Psychotherapy (SE)[a]	Experiential Dynamic Therapy (EDT)[b]	Psychodynamic-Interpersonal Therapy (PI)[c]	Time-Limited Psychotherapy (TLP)[d]
Mood disorders				
Major depression	Barber, Barrett, Gallop, Rynn, and Rickels (2011) Connolly-Gibbons et al. (2012, 2016) Soares et al. (2018)	Ajilchi Nejati, Town, Wilson, and Abbass (2016) Maina, Rosso, Crespi, and Bogetto (2007)[e] Rosso, Martini, and Maina (2012)	Barkham et al. (1996) Hardy et al. (1995) Shapiro et al. (1994)	Thyme et al. (2007)
Minor depression		Maina, Forner, and Bogetto (2005)	Barkham, Shapiro, Hardy, and Rees (1999)	
Recurrent depression	Kramer, de Roten, Perry, and Despland (2013)[e]			
Treatment resistant depression		Town, Abbass, Stride, and Bernier (2017)		
Postpartum depression		Bloch et al. (2012)		
Depression in cancer patients	Beutel et al. (2013)			
Depression in family care givers				Gallagher-Thompson and Steffen (1994)
Anxiety disorders				

Panic disorder		Martini, Rosso, Chiodelli, De Cori, and Maina (2011)[e]; Wiborg and Dahl, (1996)[e]	Brockman, Poynton, Ryle, and Watson (1987); Budman et al. (1988); Shefler, Dasberg, and Ben-Shakhar (1995)
Generalized anxiety disorder (GAD)	Crits-Christoph Gibbons, Narducci, Schamberger, and Gallop (2005); Leichsenring et al. (2009)		
Social phobia (SAD)	Leichsenring et al. (2013); Wiltink et al. (2017)	Bögels, Wijts, Oort, and Sallaerts (2014); Nader-Mohammadi Moghadam (2015)	
Mixed anxiety and depression		Bressi, Porcellana, Marinaccio, Nocito, and Magri (2010); Knekt and Lindfors (2004); Pierloot and Vinck (1978); Piper, Debbane, Bienvenu, and Garant (1984)	Shaw, Margison, Guthrie, and Tomenson (2001)
Personality disorders			
Borderline personality disorder		Reneses et al. (2013)	
Cluster C personality disorders	Emmelkamp et al. (2006); Hellerstein et al. (1998); Svartberg, Stiles, and Seltzer (2004)		

TRANSDIAGNOSTIC SHORT-TERM PSYCHODYNAMIC THERAPY MODELS

	Supportive-Expressive Psychotherapy (SE)[a]	Experiential Dynamic Therapy (EDT)[b]	Psychodynamic-Interpersonal Therapy (PI)[c]	Time-Limited Psychotherapy (TLP)[d]
Mixed personality disorders	Vinnars, Barber, Noren, Gallop, and Weinryb (2005)	Abbass, Sheldon, Gyra, and Kalpin (2008) Winston et al. (1991)		
Eating disorders				
Anorexia		Dare, Eisler, Russell, Treasure, and Dodge (2001)		
Bulimia	Garner et al. (1993)			
Severe obesity	Wiltink et al. (2007)			
Psychosomatic conditions				
Medically unexplained pain		Chavooshi Mohammadkhani, and Dolatshahee (2016a, 2016b) Chavooshi, Saberi, Tavallaie, and Sahraei (2017)		
Functional dyspepsia	Faramarzi et al. (2013)		Hamilton et al. (2000)	
Atopic dermatitis		Linnet & Jemec (2001)		
Peptic ulcers		Sjödin, Svedlund, Ottosson, and Dotevall (1986)		

Irritable bowel syndrome		Svedlund, Sjodin, Ottosson, and Dotevall (1983)	Guthrie, Creed, Dawson, and Tomenson (1991) Creed et al. (2003)
Psychogenic moment disorder		Kompoliti, Wilson, Stebbins, Bernard, and Hinson (2013)	
Motor conversion and non-epileptic seizures			Hubschmid et al. (2015)
Fibromyalgia			Scheidt et al. (2013)
Urethral syndrome		Baldoni, Baldaro, and Trombini (1995)	
Mixed somatoform disorder			Sattel et al. (2011)
Substance related problems			
Alcohol dependence	Öjehagen et al. (1992)		
Cocaine dependence	Crits-Christoph et al. (1999)		
Cocaine abuse	Kleinman et al. (1990)		
Opiate dependence	Woody et al. (1983) Woody McLellan, Luborsky, and Brien (1995)		

TRANSDIAGNOSTIC SHORT-TERM PSYCHODYNAMIC THERAPY MODELS

	Supportive-Expressive Psychotherapy (SE)[a]	Experiential Dynamic Therapy (EDT)[b]	Psychodynamic-Interpersonal Therapy (PI)[c]	Time-Limited Psychotherapy (TLP)[d]
Other disorders and conditions				
Adjustment disorder		Ben-Itzhak et al. (2012)		
Deliberate self-poisoning			Guthrie et al. (2001)	
High utilizers of psychiatric services			Guthrie et al. (1999)	

Notes: Only studies of individual therapy with adults are included. See References for complete citation information.

[a]Treatment principles based on the core conflictual relationship theme (CCRT), originally described by Luborsky (1984) and later elaborated in works by Book (1998) and Leichsenring and Leibing (2007).

[b]Treatment principles based on "Malan's triangles" originally described in Malan (1979) and Davanloo (1980). Expanded and elaborated in later works by Malan and Osmio (1992), McCullough et al. (2003), Davanloo (1990, 2000, 2005), and Abbass (2015).

[c]Treatment principles originally described in Hobson (1985) and elaborated by Guthrie and Moghavemi (2013).

[d]Treatment principles originally described by Mann (1973) and elaborated by Shefler (2001).

[e]Combined with medication.

PSYCHODYNAMIC THERAPY MANUALS AND MODELS FOR SPECIFIC DISORDERS

		PSYCHODYNAMIC THERAPY MODELS FOR SPECIFIC DISORDERS			
Condition	Depression	Panic Disorder	Posttraumatic Stress Disorder (PTSD)	Borderline Personality Disorder	Borderline Personality Disorder
Model	Short-Term Supportive Psychoanalytic Psychotherapy (SPP)[a]	Panic Focused Psychodynamic Psychotherapy (PFPP)[b]	Brief Psychodynamic Therapy for PTSD[c]	Transference-Focused Psychotherapy (TFP)[d]	Mentalization-Based Therapy (MBT)[e]
Study references	De Jonge (2001,[f] 2004) Dekker, Molenaar, Kool, Van Aalst, Peen, and de Jonghe (2005)[f] Dekker et al. (2008) Driessen et al. (2013) Kool, Dekker, and Duijsens (2003)[f]	Beutel et al. (2013b) Milrod et al. (2007, 2015)	Brom, Kleber, and Defares (1989)	Clarkin, Levy, Lenzenweger, and Kern (2007) Doering et al. (2010) Giesen-Bloo et al. (2006)	Bateman and Fonagy (1999, 2009) Jörgensen, Freund, Bøye, Jordet, Andersen, and Kjølbye (2012) Laurenssen et al. (2018)

Notes: Only studies of individual therapy with adults included. See References for complete citation information.

[a]Treatment principles described in De Jonghe, Rijnisre, and Janssen (2015).

[b]Treatment principles described in Milrod, Busch Cooper, and Shapiro (1997) and elaborated and extended in Busch et al. (2012).

[c]Treatment principles originally described by Horowitz (1976).

[d]Treatment principles originally described by Kernberg (1984) and elaborated by Yeomans, Clarkin, and Kernberg (2015).

[e]Treatment principles described by Bateman and Fonagy (2006, 2016).

[f]Combined with medication.

Abbass, A. (2015). *Reaching through resistance: Advanced psychotherapy techniques.* Kansas City, MO: Seven Leaves.

Abbass, A. A., & Katzman, J. W. (2013). The cost-effectiveness of intensive short-term dynamic psychotherapy. *Psychiatric Annals, 43,* 496–501.

Abbass, A., Sheldon, A., Gyra, J., & Kalpin, A. (2008). Intensive short-term dynamic psychotherapy for DSM-IV personality disorders: a randomized controlled trial. *Journal of Nervous and Mental Disease, 196,* 211–216.

Abend, S. M. (1982). Some observations on reality testing as a clinical concept. *Psychoanalytic Quarterly, 51,* 218–238.

The Accreditation Council for Graduate Medical Education & the American Board of Psychiatry and Neurology. (2015). *The psychiatry milestone project.* http://www.acgme.org/Portals/0/PDFs/Milestones/PsychiatryMilestones.pdf?ver=2015-11-06-120520-753

Adler, G., & Myerson, P. G. (Eds.). (1973). *Confrontation in psychotherapy.* Northvale, NJ: Jason Aronson.

Ainslie, G. (1986). Manipulation: History and theory. In M. Nichols & T. J. Paolino (Eds.), *Basic techniques of psychodynamic psychotherapy* (pp. 127–166). Northvale, NJ: Jason Aronson.

Ajilchi, B., Nejati, V., Town, J. M., Wilson, R., & Abbass, A. (2016). Effects of intensive short-term dynamic psychotherapy on depressive symptoms and executive functioning in Major Depression. *Journal of Nervous and Mental Disease, 204,* 500–505.

Akkerman, K., Carr, V., & Lewin, T. (1992). Changes in ego defenses with recovery from depression. *Journal of Nervous and Mental Disease, 180,* 634–638.

Akkerman, K., Lewin, T. J., & Carr, V. J. (1999). Long-term changes in defense style among patients recovering from major depression. *Journal of Nervous and Mental Disease, 187*(2), 80–87.

Alexander, F. G., & French, T. M. (1946). *Psychodynamic therapy: Principles and applications.* New York, NY: Ronald Press.

American Psychiatric Association. (1980). *Diagnostic and statistical manual of mental disorders* (3rd ed.). Washington, DC: Author.

American Psychiatric Association. (1995). *Diagnostic and statistical manual of mental disorders* (4th ed.). Washington, DC: Author.

American Psychiatric Association. (2013). *Diagnostic and statistical manual of mental disorders: DSM-V* (5th ed.). Arlington, VA: Author.

American Psychological Association. (2012, August). Recognition of psychotherapy effectiveness. http://www.apa.org/about/policy/resolution-psychotherapy.aspx

Anderson, T., & Hill, C. E. (2017). The role of therapist skills in therapist effectiveness. In L. G. Castonguay & C. E. Hill (Eds.), *How and why are some therapists better than others? Understanding therapist effects* (pp. 139–158). Washington, DC: American Psychological Association.

Anderson, T., Ogles, B. M., Patterson, C. L., Lambert, M. J., & Vermeersch, D. A. (2009). Therapist effects: Facilitative interpersonal skills as a predictor of therapist success. *Journal of Clinical Psychology, 65,* 755–768.

Andreasen, N. C., O'Leary, D. S., Cizadlo, T., Arndt, S., Rezai, K., Watkins, G. L., . . . Hichwa, R. D. (1995). Remembering the past: Two facets of episodic memory explored with positron emission tomography. *American Journal of Psychiatry, 152,* 1576–1585.

Andrusyna, T. P., Luborsky, L., Pham, T., & Tang, T. Z. (2006). The mechanisms of sudden gains in supportive-expressive therapy for depression. *Psychotherapy Research, 16,* 526–536.

Aristotle. (1984). Nichomachean ethics. In J. Barnes (Ed.), *The complete works of Aristotle: The revised Oxford translation* (pp. 1729–1867). Princeton, NJ: Princeton University Press.

Arvidson, R. (1973). Aspects of confrontation. In G. Adler & P. G. Myerson (Eds.), *Confrontation in psychotherapy* (pp. 163–180). Northvale, NJ: Jason Aronson.

Azim, H. F., Piper, W. E., Segal, P. M., Nixon, G. W., & Duncan, S. C. (1991). The quality of object relations scale. *Bulletin of the Menninger Clinic, 55,* 323–343.

Baldoni, F., Baldaro, B., & Trombini, G. (1995). Psychotherapeutic perspectives in urethral syndrome. *Stress Medicine, 11,* 79–84.

Barber, J. P., & Sharpless, B. A. (2010). Supportive-expressive therapy. In I. B. Weiner & W. E. Craighead (Eds.), *The Corsini encyclopedia of psychology* (4th ed., pp. 1739–1741). New York, NY: Wiley.

Barber, J. P., & Sharpless, B. A. (2015). On the future of psychodynamic therapy research. *Psychotherapy Research, 25,* 309–320.

Barber, J. P., Khalsa, S., & Sharpless, B. A. (2010). The validity of the alliance as a predictor of psychotherapy outcome. In J. C. Muran & J. P. Barber (Eds.), *The therapeutic alliance: An evidence-based guide to practice* (pp. 29–43). New York, NY: Guilford.

Barber, J. P., Muran, J. C., McCarthy, K. S., & Keefe, R. J. (2013). Research on psychodynamic therapies. In M. J. Lambert (Ed.), *Bergin and Garfield's handbook of psychotherapy and behavior change* (6th ed., pp. 443–494). New York, NY: Wiley.

Barber, J. P., Barrett, M. S., Gallop, R., Rynn, M. A., & Rickels, K. (2011). Short-term dynamic psychotherapy versus pharmacotherapy for major depressive disorder: a randomized, placebo-controlled trial. *Journal of Clinical Psychiatry, 73,* 66–73.

Bargh, J. A., Schwader, K. L., Hailey, S. E., Dyer, R. L., & Boothby, E. J. (2012). Automaticity in social-cognitive processes. *Trends in Cognitive Sciences, 16,* 593–605.

Barkham, M., Rees, A., & Shapiro, D. A. (1996). Outcomes of time-limited psychotherapy in applied settings: Replicating the second Sheffield psychotherapy project. *Journal of Consulting and Clinical Psychology, 64,* 1079–1085.

Barkham, M., Shapiro, D. A., Hardy, G. E., & Rees, A. (1999). Psychotherapy in two-plus-one sessions: Outcomes of a randomized controlled trial of cognitive-behavioral and psychodynamic-interpersonal therapy for subsyndromal depression. *Journal of Consulting and Clinical Psychology, 67,* 201–211.

Barlow, D. H. (Ed.). (2014). *Clinical handbook of psychological disorder: A step-by-step treatment manual* (5th ed.). New York, NY: Guilford.

Bateman, A., & Fonagy, P. (1999). Effectiveness of partial hospitalization in the treatment of borderline personality disorder: a randomized controlled trial. *American Journal of Psychiatry, 156,* 1563–1569.

Bateman, A., & Fonagy, P. (2006). *Mentalization-based treatment for borderline personality disorder: A practical guide.* Oxford, England: Oxford University Press.

Bateman, A., & Fonagy, P. (2008). 8-year follow-up of patients treated for borderline personality disorder: Mentalization-based treatment versus treatment as usual. *American Journal of Psychiatry, 165,* 631–638.

Bateman, A., & Fonagy, P. (2009). Randomized controlled trial of outpatient mentalization-based treatment versus structured clinical management for borderline personality disorder. *American Journal of Psychiatry, 166,* 1355–1364.

Bateman, A., & Fonagy, P. (2016). *Mentalization-based treatment for personality disorders: A practical guide* (1st ed.). Oxford, England: Oxford University Press.

Beck, A. T., Rector, N. A., Stolar, N., & Grant, P. (2009). *Schizophrenia: Cognitive theory, research, and therapy.* New York, NY: Guilford.

Beck, J. S. (2011). *Cognitive behavior therapy: Basics and beyond* (2nd ed.). New York, NY: Guilford.

Beck, R. (2015). *We believe the children: A moral panic in the 1980s.* Philadelphia, PA: Public Affairs.

Bellak, L., Hurvich, M., & Gediman, H. K. (1973). *Ego functions in schizophrenics, neurotics, and normals: A systematic study of conceptual, diagnostic, and therapeutic aspects.* New York, NY: Wiley.

Bellak, L., Chassan, J. B., Gediman, H. K., & Hurvich, M. (1973). Ego function assessment of analytic psychotherapy combined with drug therapy. *Journal of Nervous and Mental Disease, 157,* 465–469.

Ben-Itzhak, S., Bluvstein, I., Schreiber, S., Aharonov-Zaig, I., Maor, M., Lipnik, R., & Bloch, M. (2012). The effectiveness of brief versus intermediate duration psychodynamic psychotherapy in the treatment of adjustment disorder. *Journal of Contemporary Psychotherapy, 42,* 249–256.

Benjamin, L. S., & Gushing, G. (2000). *Manual for coding social interactions in terms of structural analysis of social behavior.* Salt Lake City, UT: University of Utah.

Bernstein, R. J. (1983). *Beyond objectivism and relativism: Science, hermeneutics, and praxis.* Philadelphia, PA: University of Pennsylvania Press.

Bernstein, D. A., Borkovec, T. D., & Hazlett-Stevens, H. (2000). *New directions in progressive relaxation training: A guide for helping professionals.* Westport, CT: Praeger.

Beutel, M. E., Weissßlog, G., Leuteritz, K., Wiltink, J., Haselbacher, A., Ruckes, C., . . . Brähler, E. (2013a). Efficacy of short-term psychodynamic psychotherapy (STPP) with depressed breast cancer patients: results of a randomized controlled multicenter trial. *Annals of Oncology, 25,* 378–384.

Beutel, M. E., Scheurich, V., Knebel, A., Michal, M., Wiltink, J., Graf-Morgenstern, M., . . . Subic-Wrana, C. (2013b). Implementing panic-focused psychodynamic psychotherapy into clinical practice. *Canadian Journal of Psychiatry, 58,* 326–334.

Bhagavad Gita (2009). (C. K Chapple, Ed., W. Sargeant, Trans., 25th Anniversary ed.). Albany, NY: State University of New York Press.

Bibring, E. (1953). The mechanics of depression. In P. Greenarcre (Ed.), *Affective disorders: Psychoanalytic contributions to their study* (pp. 13–48). New York, NY: International Universities Press.

Bibring, E. (1954). Psychoanalysis and the dynamic psychotherapies. *Journal of the American Psychoanalytic Association, 2,* 745–770.

Binswanger, L. (1968). *Being-in-the-world: Selected papers of Ludwig Binswanger.* New York, NY: Harper & Row.

Blagys, M., & Hilsenroth, M. (2000). Distinctive features of short-term psychodynamic-interpersonal therapy: An empirical review of the comparative psychotherapy process literature. *Clinical Psychology: Science and Practice, 7,* 167–188.

Blanchard, M., & Farber, B. A. (2015). Lying in psychotherapy: Why and what clients don't tell their therapists about therapy and their relationship. *Counseling Psychology Quarterly, 29,* 90–112.

Blatt, S. (1974). Levels of object representation in anaclitic and introjective depression. *Psychoanalytic Study of the Child, 29,* 107–157.

Bloch, M., Meiboom, H., Lorberblatt, M., Bluvstein, I., Aharonov, I., & Schreiber, S. (2012). The effect of sertraline add-on to brief dynamic psychotherapy for the treatment of postpartum depression: a randomized, double-blind, placebo-controlled study. *Journal of Clinical Psychiatry, 73,* 235–241.

Blomberg, J., Lazar, A., & Sandell, R. (2001). Long-term outcome of long-term psychoanalytically oriented therapies: First findings of the Stockholm outcome of psychotherapy and psychoanalysis study. *Psychotherapy Research, 11,* 361–382.

Bo, S., Sharp, C., Beck, E., Pedersen, J., Gondan, M., & Simonsen, E. (2017). First empirical evaluation of outcomes for mentalization-based group therapy for adolescents with BPD. *Personality Disorders, 8,* 396–401.

Bögels, S., Wijts, P., Oort, F., & Sallaerts, S. J. (2014). Psychodynamic psychotherapy versus cognitive-behavior therapy for social anxiety disorder: An efficacy and partial effectiveness trial. *Depression and Anxiety, 31,* 363–373.

Book, H. E. (1998). *How to practice brief psychodynamic psychotherapy.* Washington, DC: American Psychological Association.

Bordin, E. (1979). The generalizability of the psychoanalytic concept of the working alliance. *Psychology and Psychotherapy: Theory, Research, and Practice, 16,* 252–260.

Boris, H. (1973). Confrontation in the analysis of transference resistance. In G. Adler & P. G. Myerson (Eds.), *Confrontation in psychotherapy* (pp. 181–206). Northvale, NJ: Jason Aronson.

Boris, H. N. (1986). Interpretation: History and theory. In M. Nichols & T. Paolino (Eds.), *Basic techniques of psychodynamic psychotherapy* (pp. 287–308). Northvale, NJ: Jason Aronson.

Borkovec, T. D. (2002). Training clinic research and the possibility of a national training clinics practice research network. *Behavior Therapist, 25*(5–6), 98–103.

Borkovec, T. D., & Sharpless, B. (2004). Generalized anxiety disorder: Bringing cognitive-behavioral therapy into the valued present. *Mindfulness and acceptance: Expanding the cognitive-behavioral tradition* (pp. 209–242). New York, NY: Guilford.

Boswell, J. F., Sharpless, B. A., Greenberg, L. G., Heatherington, L., Huppert, J. D., Barber, J. P., . . . Castonguay, L. G. (2010). Schools of psychotherapy and the beginnings of a scientific approach. In D. H. Barlow (Ed.), *The Oxford Handbook of Clinical Psychology* (pp. 98–127). New York, NY: Oxford University Press.

Bowlby, J. (1969). *Attachment and loss*. New York, NY: Basic Books.

Bowlby, R., & King, P. (2004). *Fifty years of attachment theory*. London, England: Karnac on behalf of the Winnicott Clinic of Psychotherapy.

Bressi, C., Porcellana, M., Marinaccio, P. M., Nocito, E. P., & Magri, L. (2010). Short-term psychodynamic psychotherapy versus treatment as usual for depressive and anxiety disorders: a randomized clinical trial of efficacy. *Journal of Nervous and Mental Disease, 198,* 647–652.

Breuer, J., & Freud, S. (1955). Studies on hysteria. In J. Strachey (Ed. & Trans.), *The standard edition of the complete psychological works of Sigmund Freud* (Vol. 2, pp. 1–312). London, England: Hogarth.

Brewin, C. R., & Andrews, B. (2017). Creating memories for false autobiographical events in childhood: A systematic review. *Applied Cognitive Psychology, 31,* 2–23.

Brightman, B. K. (1984). Narcissistic issues in the training experience of the psychotherapist. *International Journal of Psychoanalytic Psychotherapy, 10,* 293–317.

Brockman, B., Poynton, A., Ryle, A., & Watson, J. P. (1987). Effectiveness of time-limited therapy carried out by trainees: Comparison of two methods. *British Journal of Psychiatry, 151,* 602–610.

Brom, D., Kleber, R. J., & Defares, P. B. (1989). Brief psychotherapy for posttraumatic stress disorders. *Journal of Consulting and Clinical Psychology, 57,* 607–612.

Brotherton, R., & French, C. C. (2017). Conspiracy theories. In D. Groome & R. Roberts (Eds.), *Parapsychology: The science of unusual experience* (2nd ed., pp. 158–176). New York, NY: Routledge.

Brown, H. N. (1986). Clarification: History and theory. In M. P. Nichols & T. J. Paolino (Eds.), *Basic techniques of psychodynamic psychotherapy* (pp. 237–263). Northvale, NJ: Gardner.

Brown, T. A., & Barlow, D. H. (2014). *Anxiety and related disorders interview schedule for DSM-5: Lifetime version*. New York: NY: Oxford University Press.

Budman, S. H., Demby, A., Redondo, J. P., Hannan, M., Feldstein, M., Ring, J., & Springer, T. (1988). Comparative outcome in time-limited individual and group psychotherapy. *International Journal of Group Psychotherapy, 38,* 63–86.

Buie, D. H., & Adler, G. (1973). The uses of confrontation in the psychotherapy of borderline cases. In G. Adler & P. G. Myerson (Eds.), *Confrontations in psychotherapy* (pp. 123–146). Northvale, NJ: Jason Aronson.

Bull, E. (1991). *Bone dance*. New York, NY: Ace Books.

Busch, F. N., Milrod, B. L., Singer, M. B., & Aronson, A. C. (2012). *Manual of panic focused psychodynamic psychotherapy—eXtended range*. New York, NY: Routledge.

Busch, F. N., Rudden, M., & Shapiro, T. (2016). *Psychodynamic treatment of depression* (2nd ed.). Arlington, VA: American Psychiatric Association.

Butcher, J. N., Graham, J. R., Ben-Porath, Y. S., Tellegen, A., Dahlstrom, W. G., & Kramer, B. (2001). *Minnesota multiphasic personality inventory-2 (MMPI-2) manual*. San Antonio, TX: Pearson.

Cabaniss, D. L., Cherry, S., Douglas, C. J., & Schwartz, A. R. (2011). *Psychodynamic psychotherapy: A clinical manual*. Chichester, England: Wiley-Blackwell.

Carsky, M. (2013). Supportive psychoanalytic therapy for personality disorders. *Psychotherapy, 50,* 443–448.

Caspar, F. (2017). Professional expertise in psychotherapy. In L. G. Castonguay & C. E. Hill (Eds.), *How and why are some therapists better than others? Understanding therapist effects* (pp. 193–214). Washington, DC: American Psychological Association.

Cassidy, J., & Shaver, P. R. (Eds.). (2016). *Handbook of attachment: Theory, research, and clinical applications* (3rd ed.). NY: Guilford.

Castonguay, L. G., & Hill, C. E. (2012). *Transformation in psychotherapy: Corrective experiences across cognitive behavioral, humanistic, and psychodynamic approaches.* Washington, DC: American Psychological Association.

Castonguay, L. G., & Hill, C. E. (2017). *How and why are some therapists better than others? Understandnig therapist effects.* Washington, DC: American Psychological Association.

Castonguay, L. G., Barkham, M., Lutz, W., & McAleavey, A. A. (2013). Practice-oriented research: Approaches and application. In M. J. Lambert (Ed.), *Bergin and Garfield's handbook of psychotherapy and behavior change* (6th ed., pp. 85–133). New York, NY: Wiley.

Chavooshi, B., Mohammadkhani, P., & Dolatshahee, B. (2016a). Efficacy of intensive short-term dynamic psychotherapy for medically unexplained pain: A pilot three-armed randomized controlled trial comparison with mindfulness-based stress reduction. *Psychotherapy and Psychosomatics, 85,* 123–125.

Chavooshi, B., Mohammadkhani, P., & Dolatshahee, B. (2016b). Telemedicine vs. in-person delivery of intensive short-term dynamic psychotherapy for patients with medically unexplained pain: A 12-month randomized, controlled trial. *Journal of Telemedicine and Telecare, 23,* 133–141.

Chavooshi, B., Saberi, M., Tavallaie, S. A., & Sahraei, H. (2017). Psychotherapy for medically unexplained pain: A randomized clinical trial comparing intensive short-term dynamic psychotherapy and cognitive-behavior therapy. *Psychosomatics, 58,* 506–518.

Chodoff, P. (2009). The abuse of psychiatry. In S. Bloch & S. Green (Eds.), *Psychiatric ethics* (4th ed., pp. 99–110). New York, NY: Oxford University Press.

Chow, D. L., Miller, S. D., Seidel, J. A., Kane, R. T., Thornton, J. A., & Andrews, W. P. (2015). The role of deliberate practice in the development of highly effective psychotherapists. *Psychotherapy (Chicago), 52,* 337–345.

Clarkin, J. F., Yeomans, F. E., & Kernberg, O. F. (1999). *Psychotherapy for borderline personality.* New York, NY: John Wiley & Sons.

Clarkin, J. F., Yeomans, F. E., & Kernberg, O. F. (2006). *Psychotherapy for borderline personality focusing on object relations.* Arlington, VA: American Psychiatric Publishing.

Clarkin, J. F., Levy, K. N., Lenzenweger, M. F., & Kernberg, O. F. (2007). Evaluating three treatments for borderline personality disorder: A multiwave study. *American Journal of Psychiatry, 164,* 922–928.

Clay, R. A. (2011). Advocating for psychotherapy. *APA Monitor, 42*(8), 48.

Connolly Gibbons, M. B., Crits-Christoph, P., Barber, J. P., & Schamberger, M. (2007). Insight in psychotherapy: A review of the empirical literature. In L. G. Castonguay & C. E. Hill (Eds.), *Insight in psychotherapy* (pp. 143–165). Washington, DC: American Psychological Association.

Connolly, M. B., Crits-Christoph, P., Shelton, R. C., Hollon, S., Kurtz, J., & Barber, J. P. (1999). The reliability and validity of a measure of self-understanding of interpersonal patterns. *Journal of Consulting and Clinical Psychology, 46,* 472–482.

Connolly Gibbons, M. B., Thompson, S. M., Scott, K., Schauble, L. A., Mooney, T., Thompson, D., . . . Crits-Christoph, P. (2012). Supportive-expressive dynamic psychotherapy in the community mental health system: A pilot effectiveness trial for the treatment of depression. *Psychotherapy (Chicago), 49,* 303–316.

Connolly Gibbons, M. B., Gallop, R., Thompson, D., Luther, D., Crits-Christoph, K., Jacobs, J., . . . Crits-Christoph, P. (2016). Comparative effectiveness of cognitive therapy and dynamic psychotherapy for major depressive disorder in a community mental health setting. *JAMA Psychiatry, 73,* 904–911.

Corwin, H. A. (1973). Therapeutic confrontation from routine to heroic. In G. Adler & P. G. Myerson (Eds.), *Confrontations in psychotherapy* (pp. 67–96). Northvale, NJ: Jason Aronson.

Craft, K. (2014). *Infamous lady: The true story of countess Erzsebet Bathory* (2nd ed.). Middleton, DE: CreateSpace.

Creed, F., Fernandes, L., Guthrie, E., Palmer, S., Ratcliffe, J., Read, N., . . . Tomenson, B; North of England IBS Research Group. (2003). The cost-effectiveness of psychotherapy and paroxetine for severe irritable bowel syndrome. *Gastroenterology, 124,* 303–317.

Crits-Christoph, P., Crits-Christoph, K., & Connolly Gibbons, M. B. (2010). Training in alliance-fostering techniques. In J. C. Muran & J. P. Barber (Eds.), *The therapeutic alliance: An evidence-based guide to practice* (pp. 304–319). New York, NY: Guilford.

Crits-Christoph, P., Cooper, A., & Luborsky, L. (1988). The accuracy of therapists' interpretations and the outcome of dynamic psychotherapy. *Journal of Consulting and Clinical Psychology, 56,* 490–495.

Crits-Christoph, P., Gibbons, M., & Mukherjee, D. (2013). Psychotherapy process-outcome research. In M. J. Lambert (Ed.), *Bergin and Garfield's handbook of psychotherapy and behavioral change* (6th ed., pp. 298–340). New York, NY: Wiley.

Crits-Christoph, P., Gibbons, M. B. C., Narducci, J., Schamberger, M., & Gallop, R. (2005). Interpersonal problems and the outcome of interpersonally oriented psychodynamic treatment of GAD. *Psychotherapy: Theory, Research, Practice, Training, 42,* 211–224.

Crits-Christoph, P., Siqueland, L., Blaine, J., Frank, A., Luborsky, L., Onken, L. S., . . . Beck, A. T. (1999). Psychosocial treatments for cocaine dependence: National institute on drug abuse collaborative cocaine treatment study. *Archives of General Psychiatry, 56,* 493–502.

Cuijpers, P. (2016). *Meta-analyses in mental health research: A practical guide.* Amsterdam, The Netherlands: Vrije Universiteit Amsterdam.

Curtis, H. C. (1979). The concept of therapeutic alliance: Implications for the "widening scope." *Journal of the American Psychoanalytic Association, 27*(Suppl), 159–192.

Dare, C., Eisler, I., Russell, G., Treasure, J., & Dodge, L. (2001). Psychological therapies for adults with anorexia nervosa: Randomised controlled trial of out-patient treatments. *British Journal of Psychiatry, 178,* 216–221.

Davanloo, H. (1980). *Short-term dynamic psychotherapy.* New York, NY: Jason Aronson.

Davanloo, H. (1990). *Unlocking the unconscious.* Chichester, England: Wiley.

Davanloo, H. (2000). *Intensive short-term dynamic psychotherapy—Selected papers of Habib Davanloo.* Chichester, England: Wiley.

Davanloo, H. (2005). Intensive short-term dynamic psychotherapy. In H. Kaplan & B. Sadock (Eds.), *Comprehensive Textbook of Psychiatry.* Philadelphia, PA: Lippincott Williams & Wilkins.

De Carvalho, R. J. (1999). Otto Rank, the Rankian circle in Philadelphia, and the origins of Carl Rogers' person-centered psychotherapy. *History of Psychology, 2,* 132–148.

De Jonghe, F., Hendriksen, M., van Aalst, G., Kool, S., Peen, V., Van, R., . . . Dekker, J. (2004). Psychotherapy alone and combined with pharmacotherapy in the treatment of depression. *British Journal of Psychiatry, 185,* 37–45.

De Jonghe, F., Kool, S., van Aalst, G., Dekker, J., & Peen, J. (2001). Combining psychotherapy and antidepressants in the treatment of depression. *Journal of Affective Disorders, 64*, 217–229.

De Jonghe, F., Rijnisre, P., & Janssen, R. (2015). Psychoanalytic supportive psychotherapy. *Journal of the American Psychoanalytic Association, 42*, 421–446.

Dekker, J., Koelen, J. A., Van, H. L., Schoevers, R. A., Peen, J., Hendriksen, M., . . . De Jonghe, F. (2008). Speed of action: The relative efficacy of short psychodynamic supportive psychotherapy and pharmacotherapy in the first 8 weeks of a treatment algorithm for depression. *Journal of Affective Disorders, 109*, 183–188.

Dekker, J., Molenaar, P. J., Kool, S., Van Aalst, G., Peen, J., & de Jonghe, F. (2005). Dose-effect relations in time-limited combined psycho-pharmacological treatment for depression. *Psychological Medicine, 35*, 47–58.

Del Re, A. C., Fluckiger, C., Horvath, A. O., Symonds, D., & Wampold, B. E. (2012). Therapist effects in the therapeutic alliance-outcome relationship: A restricted-maximum likelihood meta-analysis. *Clinical Psychology Review, 32*, 642–649.

Devereaux, P. J. (1951). Some criteria for the timing of confrontations and interpretations. *International Journal of Psychoanalysis, 32*, 19–24.

Dewald, P. A. (1971). *Psychotherapy, a dynamic approach* (2nd ed.). New York: Basic Books.

Diener, M. J., Hilsenroth, M. J., & Weinberger, J. (2007). Therapist affect focus and patient outcomes in psychodynamic psychotherapy: A meta-analysis. *American Journal of Psychiatry, 164*, 936–941.

Driessen, E., Hegelmaier, L. M., Abbass, A. A., Barber, J. P., Dekker, J. J., Van, H. L., . . . Cuijpers, P. (2015). The efficacy of short-term psychodynamic psychotherapy for depression: A meta-analysis update. *Clinical Psychology Review, 42*, 1–15.

Doering, S., Hörz, S., Rentrop, M., Fischer-Kern, M., Schuster, P., Benecke, C., . . Buchheim, P. (2010). Transference-focused psychotherapy v. treatment by community psychotherapists for borderline personality disorder: Randomized controlled trial. *British Journal of Psychiatry, 196*, 389–395.

Driessen, E., Van, L. H., Don, F. J., Peen, J., Kool, S., Westra, D., . . . Dekker, J. J. (2013). The efficacy of cognitive-behavioral therapy and psychodynamic therapy in the outpatient treatment of major depression: A randomized clinical trial. *American Journal of Psychiatry, 170*, 1041–1050.

du Bois-Reymond, E. (1883). Darwin and Copernicus. *Nature, 27*, 557–558.

Egger, N., Wild, B., Zipfel, S., Junne, F., Konnopka, A., Schmidt, U., . . . Konig, H. H. (2016). Cost-effectiveness of focal psychodynamic therapy and enhanced cognitive-behavioural therapy in out-patients with anorexia nervosa. *Psychological Medicine, 46*, 3291–3301.

Eikenaes, I., Hummelen, B., Abrahamsen, G., Andrea, H., & Wilberg, T. (2013). Personality functioning in patients with avoidant personality disorder and social phobia. *Journal of Personality Disorders, 27*, 746–763.

Eissler, K. R. (1953). The effect of the structure of the ego on psychoanalytic technique. *Journal of the American Psychoanalytic Association, 1*, 104–143.

Ekeblad, A., Falkenstrom, F., & Holmqvist, R. (2016). Reflective functioning as predictor of working alliance and outcome in the treatment of depression. *Journal of Consulting and Clinical Psychology, 84*, 67–78.

Elliott, R., Shapiro, D. A., Firth-Cozens, J., Stiles, W. B., Hardy, G. E., Llewelyn, S. P., & Margison, F. R. (1994). Comprehensive process analysis of insight events in cognitive-behavioral and psychodynamic-interpersonal psychotherapies. *Journal of Counseling Psychology, 41,* 449–463.

Emmelkamp, P. M. G., Benner, A., Kuipers, Feiertag, G. A., Koster, H. C., & van Apeldoorn, F. J. (2006). Comparison of brief dynamic and cognitive-behavioral therapies in avoidant personality disorder. *British Journal of Psychiatry, 189,* 60–64.

Erikson, E. H. (1963). *Childhood and society* (2nd ed.). New York, NY: Norton.

Etchegoyen, R. H. (2012). *Fundamentals of psychoanalytic technique.* London, England: Karnac Books.

Eubanks, C. F., Burckell, L. A., & Goldfried, M. R. (2018). Clinical consensus strategies to repair ruptures in the therapeutic alliance. *Journal of Psychotherapy Integration, 28,* 60–76.

Eubanks-Carter, C., Muran, J. C., & Safran, J. D. (2015a). Alliance-focused training. *Psychotherapy (Chicago), 52,* 169–173.

Eubanks-Carter, C. F., Muran, J. C., & Safran, J. D. (2015b). *Rupture resolution rating system (3RS).* New York, NY: Mount Sinai-Beth Israel Medical Center.

Fairbairn, W. R. D., Scharff, D. E., & Birtles, E. F. (1994). *From instinct to self: Selected papers of W. R. D. Fairbairn.* Northvale, NJ: J. Aronson.

Faramarzi, M., Azadfallah, P., Book, H. E., Tabatabaei, K. R., Taheri, H., & Shokri-shirvani, J. (2013). A randomized controlled trial of brief psychoanalytic psychotherapy in patients with functional dyspepsia. *Asian Journal of Psychiatry, 6,* 228–234.

Farber, B. A. (2006). *Self-disclosure in psychotherapy.* New York, NY: Guilford.

Fenichel, O. (1941). *Problems of psychoanalytic technique.* New York, NY: Psychoanalytic Quarterly.

Ferenczi, S. (1950). *Further contributions to the theory and technique of psycho-analysis* (2nd ed.). London, England: Hogarth.

Ferenczi, S. (1955). The elasticity of psycho-analytic technique. In M. Balint (Ed.), *Final contributions to the problems and methods of psychoanalysis* (pp. 87–101). New York: Basic Books.

Ferenczi, S., & Rank, O. (1986). *The development of psycho-analysis* [Entwicklungsziele der Psychoanalyse]. Madison, CT: International Universities Press.

Feyerabend, P. K. (2010). *Against method* (4th ed.). New York, NY: Verso Books.

Fink, B. (2007). *Fundamentals of psychoanalytic technique: A Lacanian approach.* New York, NY: Norton.

First, M. B., Williams, J. B. W., Benjamin, L. S., & Spitzer, R. L. (2016). *Structured clinical interview for DSM-5 personality disorders.* Arlington, VA: American Psychiatric Association.

First, M. B., Williams, J. B. W., Karg, R. S., & Spitzer, R. L. (2014). *Structured clinical interview for DSM-5 disorders: Patient edition.* New York, NY: Biometrics Research Department.

Fleischer, L., & Lee, E. (2016). The analytic principle and attitude: Mobilizing psychoanalytic knowledge to maximize social work students' practice competence. *Psychoanalytic Social Work, 23,* 99–118.

Foa, E. B., Hembree, E. A., & Rothbaum, B. O. (2007). *Prolonged exposure therapy for PTSD: Emotional processing of traumatic experiences: Therapist guide.* New York, NY: Oxford University Press.

Foa, E. B., Keane, T. M., Terence, M., Friedman, M. J., & Cohen, J. A. (2008). *Effective treatments for PTSD: Practice guidelines from the international society for traumatic stress studies* (2nd ed.). New York, NY: Guilford.

Fonagy, P., Target, M., Steele, H., & Steele, M. (1998). *Reflective functioning manual, version 5.0, for application to adult attachment interviews*. London, England: University College London.

Fournier, J. C., DeRubeis, R. J., Hollon, S. D., Dimidjian, S., Amsterdam, J. D., Shelton, R. C., & Fawcett, J. (2010). Antidepressant drug effects and depression severity: A patient-level meta-analysis. *Journal of the American Medical Association, 303*, 47–53.

Frankl, V. E. (2006). *Man's search for meaning* [Psycholog erlebt das Konzentrationslager] (Mini book ed.). Boston, MA: Beacon.

Frederickson, J. (1999). *Psychodynamic psychotherapy: Learning to listen from multiple perspectives*. New York, NY: Taylor & Francis.

Freud, A. (1966). *The ego and the mechanisms of defense*. New York, NY: International Universities Press.

Freud, S. (1953a). The claims of psycho-analysis to scientific interest. In J. Strachey (Ed. & Trans.), *The standard edition of the complete psychological works of Sigmund Freud* (Vol. 13, pp. 165–190). London, England: Hogarth.

Freud, S. (1953b). Fragment of an analysis of a case of hysteria. In J. Strachey (Ed. & Trans.), *The standard edition of the complete psychological works of Sigmund Freud* (pp. 7–124). London, England: Hogarth.

Freud, S. (1953c). The interpretation of dreams. In J. Strachey (Ed. & Trans.), *The standard edition of the complete psychological works of Sigmund Freud* (Vols. 4–5). London, England: Hogarth. (Original work published 1900)

Freud, S. (1955). Lines of advance in psychoanalytic therapy. In J. Strachey (Ed. & Trans.), *The standard edition of the complete psychological works of Sigmund Freud* (Vol. 17, pp. 157–168). London, England: Hogarth.

Freud, S. (1958a). The dynamics of transference. In J. Strachey (Ed. & Trans.), *The standard edition of the complete psychological works of Sigmund Freud* (Vol. 12, pp. 97–108). London, England: Hogarth.

Freud, S. (1958b). On the beginning of treatment (further recommendations on the technique of psycho-analysis I). In J. Strachey (Ed. & Trans.), *The standard edition of the complete psychological works of Sigmund Freud* (Vol. 12, pp. 121–144). London, England: Hogarth.

Freud, S. (1958c). Observations on transference-love. In J. Strachey (Ed. & Trans.), *The standard edition of the complete psychological works of Sigmund Freud* (Vol. 12, pp. 157–171). London, England: Hogarth.

Freud, S. (1958d). Papers on technique (1911–1915). In J. Strachey (Ed. & Trans.), *The standard edition of complete psychological works of Sigmund Freud* (Vol. 12, pp. 85–171). London, England: Hogarth.

Freud, S. (1958e). Recommendations to physicians practising psychoanalysis. In J. Strachey (Ed. & Trans.), *The standard edition of the complete psychological works of Sigmund Freud* (Vol. 12, pp. 109–120). London, England: Hogarth. (Original work published 1912)

Freud, S. (1960). The psychopathology of every day life. In J. Strachey (Ed. & Trans.), *The standard edition of the complete psychological works of Sigmund Freud* (J Vol. 6, pp. 1–296). London, England: Hogarth.

Freud, S. (1963). Introductory lectures on psychoanalysis. In J. Strachey (Ed. & Trans.), *The standard edition of the complete psychological works of Sigmund Freud* (Vols. 15–16). London, England: Hogarth. (Original work published 1920)

Freud, S. (1961a). The future of an illusion. In J. Strachey (Ed. & Trans.), *The standard edition of the complete psychological works of Sigmund Freud* (Vol. 21, pp. 5–58). London, England: Hogarth.

Freud, S. (1961b). Civilization and its discontents. In J. Strachey (Ed. & Trans.), *The standard edition of the complete psychological works of Sigmund Freud* (Vol. 21, pp. 59–148). New York: Norton.

Freud, S. (1964). New introductory lectures on psycho-analysis. In J. Strachey (Ed. & Trans.), *The standard edition of the Complete Psychological works of Sigmund Freud* (Vol. 22, pp. 7–184). London, England: Hogarth.

Freud, S. (1964). An outline of psycho-analysis. In J. Strachey (Ed. & Trans.), *The standard edition of the complete psychological works of Sigmund Freud* (Vol. 23, pp. 144–208). London, England: Hogarth.

Freud, S. (1964). Constructions in analysis. In J. Strachey (Ed. & Trans.), *The standard edition of the complete psychological works of Sigmund Freud* (Vol. 23, pp. 255–270). London, England: Hogarth.

Freud, S. (1974). *Standard edition of the complete psychological works of Sigmund Freud* (J. Strachey, Ed. & Trans., Vol. 24). London, England: Hogarth.

Friedlander, M. L., Sutherland, O., Sandler, S., Kortz, L., Bernardi, S., Lee, H. H., & Drozd, A. (2012). Exploring corrective experiences in a successful case of short-term dynamic psychotherapy. *Psychotherapy (Chicago), 49*, 349–363.

Fruzzetti, A. R., & Fruzzetti, A. (2008). Dialectics in cognitive and behavior therapy. In W. T. O'Donohue & J. E. Fisher (Eds.), *Cognitive behavior therapy: Applying empirically supported techniques in your practice* (2nd ed., pp. 132–141). Hoboken, NJ: Wiley.

Gabbard, G. O. (2010). *Long-term psychodynamic psychotherapy*. Arlington, VA: American Psychiatric Publishing.

Gabbard, G. O. (2014). *Psychodynamic psychiatry in clinical practice* (5th ed.). Washington, DC: American Psychiatric Publishing.

Gabbard, G. O., Horwitz, L., Allen, J. G., Frieswyk, S., Newsom, G., Colson, D. B., & Coyne, L. (1994). Transference interpretation in the psychotherapy of borderline patients: A high-risk, high-gain phenomenon. *Harvard Review of Psychiatry, 2*(2), 59–69.

Gadamer, H. (1975). *Truth and method* [Wahrheit und methode] (J. Wiensheimer & D. Marshall, Trans., 2nd ed.). New York, NY: Continuum.

Gallagher-Thompson, D., & Steffen, A. M. (1994). Comparative effects of cognitive-behavioral and brief psychodynamic psychotherapies for depressed family caregivers. *Journal of Consulting and Clinical Psychology, 62*, 543–549.

Garner, D. M., Rockert, W., Davis, R., Garner, M. V., Olmsted M., & Eagle M. (1993). Comparison of cognitive-behavioral and supportive-expressive therapy for bulimia nervosa. *American Journal of Psychiatry, 150*, 37–46.

Gaston, L. (1995). Dynamic therapy for post-traumatic stress disorder. In J. P. Barber & P. Crits-Christoph (Eds.), *Dynamic therapies for psychiatric disorders: Axis-I* (pp. 161–192). New York, NY: Basic Books.

Geller, J., & Farber, B. (1993). Factors influencing the process of internalization in psychotherapy. *Psychotherapy Research, 3*, 166–180.

Gelso, C. J., & Carter, J. A. (1994). Components of the psychotherapy relationship: Their interaction and unfolding during treatment. *Journal of Counseling Psychology, 41*, 296–306.

George, C., Kaplan, N., & Main, M. (1996). *Adult attachment interview* (3rd ed.). Berkeley, CA: Department of Psychology, University of California.

Gerber, A. J., Kocsis, J. H., Milrod, B. L., Roose, S. P., Barber, J. P., Thase, M. E., . . . Leon, A. C. (2011). A quality-based review of randomized controlled trials of psychodynamic psychotherapy. *American Journal of Psychiatry, 168*, 19–28.

Giesen-Bloo, J., Van Dyck, R., Spinhoven, P., van Tilburg, W., Dirksen, C., van Asselt, T., . . . Arntz, A. (2006). Outpatient psychotherapy for borderline personality disorder: Randomized trial of schema-focused therapy vs transference-focused psychotherapy. *Archives of General Psychiatry, 63*, 649–658.

Gilbert, P. (2014). The origins and nature of compassion focused therapy. *British Journal of Clinical Psychology, 53*, 6–41.

Glover, E. (1955). *The technique of psychoanalysis*. London, England: Bailliere Tindall & Cox.

Gray-Little, B. (2009). The assessment of psychopathology in racial and ethnic minorities. In J. N. Butcher (Ed.), *Oxford handbook of personality assessment* (pp. 396–414). New York, NY: Oxford University Press.

Greenberg, J. R., & Mitchell, S. A. (1983). *Object relations in psychoanalytic theory*. Cambridge, MA: Harvard.

Greenson, R. R. (1967). *The technique and practice of psychoanalysis*. New York, NY: International Universities Press.

Grunbaum, A. (1984). *The foundations of psychoanalysis: A philosophical critique*. Berkeley, CA: University of California Press.

Guthrie, E., Creed, F., Dawson, D., & Tomenson, B. (1991). A controlled trial of psychological treatment for the irritable bowel syndrome. *Gastroenterology, 100*, 450–457.

Guthrie, E., Kapur, N., Mackway-Jones, K., Chew-Graham, C., Moorey, J., Mendel, E., . . . Tomenson, B. (2001). Randomized controlled trial of brief psychological intervention after deliberate self poisoning. *British Medical Journal, 323*, 135–138.

Guthrie, E., & Moghavemi, A. (2013). Psychodynamic-interpersonal therapy: an overview of the treatment approach and evidence base. *Psychodynamic Psychiatry, 41*, 619–635.

Guthrie, E., Moorey, J., Margison, F., Barker, H., Palmer, S., McGrath, G., . . . Creed, F. (1999). Cost-effectiveness of brief psychodynamic-interpersonal therapy in high utilizers of psychiatric services. *Archives of General Psychiatry, 56*, 519–526.

Habarth, J., Hansell, J., & Grove, T. (2011). How accurately do introductory psychology textbooks present psychoanalytic theory? *Teaching of Psychology, 38*, 16–21.

Habermas, J. (1971). *Knowledge and human interest* (J. J. Shapiro, Trans.). Boston, MA: Beacon.

Hamilton, J., Guthrie, E., Creed, F., Thompson, D., Tomenson, B., Bennett, R., . . . Liston, R. (2000). A randomized controlled trial of psychotherapy in patients with chronic functional dyspepsia. *Gastroenterology, 119*, 661–669.

Hardy, G. E., Barkham, M., Shapiro, D. A., Stiles, W. B., Rees, A., & Reynolds, S. (1995). Impact of Cluster C personality disorders on outcomes of contrasting brief psychotherapies for depression. *Journal of Consulting and Clinical Psychology, 63*, 997–1004.

Hartmann, H. (1939). *Ego psychology and the problem of adaptation*. New York, NY: International Universities Press.

Heidegger, M. (2010). *Being and time: A revised edition of the Stambaugh translation* (J. Stambaugh, Trans. & D. J. Schmidt, Ed.). Albany, NY: State University of New York Press.

Heldt, E., Blaya, C., Kipper, L., Salum, G. A., Otto, M. W., & Manfro, G. G. (2007). Defense mechanisms after brief cognitive-behavior group therapy for panic disorder: One-year follow-up. *Journal of Nervous and Mental Disease, 195,* 540–543.

Heller, D. (1985). *Power in psychotherapeutic practice.* New York, NY: Human Sciences Press.

Hellerstein, D. J., Pinsker, H., Rosenthal, R. N., & Klee, S. (1994). Supportive therapy as the treatment model of choice. *Journal of Psychotherapy Practice and Research, 3,* 300–306.

Hellerstein, D. J., Rosenthal, R. N., Pinsker, H., Wallner Samstag, L. Muran, J. C., & Winston, A. (1998). A randomized prospective study comparing supportive and dynamic therapies. Outcome and alliance. *Journal of Psychotherapeutic Practice and Research, 7,* 261–271.

Henretty, J. R., & Levitt, H. M. (2010). The role of therapist self-disclosure in psychotherapy: A qualitative review. *Clinical Psychology Review, 30,* 63–77.

Hergenhahn, B. R., & Henley, T. B. (2014). *An introduction to the history of psychology* (7th ed.). Belmont, CA: Wadsworth.

Hirsch, I. (1998). The concept of enactment and theoretical convergence. *Psychoanalytic Dialogues, 4,* 171–192.

Hitchens, C. (2003). Mommie dearest. *Slate,* April 4, 2018.

Hobbes, T. (1997). *Leviathan: Or the matter, forme, and power of a commonwealth ecclesiasticall and civil* (M. Oakeshott, Ed.). New York, NY: Touchstone.

Hobson, R. F. (1985). *Forms of feeling. The heart of psychotherapy.* London: Tavistock Routledge.

Hoffart, A., Versland, S., & Sexton, H. (2002). Self-understanding, empathy, guided discovery, and schema belief in schema-focused cognitive therapy of personality problems: A process-outcome. *Cognitive Therapy and Research, 26,* 199–219.

Hoffer, W. (1950). Three psychological criteria for the termination of treatment. *International Journal of Psychoanalysis, 31,* 194–195.

Hoglend, P., Bogwald, K. P., Amlo, S., Heyerdahl, O., Sorbye, O., Marble, A., . . . Bentsen, H. (2000). Assessment of change in dynamic psychotherapy. *Journal of Psychotherapy Practice and Research,* 9, 190–199.

Hoglend, P., Hersoug, A. G., Bogwald, K. P., Amlo, S., Marble, A., Sorbye, O., , . . Crits-Christoph, P. (2011). Effects of transference work in the context of therapeutic alliance and quality of object relations. *Journal of Consulting and Clinical Psychology, 79,* 697–706.

Holland, S. J., Roberts, N. E., & Messer, S. B. (1998). Reliability and validity of the Rutgers psychotherapy progress scale. *Psychotherapy Research, 8,* 104–110.

Hollon, S. D., DeRubeis, R. J., Shelton, R. C., Amsterdam, J. D., Salomon, R. M., O'Reardon, J. P., . . . Gallop, R. (2005). Prevention of relapse following cognitive therapy vs medications in moderate to severe depression. *Archives of General Psychiatry, 62,* 417–422.

Horney, K. (1950). Neurosis and human growth. In *The collected works of Karen Horney* (Vol. 2, pp. 1–389). New York, NY: Norton.

Horowitz, M. J. (1976). *Stress response syndromes.* New York, NY: Aronson.

Horowitz, L. M., Alden, L. E., Wiggins, J. S., & Pincus, A. L. (2000). *Inventory of interpersonal problems manual*. Odessa, FL: Psychological Corporation.

Horowitz, L. M., Rosenberg, S. E., Baer, B. A., Ureno, G., & Villasenor, V. S. (1988). Inventory of interpersonal problems: Psychometric properties and clinical applications. *Journal of Consulting and Clinical Psychology, 56,* 885–892.

Horvath, A. O., & Greenberg, L. S. (1989). Development and validation of the working alliance inventory. *Journal of Counseling Psychology, 36,* 223–233.

Hubschmid, M., Aybek, S., Maccaferri, G. E., Chocron, O., Gholamrezaee, M. M., Rossetti, A. O., . . . Berney, A (2015). Efficacy of brief interdisciplinary psychotherapeutic intervention for motor conversion disorder and nonepileptic attacks. *General Hospital Psychiatry, 37,* 448–455.

Huprich, S. K. (2009). *Psychodynamic therapy: Conceptual and empirical foundations.* New York, NY: Routledge.

Huprich, S. K. (2015). *Rorschach assessment of the personality disorders.* New York, NY: Routledge.

International Psychoanalytic Association. (2018). IPA training institutes. http://www.ipa.world/IPA/ipso/Aboutus/InstituteAlphaList.aspx

Irvine, W. B. (2009). *A guide to the good life: The ancient art of stoic joy.* Oxford, England: Oxford University Press.

Isaacs, S. (1939). Criteria for interpretation. *International Journal of Psycho-Analysis, 20,* 160.

Johansen, P. O., Krebs, T. S., Svartberg, M., Stiles, T. C., & Holen, A. (2011). Change in defense mechanisms during short-term dynamic and cognitive therapy in patients with cluster C personality disorders. *Journal of Nervous and Mental Disease, 199,* 712–715.

Joiner, T. (2009). *The interpersonal theory of suicide: Guidance for working with suicidal clients.* Washington, DC: American Psychological Association.

Jones, E. (1953). The god complex. *Essays in applied psychoanalysis* (Vol. 2, pp. 244–265). London, England: Hogarth. (Original work published 1913)

Jones, E. E., Parke, L. A., & Pulos, S. M. (1992). How therapy is conducted in the private consulting room: A multidimensional description of brief psychodynamic treatments. *Psychotherapy Research, 2,* 16–30.

Jørgensen, C. R., Freund, C., Bøye, R., Jordet, H., Andersen, D., & Kjølbye, M. (2012). Outcome of mentalization-based and supportive psychotherapy in patients with borderline personality disorder: a randomized trial. *Acta Psychiatrica Scandinavica, 127,* 305–317.

Jung, C. G. (1969). Aion. In H. Read, M. Fordham, G. Adler, & W. McGuire (Eds.), *The collected works of C. G. Jung* (R. F. C. Hull, Trans., 2nd ed., Vol. 9, part 2). Princeton, NJ: Princeton University Press.

Kant, I. (1996). *Critique of pure reason* [Kritik der reinen Vernunft.] (Unifi ed.). Indianapolis, IN: Hackett.

Kant, I., (2002). *Critique of practical reason* [Kritik der praktischen Vernunft.]. Indianapolis, IN: Hackett.

Karpf, R. J. (1986). Confrontations: History and theory. In M. Nichols & T. J. Paolino (Eds.), *Basic techniques of psychodynamic psychotherapy* (pp. 187–206). Northvale, NJ: Jason Aronson.

Kelman, H. C., & Parloff, M. B. (1957). Interrelations among three criteria for improvement in group therapy. *Journal of Abnormal and Social Psychology, 54,* 281–288.

Kernberg, O. (1965). Notes on countertransference. *Journal of the American Psychoanalytic Association, 13,* 38–56.

Kernberg, O. F. (1975). *Borderline conditions and pathological narcissism.* New York, NY: J. Aronson.

Kernberg, O. F. (1984). *Severe personality disorders: Psychotherapeutic strategies.* New Haven, CT: Yale University Press.

Kernberg, O. F. (1992). *Aggression in personality disorders and perversions.* Binghamton, NY: Vail-Ballou.

Khan, A., & Brown, W. A. (2015). Antidepressants versus placebo in major depression: An overview. *World Psychiatry, 14,* 294–300.

Kierkegaard, S. A. (1980). *The concept of anxiety: A simple psychological orienting deliberation on the dogmatic issue of hereditary sin* (H. Hong & E. Hong, Trans.). Princeton, NJ: Princeton University Press.

Kierkegaard, S. (1983). *Fear and trembling; repetition.* Princeton, NJ: Princeton University Press.

Kivlighan, D. M., Multon, K. D., & Patton, M. J. (2000). Insight and symptom reduction in time-limited psychoanalytic counseling. *Journal of Counseling Psychology, 47,* 50–58.

Klein, M. (1949). *The psycho-analysis of children* (3th ed.). London, England: Hogarth.

Klein, C., Milrod, B., Busch, F., Levy, K., & Shapiro, T. (2003). A preliminary study of clinical process in relation to outcome in psychodynamic psychotherapy for panic disorder. *Psychoanalytic Inquiry, 23,* 308–331.

Kleinman, P. H., Woody, G. E., Todd, T. C., Millman, R. B., Kang, S. Y., Kemp, J., & Lipton, D. S. (1990). Crack and cocaine abusers in outpatient psychotherapy. *NIDA Research Monograph, 104,* 24–35.

Knekt, P., & Lindfors, O. (2004). *A randomized trial of the effect of four forms of psychotherapy on depressive and anxiety disorders.* Helsinki, Finland: Kela.

Koch, S. (1999). The limits of psychological knowledge: Lessons of a century qua "science." In D. Finkelman & F. Kessel (Eds.), *Psychology in human context: Essays in dissidence and reconstruction* (pp. 395–416). Chicago, IL: University of Chicago Press.

Koch, S., Finkelman, D., & Kessel, F. S. (1999). *Psychology in human context: Essays in dissidence and reconstruction.* Chicago, IL: University of Chicago Press.

Kohut, H. (1977). *The restoration of the self.* New York, NY: International Universities Press.

Kohut, H. (1984). *How does analysis cure?: Contributions to the psychology of the self.* Chicago, IL: University of Chicago Press.

Kohut, H. (2001). *The analysis of the self: A systematic approach to the psychoanalytic treatment of narcissistic personality disorders.* Madison, CT: International Universities Press.

Kolmes, K., & Taube, D. O. (2016). Client discovery of psychotherapist personal information online. *Professional Psychology: Research and Practice, 47,* 147–154.

Kompoliti, K., Wilson, B., Stebbins, G., Bernard, B., & Hinson, V. (2013). Immediate vs. delayed treatment of psychogenic movement disorders with short-term psychodynamic psychotherapy: Randomized clinical trial. *Parkinsonism & Related Disorders, 20,* 60–63.

Kool, S., Dekker, J., & Duijsens, I. (2003). Efficacy of combined therapy and pharmacotherapy for depressed patients with or without personality disorders. *Harvard Review
of Psychiatry, 11,* 133–142.

Kramer, R. (1995). The birth of client-centered therapy: Carl rogers, Otto Rank, and "the
beyond." *Journal of Humanistic Psychology, 35*(4), 54–110.

Kramer, U., Despland, J. N., Michel, L., Drapeau, M., & de Roten, Y. (2010). Change
in defense mechanisms and coping over the course of short-term dynamic psychotherapy for adjustment disorder. *Journal of Clinical Psychology, 66,* 1232–1241.

Kramer, U., de Roten, Y., Perry, J. C., & Despland, J. N. (2013). Change in defense
mechanisms and coping patterns during the course of 2-year-long psychotherapy
and psychoanalysis for recurrent depression: a pilot study of a randomized controlled
trial. *Journal of Nervous and Mental Disease, 201,* 614–620.

Krause, D. R., & Seligman, D. A. (2005). Validation of a behavioral health treatment outcome and assessment tool for naturalistic settings: The treatment outcome package.
Journal of Clinical Psychology, 61, 285–314.

Lacan, J. (1976). Conferences et entretiens dans des universites nord-americaines
[Lectures and interviews at North American universities] *Scilicet, 6–7,* 5–63.

Lakatos, I., & Musgrave, A. (Eds.). (1970). *Criticism and the growth of knowledge.*
Cambridge, England: Cambridge University Press.

Lambert, M. J. (2013). The efficacy and effectiveness of psychotherapy. In M. J. Lambert
(Ed.), *Bergin and Garfield's handbook of psychotherapy and behavior change* (6th ed.,
pp. 169–218). Hoboken, NJ: Wiley.

Lambert, M. J., Kahler, M., Harmon, C., Shimokawa, K., & Burlingame, G. M. (2011).
Administration and scoring manual for the outcome questionnaire (OQ-45.2). Orem,
UT: American Professional Credentialing Services.

Lambert, M. J., Burlingame, G. M., Umphress, V. , Hansen, N. B., Vermeersch, D. A.
... Yanchar, S. C. (1996), The reliability and validity of the Outcome Questionnaire.
Clinical Psychology and Psychotherapy, 3, 249–258.

La Mettrie, J. O. (1912). *Man a machine* (G. C. Bussey, Ed. & Trans.). La Salle, IL:
Open Court.

Langs, R. (1973). *The technique of psychoanalytic psychotherapy.* New York: Aronson.

Laurenssen, E. M. P., Luyten, P., Kikkert, M. J., Westra, D., Peen, J. Soons, M. B. J. .
. . Dekker, J. J. M. (2018). Day hospital mentalization-based treatment v. specialist
treatment as usual in patients with borderline personality disorder: Randomized
controlled trial. *Psychological Medicine, 48,* 2522–2539.

Leahy, R. L. (2017). *Cognitive therapy techniques: A practitioner's guide* (2nd ed.).
New York, NY: Guilford.

Leichsenring, F., & Leibing, E. (2003). The effectiveness of psychodynamic therapy and
cognitive behavior therapy in the treatment of personality disorders: A meta-analysis.
American Journal of Psychiatry, 160, 1223–1232.

Leichsenring, F., & Leibing, E. (2007). Supportive-expressive (SE) psychotherapy: An
update. *Current Psychiatry Reviews, 3,* 57–64.

Leichsenring, F., & Rabung, S. (2008). Effectiveness of long-term psychodynamic psychotherapy: A meta-analysis. *JAMA, 300,* 1551–1565.

Leichsenring, F., Rabung, S., & Leibing, E. (2004). The efficacy of short-term psychodynamic psychotherapy in specific psychiatric disorders: A meta-analysis. *Archives of
General Psychiatry, 61,* 1208–1216.

Leichsenring, F., Steinert, C., & Crits-Christoph, P. (2018). On mechanisms of change in psychodynamic therapy. *Zeitschrift Fur Psychosomatische Medizin Und Psychotherapie, 64,* 16–22.

Leichsenring, F., Salzer, S., Beutel, M. E., Herpertz, S., Hiller, W., Hoyer, J., . . . Leibing, E. (2013). Psychodynamic therapy and cognitive-behavioral therapy in social anxiety disorder: A multicenter randomized controlled trial. *American Journal of Psychiatry, 170,* 759–767.

Leichsenring, F., Salzer, S., Jaeger, U., Kächele, H., Kreische, R., Leweke, F., . . . Leibing, E. (2009). Short-term psychodynamic psychotherapy and cognitive-behavioral therapy in generalized anxiety disorder: A randomized, controlled trial. *American Journal of Psychiatry, 166,* 875–881.

Leichsenring, F., Salzer, S., Beutel, M. E., Herpertz, S., Hiller, W., Hoyer, J., . . . Leibing, E. (2014). Long-term outcome of psychodynamic therapy and cognitive-behavioral therapy in social anxiety disorder. *American Journal of Psychiatry, 171,* 1074–1082.

Lemma, A., Roth, A., & Pilling, S. (2008). *The competencies required to deliver effective psychoanalytic/psychodynamic therapy.* London, England: Research Department of Clinical, Educational, and Health Psychology, University College London.

Levin, S. (1973). Confrontation as a demand for change. In G. Adler & P. G. Myerson (Eds.), *Confrontation in psychotherapy* (pp. 303–318). Northvale, NJ: Jason Aronson.

Levy, K., & Anderson, T. (2013). Is clinical psychology doctoral training becoming less intellectually diverse? and if so, what can be done? *Clinical Psychology: Science and Practice, 20,* 211–220.

Levy, K. N., Meehan, K. B., Kelly, K. M., Reynoso, J. S., Weber, M., Clarkin, J. F., & Kernberg, O. F. (2006). Change in attachment patterns and reflective functioning in a randomized control trial of transference-focused psychotherapy for borderline personality disorder. *Journal of Consulting and Clinical Psychology, 74,* 1027–1040.

Levy, S. T. (1990). *Principles of interpretation.* Northvale, NJ: Aronson.

Lilliengren, P., Johansson, R., Town, J. M., Kisely, S., & Abbas, A. (2017). Intensive short-term dynamic psychotherapy for generalized anxiety disorder: A pilot effectiveness and process-outcome study. *Clinical Psychology & Psychotherapy, 24,* 1313–1354.

Lindgren, A., Werbart, A., & Philips, B. (2010). Long-term outcome and post-treatment effects of psychoanalytic psychotherapy with young adults. *Psychology and Psychotherapy, 83*(Pt 1), 27–43.

Lingiardi, V., & McWilliams, N. (2017). *Psychodynamic diagnostic manual: PDM-2* (2nd ed.). New York, NY: Guilford.

Linnet, J., & Jemec, G. B. (2001). Anxiety level and severity of skin condition predicts outcome of psychotherapy in atopic dermatitis patients. *International Journal of Dermatology, 40,* 632–636.

Loewald, H. W. (1960). On the therapeutic action of psychoanalysis. *Journal of the American Psychoanalytic Association, 41,* 16–33.

Loranger, A. (1999). *International personality disorders examination (IPDE) manual.* Odessa, FL: Psychological Assessment Resources.

Lothane, Z. (1986). Confrontation: Clinical application. In M. P. Nichols & T. J. Paolino (Eds.), *Basic techniques of psychodynamic psychotherapy* (pp. 207–236). Northvale, NJ: Gardner.

Lothane, Z. (2002). Requiem or reveille: A response to Robert F. Bornstein (2001). *Psychoanalytic Psychology, 19,* 572–579.

Luborsky, L. (1984). *Principles of psychoanalytic psychotherapy: A manual for supportive-expressive treatment*. New York, NY: Basic Books.

Luborsky, L., Mintz, J., Auerbach, A., Christoph, P., Bachrach, H., Todd, T., . . . O'Brien, C. P. (1980). Predicting the outcome of psychotherapy. Findings of the Penn Psychotherapy Project. *Archives of General Psychiatry, 37,* 471–481.

Mallinckrodt, B., Choi, G., & Daly, K. D. (2015). Pilot test of a measure to assess therapeutic distance and its association with client attachment and corrective experience in therapy. *Psychotherapy Research, 25,* 505–517.

Maina, G., Forner, F., & Bogetto, F. (2005). Randomized controlled trial comparing brief dynamic and supportive therapy with waiting list condition in minor depressive disorders. *Psychotherapy and Psychosomatics, 74,* 43–50.

Maina, G., Rosso, G., Crespi, C., & Bogetto, F. (2007). Combined brief dynamic therapy and pharmacotherapy in the treatment of major depressive disorder: A pilot study. *Psychotherapy and Psychosomatics, 76,* 298–305.

Malan, D. (1979). *Individual psychotherapy and the science of psychodynamics*. London, England: Butterworth.

Malan, D. M., & Osimo, F. (1992). *Psychodynamics, training, and outcome in brief psychotherapy*. London, England: Butterworth-Heinemann.

Mann, J. (1973). *Time-limited psychotherapy*. Cambridge, MA: Harvard University Press.

Mann, J. (1973). Confrontation as a mode of teaching. In G. Adler & P. G. Myerson (Eds.), *Confrontation in psychotherapy* (pp. 39–48). Northvale, NJ: Jason Aronson.

Maroda, K. J. (2010). *Psychodynamic techniques: Working with emotion in the therapeutic relationship*. New York, NY: Guilford.

Martini, B., Rosso, G., Chiodelli, D. F., De Cori, D., & Maina, G. (2011). Brief dynamic therapy combined with pharmacotherapy in the treatment of panic disorder with concurrent depressive symptoms. *Clinical Neuropsychiatry, 8,* 204–221.

Maxwell, H., Tasca, G. A., Grenon, R., Faye, M., Ritchie, K., Bissada, H., & Balfour, L. (2017). Change in attachment dimensions in women with binge-eating disorder following group psychodynamic interpersonal psychotherapy. *Psychotherapy Research, 28,* 887–901.

May, R. (1983). *The discovery of being: Writings in existential psychology*. New York, NY: Norton.

McCarthy, K. S., Connolly Gibbons, M. B., & Barber, J. P. (2008). The relation of rigidity across relationships with symptoms and functioning: An investigation with the revised central relationship questionnaire. *Journal of Counseling Psychology, 55,* 346–358.

McCullough, L., Kuhn, N., Andrews, S., Kaplan, A., Wolf, J., & Hurley, C. L. (2003). *Treating affect phobia: A manual for short-term dynamic psychotherapy*. New York, NY: Guilford.

McCullough, L., Winston, H. A., Farber, B. A., Porter, F., Pollack, J., Vingiano, W., . . . Trujillo, M. (1991). The relationship of patient-therapist interaction to the outcome in brief dynamic psychotherapy. *Psychotherapy: Theory, Practice, Research, Training, 28,* 525–533.

McMullin, R. E. (2000). *The new handbook of cognitive therapy techniques* (Rev ed.). New York, NY: Norton.

McNally, R. T. (1983; 1983). *Dracula was a woman*. New York, NY: McGraw-Hill.

McWilliams, N. (1999). *Psychoanalytic case formulation*. New York, NY: Guilford.

McWilliams, N. (2004). *Psychoanalytic psychotherapy: A practitioner's guide.* New York, NY: Guilford.

McWilliams, N. (2011). *Psychoanalytic diagnosis* (2nd ed.). New York, NY: Guilford.

Meissner, W. W. (1979). Narcissistic personalities and borderline conditions: A differential diagnosis. *Annual Review of Psychoanalysis, 7,* 171–202.

Menninger, K. (1958). *Theory of psychoanalytic technique.* New York: NY: Basic Books.

Messer, S. B., & McWilliams, N. (2007). Insight in psychodynamic therapy: Theory and assessment. In L. G. Castonguay & C. E. Hill (Eds.), *Insight in psychotherapy* (pp. 9–30). Washington, DC: American Psychological Association.

Messer, S. B., & Winokur, M. (1984). Ways of knowing and visions of reality in psychoanalytic and behavior therapy. In S. B. Messer & H. Arkowitz (Eds.), *Psychoanalytic therapy and behavior therapy: Is integration possible* (pp. 63–100). New York, NY: Plenum.

Messer, S. B., Sass, L. A., & Woolfolk, R. L. (1988). *Hermeneutics and psychological theory: Interpretive perspectives on personality, psychotherapy, and psychopathology.* New Brunswick, NJ: Rutgers University Press.

Meulemeester, C. D., Vansteelandt, K., Luyten, P., & Lowyck, B. (2018). Mentalizing as a mechanism of change in the treatment of patients with borderline personality disorder: A parallel process growth modeling approach. *Personality Disorders: Theory, Research, and Treatment, 9,* 22–29.

Midgley, N., O'Keefe, S. O., French, L., & Kennedy, E. (2017). Psychodynamic psychotherapy for children and adolescents: An updated narrative review of the evidence base. *Journal of Child Psychotherapy, 43,* 307–329.

Milbrath, C., Bond, M., Cooper, S., Znoj, H. J., Horowitz, M. J., & Perry, J. C. (1999). Sequential consequences of therapist's interventions. *Journal of Psychotherapy Practice and Research, 8,* 40–54.

Milhorn, T. H. (2018). *Substance use disorders: A guide for the primary care provider.* Cham, Switzerland: Springer.

Miller, A. (1981). *Prisoners of childhood: The drama of the gifted child and the search for the true self* [Drama des begabten Kindes.]. New York, NY: Basic Books.

Miller, R. B. (1992). *The restoration of dialogue: Readings in the philosophy of clinical psychology.* Washington, DC: American Psychological Association.

Miller-Bottome, M., Talia, A., Safran, J. D., & Muran, J. C. (2018). Resolving alliance ruptures from an attachment-informed perspective. *Psychoanalytic Psychology, 35,* 175–183.

Milrod, B., Busch F. N., Cooper, A., & Shapiro, T. (1997). *Manual of panic focused psychodynamic psychotherapy.* Washington, DC: American Psychiatric Press.

Milrod, B., Chambless, D. L., Gallop, R., Busch, F. N., Schwalberg, M., McCarthy, K. S., . . . Barber, J. P. (2015). Psychotherapies for panic disorder: A tale of two sites. *Journal of Clinical Psychiatry, 77,* 927–935.

Milrod, B., Leon, A. C., Busch, F., Rudden, M., Schwalberg, M., Clarkin, J., . . . Shear, M. K. (2007). A randomized controlled clinical trial of psychoanalytic psychotherapy for panic disorder. *American Journal of Psychiatry, 164,* 265–272.

Misch, D. A. (2000). Basic strategies of dynamic supportive therapy. *Journal of Psychotherapy Practice and Research, 9,* 173–189.

Mischel, W., Ebbesen, E. B., & Zeiss, A. R. (1972). Cognitive and attentional mechanisms in delay of gratification. *Journal of Personality and Social Psychology, 21,* 204–218.

Mitchell, S. A., & Black, M. J. (1995). *Freud and beyond: A history of modern psychoanalytic thought*. New York, NY: Basic Books.

Mullin, A. S., Hilsenroth, M. J., Gold, J., & Farber, B. A. (2017). Changes in object relations over the course of psychodynamic psychotherapy. *Clinical Psychology & Psychotherapy, 24,* 501–511.

Mullin, A. S. J., Hilsenroth, M. J., Gold, J., & Farber, B. A. (2018). Facets of object representation: Process and outcome over the course of psychodynamic psychotherapy. *Journal of Personality Assessment, 100,* 145–155.

Muran, J. C., & Barber, J. P. (Eds.). (2010). *The therapeutic alliance: An evidence-based guide to practice*. New York, NY: Guilford.

Muran, J. C., & Safran, J. D. (2017). Therapeutic alliance ruptures. In A. E. Wenzel (Ed.), *Sage encyclopedia of abnormal and clinical psychology*. New York: Sage.

Muran, J. C., Safran, J. D., Gorman, B. S., Samstag, L. W., Eubanks-Carter, C., & Winston, A. (2009). The relationship of early alliance ruptures and their resolution to process and outcome in three time-limited psychotherapies for personality disorders. *Psychotherapy (Chicago), 46,* 233–248.

Nader-Mohammadi Moghadam, M. Atef-Vahid, M. K., Asgharnejad-Farid, A. A., Shabani, A., & Lavasni, F. (2015). Effectiveness of short-term dynamic psychotherapy versus Sertraline in Treatment of Social Phobia. *Iran Journal of Psychiatry, 9*(2), 2–6.

National Center for Health Statistics. (2016). *Health, United States, 2016: With chartbook on long-term trends in health*. Hyattsville, MD: National Center for Health Statistics.

Nichols, M. P. (1986). Introduction. In M. P. Nichols & T. J. Paolino (Eds.), *Basic techniques of psychodynamic psychotherapy* (pp. 1–20). Northvale, NJ: Gardner.

Nietzsche, F. W. (1967). *The will to power* (W. Kaufman, Ed., W. Kaufman & R. J. Hollingdale, Trans.). New York, NY: Vintage Books.

Nietzsche, F. W. (1998). *Beyond good and evil*. New York, NY: Oxford University Press.

Nietzsche, F. W. (1998). *Twilight of the idols, or, how to philosophize with a hammer*. New York, NY: Oxford University Press.

Nietzsche, F. W. (2005). Twilight of the idols, or how to philosophize with a hammer (J. Norman, Trans.). In A. Ridley & J. Norman (Eds.), *The Anti-Christ, Ecce homo, Twilight of the idols, and other writings* (pp. 153–230). Cambridge, England: Cambridge University Press.

Nissen-Lie, H. A., Monsen, J. T., Ulleberg, P., & Ronnestad, M. H. (2013). Psychotherapists' self-reports of their interpersonal functioning and difficulties in practice as predictors of patient outcome. *Psychotherapy Research, 23,* 86–104.

Nissen-Lie, H. A., Ronnestad, M. H., Hoglend, P. A., Havik, O. E., Solbakken, O. A., Stiles, T. C., & Monsen, J. T. (2017). Love yourself as a person, doubt yourself as a therapist? *Clinical Psychology & Psychotherapy, 24,* 48–60.

Ogrodniczuk, J. S., & Piper, W. E. (1999). Use of transference interpretations in dynamically oriented individual psychotherapy for patients with personality disorders. *Journal of Personality Disorders, 13,* 297–311.

Öjehagen, A., Berglund, M., Appel, C. P., Andersson, K., Nilsson, B., Skjaerris, A., & Wedlin-Toftenow, A. M. (1992). A randomized study of long-term out-patient treatment in alcoholics. Psychiatric treatment versus multimodal behavioural therapy, during 1 versus 2 years of treatment. *Alcohol Alcohol, 27,* 649–658.

OPD Task Force. (2008). *Operationalized psychodynamic diagnosis (OPD-2): Manual of diagnosis and treatment planning*. Cambridge, MA: Hogrefe & Huber.

Oswald, M. E., & Grosjean, S. (2004). Confirmation bias. In R. F. Pohl (Ed.), *Cognitive illusions: A handbook on fallacies and biases in thinking, judgment, and memory* (pp. 79–96). New York, NY: Psychology Press.

Perlis, M. L., Jungquist, C., Smith, M. T., & Posner, D. (2005). *Cognitive behavioral treatment of insomnia A session-by-session guide.* New York, NY: Springer Science + Business Media.

Perry, W., & Viglione, D. J., Jr. (1991). The ego impairment index as a predictor of outcome in melancholic depressed patients treated with tricyclic antidepressants. *Journal of Personality Assessment, 56,* 487–501.

Pierloot, R., & Vinck, J. (1978). Differential outcome of short-term dynamic psychotherapy and systematic desensitizations in the treatment of anxious outpatients: A preliminary report. *Psychologica Belgica, 18,* 87–98.

Pine, F. (1985). *Developmental theory and clinical process.* New Haven, CT: Yale University Press.

Piper, W. E., Azim, H. F., Joyce, A. S., & McCallum, M. (1991). Transference interpretations, therapeutic alliance, and outcome in short-term individual psychotherapy. *Archives of General Psychiatry, 48,* 946–953.

Piper, W. E., Debbane, E. G., Bienvenu, J. P., & Garant, J. (1984). A comparative study of four forms of psychotherapy. *Journal of Consulting and Clinical Psychology, 52,* 268–279.

Plato. (1997a). Apology. (G. M. A. Grube, Trans.). In J. M. Cooper & D. S. Hutchinson (Eds.), *Plato: Complete works* (pp. 17–36). Indianapolis, IN: Hackett.

Plato. (1997b). Republic (G. M. A. Grube & C. D. C. Reeve, Trans.) In J. M. Cooper (Ed.), *Plato: Complete works* (pp. 971–1223). Indianapolis, IN: Hackett.

Plutarch. (1931). *Plutarch's moralia III* (T. E. Page, Ed. & F. C. Babbitt, Trans.). Cambridge, England: Harvard University Press.

Plutarch. (1939). *Plutarch's moralia VI* (T. E. Page, Ed. & W. C. Helmbold, Trans.). Cambridge, England: Harvard University Press.

Popper, K. (2002). *The logic of scientific discovery.* New York, NY: Routledge.

Pyles, B. (2014). Can we thrive? *American Psychoanalyst, 48*(2), 3–4.

Racker, H. (1968). *Transference and countertransference.* London: Hogarth Press.

Rado, S. (1969). *Adaptational psychodynamics: Motivation and control.* New York, NY: Science House.

Rank, O., Taft, J., & Rank, O. (1945). *Will therapy and truth and reality.* New York, NY: Knopf.

Rapaport, D. (1967). A theoretical analysis of the superego concept. In M. Gill (Ed.), *The collected papers of David Rapaport* (pp. 685–709). New York, NY: Basic Books.

Redmond, J., & Shulman, M. (2008). Access to psychoanalytic ideas in American undergraduate institutions. *Journal of the American Psychoanalytic Association, 56,* 391–408.

Reich, W. (1990). *Character analysis* [Charakteranalyse.] New York, NY: Noonday.

Reik, T. (1948). *Listening with the third ear: The inner experience of a psychoanalyst.* New York, NY: Farrar, Straus, & Giroux.

Reneses, B., Galián, M., Serrano, R., Figuera, D., Fernandez Del Moral, A., López-Ibor, J. J., . . . Trujillo, M. (2013). A new time limited psychotherapy for BPD: Preliminary results of a randomized and controlled trial. *Actas Españolas de Psiquiatría, 41*(3), 139–148.

Rickman, J. (1950). On the criteria for termination of an analysis. *International Journal of Psychoanalysis, 31,* 200–201.

Ricoeur, P. (1970). *Freud and philosophy: An essay on interpretation* (D. Savage, Trans.). Binghamton, NY: Yale University Press.

Riso, L. P., du Toit, P. L., Stein, D. J., & Young, J. E. (Eds.). (2007). *Cognitive schemas and core beliefs in psychological problems: A scientist-practitioner guide.* Washington, DC: American Psychological Association.

Rockland, L. (1989). *Supportive therapy: A psychodynamic approach.* New York, NY: Basic Books.

Rogers, C. R. (1942). *Counseling and psychotherapy: Newer concepts in practice.* Boston: Houghton Mifflin.

Rogers, C. R. (1995). *On becoming a person: A therapist's view of psychotherapy.* Boston: Houghton Mifflin.

Rosso, G., Martini, B., & Maina, G. (2012). Brief dynamic therapy and depression severity: A single-blind, randomized study. *Journal of Affective Disorders, 147,* 101–106.

Roth, A., & Fonagy, P. (2005). *What works for whom? A critical review of psychotherapy research* (2nd ed.). New York, NY: Guilford.

Roy, C. A., Perry, C. J., Luborsky, L., & Banon, E. (2009). Changes in defensive functioning in completed psychoanalyses: The Penn psychoanalytic treatment collection. *Journal of the American Psychoanalytic Association, 57,* 399–415.

Rudden, M., Milrod, B., Target, M., Ackerman, S., & Graf, E. (2006). Reflective functioning in panic disorder patients: A pilot study. *Journal of the American Psychoanalytic Association, 54,* 1339–1343.

Ruiz, M. A., Pincus, A. L., Borkovec, T. D., Echemendia, R. J., Castonguay, L. G., & Ragusea, S. A. (2004). Validity of the inventory of interpersonal problems for predicting treatment outcome: An investigation with the Pennsylvania practice research network. *Journal of Personality Assessment, 83,* 213–222.

Safran, J. D. (2011). Theodore Reik's listening with the third ear and the role of self-analysis in contemporary psychoanalytic thinking. *Psychoanalytic Review, 98,* 205–216.

Safran, J. D., & Muran, J. C. (1996). The resolution of ruptures in the therapeutic alliance. *Journal of Consulting and Clinical Psychology, 64,* 447–458.

Safran, J. D., & Muran, J. C. (2000). *Negotiating the therapeutic alliance: A relational treatment guide.* New York, NY: Guilford.

Safran, J. D., Muran, J. C., & Eubanks-Carter, C. (2011). Repairing alliance ruptures. In J. C. Norcross (Ed.), *Psychotherapy relationships that work: Evidence-based responsiveness* (2nd ed., pp. 224–238). New York, NY: Oxford University Press.

Salzer, S., Leibing, E., Jakobsen, T., Rudolf, G., Brockmann, J., Eckert, J., . . . Leichsenring, F. (2010). Patterns of interpersonal problems and their improvement in depressive and anxious patients treated with psychoanalytic therapy. *Bulletin of the Menninger Clinic, 74,* 283–300.

Sartre, J. (2003). *Being and nothingness: An essay on phenomenological ontology.* London, England: Routledge. (Original work published 1958)

Sattel, H., Lahmann, C., Gündel, H., Guthrie, E., Kruse, J., Noll-Hussong, M., . . . (2011). Brief psychodynamic interpersonal psychotherapy for patients with multisomatoform disorder: randomized controlled trial. *British Journal of Psychiatry, 200,* 60–67.

Schafer, R. (1976). *A new language for psychoanalysis.* New Haven, CT: Yale University Press.

Scheidt, C. E., Waller, E., Endorf, K., Schmidt, S., König, R., Zeeck, A., . . . Lacour, M. (2013). Is brief psychodynamic psychotherapy in primary fibromyalgia syndrome with concurrent depression an effective treatment? A randomized controlled trial. *General Hospital Psychiatry, 35,* 160–167.

Schopenhauer, A. (1969). *The world as will and representation.* New York, NY: Dover.

Sears, R. W., Rudisill, J. R., & Mason-Sears, C. (2006). *Consultation skills for mental health professionals.* Hoboken, NJ: Wiley.

Shakespeare, W. (1988). *Hamlet* (B. Bevlington, Ed.). New York, NY: Bantam.

Shane, M. (1979). The developmental approach to "working through" in the analytic process. *International Journal of Psycho-Analysis, 60,* 375–382.

Shapiro, D. A., Barkham, M., Rees, A., Hardy, G. E., Reynolds, S., & Startup, M. (1994). Effects of treatment duration and severity of depression on the effectiveness of cognitive-behavioral and psychodynamic-interpersonal psychotherapy. *Journal of Consulting and Clinical Psychology, 62,* 522–534.

Sharpless, B. A. (2013). Kierkegaard's conception of psychology. *Journal of Theoretical and Philosophical Psychology, 33*(2), 90–106.

Sharpless, B. A. (2014). Serial killers, movie stars, and "eruptions": A case of obsessionality. In R. F. Summers & J. P. Barber (Eds.), *Practicing psychodynamic psychotherapy: A casebook* (pp. 120–138). New York, NY: Guilford.

Sharpless, B. A. (2015). The critique of eros: Freud on narcissism and the prospects for romantic love. *Psychodynamic Practice: Individuals, Groups and Organizations, 21,* 210–225.

Sharpless, B. A., & Barber, J. P. (2009a). A conceptual and empirical review of the meaning, measurement, development, and teaching of intervention competence in clinical psychology. *Clinical Psychology Review, 29,* 47–56.

Sharpless, B. A., & Barber, J. P. (2009b). The examination for professional practice in psychology (EPPP) in the era of evidence-based practice. *Professional Psychology: Research and Practice, 40,* 333–340.

Sharpless, B. A., & Barber, J. P. (2012). *Corrective emotional experiences from a psychodynamic perspective.* Washington, DC: American Psychological Association.

Sharpless, B. A., & Barber, J. P. (2015). Transference/countertransference. In R. Cautin & S. O. Lilienfeld (Eds.), *The encyclopedia of clinical psychology* (pp. 2875–2880). Malden, MA: Wiley-Blackwell.

Sharpless, B. A., & Doghramji, K. (2015). *Sleep paralysis: Historical, psychological, and medical perspectives.* New York, NY: Oxford University Press.

Sharpless, B. A., Muran, J. C., & Barber, J. P. (2010). Coda: Recommendations for practice and training. In *The therapeutic alliance: An evidence-based guide to practice* (pp. 341–354). New York, NY: Guilford.

Sharpless, B. A., Tse, J., & Ajeto, D. (2014, August). *Changes in clinical and counseling psychology programs over time: Students, faculty, and outcomes.* Paper presented at the 122nd annual meeting for the American Psychological Association, Washington, DC.

Shaw, C. M., Margison, F. R., Guthrie, E. A., & Tomenson, B. (2001). Psychodynamic interpersonal therapy by inexperienced therapists in a naturalistic setting: A pilot study. *European Journal of Psychotherapy, Counselling, and Health, 4,* 87–101.

Shedler, J. (2010). The efficacy of psychodynamic psychotherapy. *The American Psychologist, 65(2)*, 98–109.

Sherwood, M. (1969). *The logic of explanation in psychoanalysis.* New York, NY: Academic.

Shefler, G., Dasberg, H., & Ben-Shakhar, G. (1995). A randomized controlled outcome and follow-up study of Mann's time-limited psychotherapy. *Journal of Consulting and Clinical Psychology, 63*, 585–593.

Shefler, G. (2001). *Time-limited psychotherapy in practice.* London, England: Brunner-Routledge.

Sifneos, P. (1973). Confrontation in short-term, anxiety-provoking therapy. In G. Adler & P. G. Myerson (Eds.), *Confrontation in psychotherapy* (pp. 369–383). Northvale, NJ: Jason Aronson.

Silver, R. J. (1986). Manipulation: Clinical application. In M. Nichols & T. J. Paolino (Eds.), *Basic techniques of psychodynamic psychotherapy* (pp. 167–186). Northvale, NJ: Jason Aronson.

Sjödin, I., Svedlund, J., Ottosson, J. O., & Dotevall, G. (1986). Controlled study of psychotherapy in chronic peptic ulcer disease. *Psychosomatics, 27*, 187–195.

Slavin-Mulford, J., Hilsenroth, M., Weinberger, J., & Gold, J. (2011). Therapeutic interventions related to outcome in psychodynamic psychotherapy for anxiety disorder patients. *Journal of Nervous and Mental Disease, 199*, 214–221.

Slomin, D. A., Shefler, G., Gvirsman, S. D., & Tishby, O. (2011). Changes in rigidity and symptoms among adolescents in psychodynamic psychotherapy. *Psychotherapy Research, 21*, 685–697.

Sparo, S. S., Cichetti, D. V., & Saulnier, C. A. (2016). *Vineland adaptive behavior scales (Vineland-3)* (3rd ed.). San Antonio, TX: Pearson.

Soares, M. C., Mondin, T. C., Del Grande da Silva, G., Barbosa, L. P., Molina, M. L., Jansen, K. . . . da Silva, R. A. (2018). Comparison of clinical significance of cognitive-behavioral therapy and psychodynamic therapy for major depressive disorder: A randomized clinical trial. *Journal of Nervous and Mental Disease, 206*, 686–693.

Solomon, I. (1992). *The encyclopedia of evolving techniques in psychodynamic therapy.* Northvale, NJ: J. Aronson.

Spence, D. P. (1982). *Narrative truth and historical truth: Meaning and interpretation in psychoanalysis.* New York, NY: Norton.

Spielmans, G. I., Berman, M. I., & Usitalo, A. N. (2011). Psychotherapy versus second-generation antidepressants in the treatment of depression: A meta-analysis. *Journal of Nervous and Mental Disease, 199*, 142–149.

"Stance." *Oxford Living Dictionary.* Accessed October 2, 2018 at https://en.oxforddictionaries.com/definition/us/stance

Steger, M. F., Frazier, P., Oishi, S., & Kaler, M. (2006). The meaning in life questionnaire: Assessing the presence of and search for meaning in life. *Journal of Counseling Psychology, 53*, 80–93.

Steinert, C., Munder, T., Rabung, S., Hoyer, J., & Leichsenring, F. (2017). Psychodynamic therapy: As efficacious as other empirically supported treatments? A meta-analysis testing equivalence of outcomes. *American Journal of Psychiatry, 174*, 943–953.

Stigler, M., de Roten, Y., Drapeau, M., & Despland, J. N. (2007). Process research in psychodynamic psychotherapy: A combined measure of accuracy and conflictuality of interpretations. *Swiss Archives of Neurology and Psychiatry, 58*, 225–232.

Stiles, W. B., & Goldsmith, J. Z. (2010). The alliance over time. In J. C. Muran & J. P. Barber (Eds.), *The therapeutic alliance: An evidence-based guide to practice* (pp. 44–62). New York, NY: Guilford.

Stocking, M. (1973). Confrontations in psychotherapy: Considerations arising from the psychoanalytic treatment of the child. In G. Adler & P. G. Myerson (Eds.), *Confrontations in psychotherapy* (pp. 319–346). Northvale, NJ: Jason Aronson.

Stolorow, R. D., Brandschaft, B., & Atwood, G. E. (1995). *Psychoanalytic treatment: An intersubjective approach.* New York, NY: Routledge.

Strachey, J. (1934). The nature of the therapeutic action of psychoanalysis. *International Journal of Psychoanalysis, 15,* 127–159.

Stricker, G. (2010). *Psychotherapy integration.* Washington, DC: American Psychological Association.

Stricker, G., & Gold, J. (2005). Assimilative psychodynamic psychotherapy. In J. C. Norcross & M. R. Goldfried (Eds.), *Handbook of psychotherapy integration* (2nd ed., pp. 221–240). New York, NY: Oxford University Press.

Strupp, H. H., & Binder, J. L. (1984). *Psychotherapy in a new key: A guide to time-limited dynamic psychotherapy.* New York, NY: Basic Books.

Sullivan, H. S., & Perry, H. S.; William Alanson White Psychiatric Foundation. (1953). *The collected works of Harry Stack Sullivan, M.D.* New York, NY: Norton.

Summers, R. F., & Barber, J. P. (2010). *Psychodynamic therapy: A guide to evidence-based practice.* New York, NY: Guilford.

Summers, R. F., & Barber, J. P. (2015). *Practicing psychodynamic therapy: A casebook.* New York, NY: Guilford.

Svartberg, M., Stiles, T. C., & Seltzer, M. H. (2004). Randomized, controlled trial of the effectiveness of short-term dynamic psychotherapy and cognitive therapy for cluster C personality disorders. *American Journal of Psychiatry, 161,* 810–817.

Svedlund, J., Sjodin, I., Ottosson, J. O., & Dotevall, G. (1983). Controlled study of psychotherapy in irritable bowel syndrome. *Lancet, 2,* 589–592.

Target, M. (2018). 20/20 hindsight: A 25-year programme at the Anna Freud Centre of efficacy and effectiveness research on child psychoanalytic psychotherapy. *Psychotherapy Research, 28,* 30–46.

Thomä, H., & Kächele, H. (1992). *Psychoanalytic practice.* Berlin, Germany: Springer.

Thoma, N. C., McKay, D., Gerber, A. J., Milrod, B. L., Edwards, A. R., & Kocsis, J. H. (2012). A quality-based review of randomized controlled trials of cognitive-behavioral therapy for depression: An assessment and metaregression. *American Journal of Psychiatry, 169,* 22–30.

Thyme, K. E., Sundin, E. C., Stahlberg, G., Lindstrom, B., Eklof, H., & Wiberg, B. (2007). The outcome of short-term psychodynamic art therapy compared to short-term psychodynamic verbal therapy for depressed women. *Psychoanalytic Psychotherapy, 21,* 250–264.

Tsai, M., Ogrodniczuk, J. S., Sochting, I., & Mirmiran, J. (2014). Forecasting success: Patients' expectations for improvement and their relations to baseline, process and outcome variables in group cognitive-behavioural therapy for depression. *Clinical Psychology & Psychotherapy, 21*(2), 97–107.

Town, J. M., Abbass, A., Stride, C., & Bernier, D. (2017) A randomized controlled trial of Intensive Short-Term Dynamic Psychotherapy for treatment resistant depression: The Halifax depression study. *Journal of Affective Disorders, 214,* 15–25.

Vermote, R., Lowyck, B., Luyten, P., Vertommen, H., Corveleyn, J., Verhaest, Y., . . . Peuskens, J. (2010). Process and outcome in psychodynamic hospitalization-based treatment for patients with a personality disorder. *Journal of Nervous and Mental Disease, 198*(2), 110–115.

Vigo, D., Thornicroft, G., & Atun, R. (2016). Estimating the true global burden of mental illness. *Lancet Psychiatry, 3,* 171–178.

Vinnars, B., Barber, J. P., Noren, K., Gallop, R., & Weinryb, R. M. (2005). Manualized supportive-expressive psychotherapy versus nonmanualized community-delivered psychodynamic therapy for patients with personality disorders: Bridging efficacy and effectiveness. *American Journal of Psychiatry, 162,* 1933–1940.

Wachtel, P. (2011). *Therapeutic communication: Knowing what to say when* (2nd ed.). New York, NY: Guilford.

Waelder, R. (2007). The principle of multiple function: Observations on over-determination, 1936. *Psychoanalytic Quarterly, 76,* 75–92; discussion 93–117, 119–48.

Wallerstein, R. S. (1989). The psychotherapy research project of the Menninger foundation: An overview. *Journal of Consulting and Clinical Psychology, 57,* 195–205.

Wampold, B. E., & Imel, Z. E. (2015). *The great psychotherapy debate: The evidence for what makes psychotherapy work* (2nd ed.). New York, NY: Routledge.

Wampold, B. E., Baldwin, S. A., Holtforth, M. G., & Imel, Z. E. (2017). What characterizes effective therapists? In L. G. Castonguay & C. E. Hill (Eds.), *How and why are some therapists better than others? understanding therapist effects* (pp. 37–54). Washington, DC: American Psychological Association.

Weisman, A. (1973). Confrontation, countertransference, and context. In G. Adler & P. G. Myerson (Eds.), *Confrontation in psychotherapy* (pp. 97–122). Northvale, NJ: Jason Aronson.

Welpton, D. F. (1973). Confrontation in the therapeutic process. In G. Adler & P. G. Myerson (Eds.), *Confrontation in psychotherapy* (pp. 249–270). Northvale, NJ: Jason Aronson.

Werman, D. S. (1984). *The practice of supportive psychotherapy.* New York, NY: Brunner/Mazel.

Westen, D. (1999). The scientific status of unconscious processes: Is Freud really dead? *Journal of the American Psychoanalytic Association, 47,* 1061–1106.

Wiborg, I. M., & Dahl, A. A. (1996). Does brief dynamic psychotherapy reduce the relapse rate of panic disorder? *Archives of General Psychiatry, 53,* 689–694.

Wilczek, A., Weinryb, R. M., Barber, J. P., Gustavsson, J. P., & Asberg, M. (2004). Change in the core conflictual relationship theme after long-term dynamic psychotherapy. *Psychotherapy Research, 14,* 107–125.

Wiltink, J., Dippel, A., Szczepanski, M., Thiede, R., Alt, C., & Beutel, M. E. (2007). Long-term weight loss maintenance after inpatient psychotherapy of severely obese patients based on a randomized study: Predictors and maintaining factors of health behavior. *Journal of Psychosomatic Research, 62,* 691–698.

Wiltink, J., Ruckes, C., Hoyer, J., Leichsenring, F., Joraschky, P., Leweke, F., . . . Beutel, M. E. (2017). Transfer of manualized short term psychodynamic psychotherapy (STPP) for social anxiety disorder into clinical practice: Results from a cluster-randomized controlled trial. *BMC Psychiatry, 17,* 92.

Winnicott, D. W. (1955). Metapsychological and clinical aspects of regression within the psycho-analytical set-up. *International Journal of Psycho-Analysis, 36,* 16–26.

Winnicott, D. W. (1989). In C. Winnicott, R. Shepherd, & M. Davis (Eds.), *Psychoanalytic explorations*. Cambridge, MA: Harvard University Press.

Winston, A. (2014). Supportive psychotherapy. In R. E. Hales, S. C. Yudofsky, & L. W. Roberts (Eds.), *The American psychiatric publishing textbook of psychiatry* (6th ed., pp. 1161–1188). Washington, DC: American Psychiatric Publishing.

Winston, A., Rosenthal, R. N., & Pinsker, H. (2012). *Learning supportive psychotherapy: An illustrated guide*. Arlington, VA: American Psychiatric Association.

Winston, A., Pollack, J., McCullough, L., Flegenheimer, W., Kestenbaum, R., & Trujillo, M. (1991). Brief psychotherapy of personality disorders. *Journal of Nervous and Mental Diseases, 179,* 188–193.

Woody, S. R., & Ollendick, T. H. (2006). Technique factors in treating anxiety disorders. In L. G. Castonguay & L. E. Beutler (Eds.), *Principles of therapeutic change that work* (pp. 167–186). New York, NY: Oxford University Press.

Woody, G. F., Luborsky, L., McLellan, A. T., O'Brien, C. P., Beck, A. T., Blaine, J., . . . Hole, A. (1983). Psychotherapy for opiate addicts: Does it help? *Archives of General Psychiatry, 40,* 639–645.

Woody, G. E., McLellan, A. T., Luborsky, L., & O Brien, C. P. (1995). Psychotherapy in community methadone programs: A validation. *American Journal of Psychiatry, 152,* 1302–1308.

World Health Organization. (1990). *International classification of diseases* (10th ed.). Geneva: Author.

World Health Organization. (2018). *International classification of diseases* (11th ed.). Geneva: Author.

Yeomans, F. E., Clarkin, J. F., & Kernberg, O. F. (2015). *Transference-focused psychotherapy for borderline personality disorder: A clinical guide*. Arlington, VA: American Psychiatric Association.

Yeomans, F. E., Selzer, M. A., & Clarkin, J. F. (1992). *Treating the borderline patient: A contract-based approach*. New York, NY: Basic Books.

Zalaznik, D., Weiss, M., & Huppert, J. D. (2017). Improvement in adult anxious and avoidant attachment during cognitive behavior therapy for panic disorder. *Psychotherapy Research*. doi: 10.1080/10503307.2017.1365183

Zilcha-Mano, S. (2017). Is the alliance really therapeutic? revisiting this question in light of recent methodological advances. *American Psychologist, 72,* 311–325.